D0919899

EFFICIENCY AND UPLIFT

EFFICIENCY
AND
UPLIFT

Scientific Management
in the Progressive Era
1890-1920

SAMUEL HABER

THE UNIVERSITY OF CHICAGO PRESS
Chicago & London

Library of Congress Catalog Card Number: 64-15828

THE UNIVERSITY OF CHICAGO PRESS, CHICAGO & LONDON
The University of Toronto Press, Toronto 5, Canada

Printed in the United States of America

To Janice

• ACKNOWLEDGMENTS

I want to thank Professor Henry F. May, who suggested that I study the history of scientific management in the progressive era, and who read and criticized the entire manuscript. I have benefited greatly not only from his astute comments but also from the example of his own work, which sets high standards for scholarship in American intellectual history. Professors F. Hunter Dupree and Reinhard Bendix of the University of California read the manuscript and offered many helpful suggestions, as did Professor Herman E. Michl of the Department of Economics of the University of Delaware.

My debt to Dr. Lucille Birnbaum is great and abiding. She gave me the benefit of an enthusiastic and thoughtful line-by-line commentary on the manuscript. Mr. Arthur Lipow read the first three chapters, and our many wide-ranging conversations were extremely helpful.

I must thank Professor Samuel Williams and Miss Frances I. Duck for access to the Frederick W. Taylor Collection at the Stevens Institute of Technology in Hoboken, New Jersey. I should also like to thank Mrs. Pearl W. Von Allmen of the University of Louisville School of Law for admitting me to the Louis D. Brandeis Collection; Mr. Roland Baughman of the Department of Special Collections of Columbia University Libraries for access to the Melville Dewey Papers, the Lincoln Steffens Papers, and the Randolph Bourne Papers; and Professor Hammond of the Bancroft Library, University of California, Berkeley, for access to the Francis J. Heney Papers. I am very grateful to Mr. J. Christian Barth who patiently answered questions about his father and sent copious quotes from his own collection of Carl G. Barth's personal papers. The Social Science Research Council provided funds for a full year's research; the University of Delaware's Summer

Faculty Fellowship Committee and the University of California's Committee on Research granted funds for my work. The Harvard Graduate School of Business Administration awarded a research grant that enabled me to study the Carl G. Barth papers at the Baker Library.

My wife read the manuscript at every stage and I have relied upon her judgment at many points. She was my severest critic and greatest help. Though my account as it stands owes much to everyone mentioned and to many others, they, of course, are not responsible for my errors.

• INTRODUCTION

We are often told that Americans love efficiency. In fact, we are told this so often that some serious students of American character have come to see such statements as commonplaces deadening our understanding of America and Americans rather than enlivening it. Yet if we give these commonplaces specificity, if we look closely at Americans professing the love of efficiency (and to a lesser extent acting upon it), we may come away from such study with a better understanding of our country and our ways.

The progressive era is almost made to order for the study of Americans in love with efficiency. For the progressive era gave rise to an efficiency craze — a secular Great Awakening, an outpouring of ideas and emotions in which a gospel of efficiency was preached without embarrassment to businessmen, workers, doctors, housewives, and teachers, and yes, preached even to preachers. Men as disparate as William Jennings Bryan and Walter Lippmann discoursed enthusiastically on efficiency. Efficient and good came closer to meaning the same thing in these years than in any other period of American history.

If we sift through the vast literature of efficiency that the progressive era produced, we can discover at least four principal ways in which the word efficiency was used. First of all, it described a personal attribute. An efficient person was an effective person, and that characterization brought with it a long shadow of latent associations and predispositions; a turning toward hard work and away from feeling, toward discipline and away from sympathy, toward masculinity and away from femininity. Second, the word signified the energy output-input ratio of a machine. This was a more recent use than that describing a trait of character. (However, mechanical efficiency may have added coloring to personal efficiency; a machine does, but does not feel.) The concept of mechanical efficiency developed out of the application of the laws of thermodynamics to the technology of the steam engine in the last quarter of the nineteenth century, and it soon became a central concept of engineering.

The machine whose efficiency the engineer calculated, however, was often owned by a business enterprise interested in profit. Commercial efficiency, the output-input ratio of dollars, was a third meaning common in the progressive era, and a meaning which engineers who were concerned with the delicate adjustment of material means to ends could not ignore. Finally, efficiency not only signified a personal quality, a relationship between materials, and a relationship between investment and revenue, but, most important, it signified a relationship between men. Efficiency meant social harmony and the leadership of the "competent." Progressives often called this social efficiency. And it is this meaning that has particular importance for the understanding of the progressive era.

At the very center of the efficiency craze was Frederick W. Taylor's program of industrial management. The four meanings of efficiency that the craze brought to view were all contained within Taylor's system. Taylor promised to bestow hard work and ample profits and to make "each workman's interest the same as that of his employers." Taylor's factory was to be one big machine, with all tasks organized and distributed accordingly, and with men of special training placed to see that the gears meshed. Unexpectedly, scientific management's promises of commercial efficiency were the least convincing. The checkered career of the Taylor System in the world of business might have been completely disheartening to the Taylorites had it not been for the fulness of response that scientific management found among the reformers and their public.

Taylor fashioned his methods after the exact sciences — experiment, measurement, generalization — in the hope of discovering laws of management which, like laws of nature, would be impartial and above class prejudice. Of course, Taylor's science obscured his bias rather than eliminated it.

Yet many who vigorously disparaged his accomplishment came to share his aspiration. He proposed a neat, understandable world in the factory, an organization of men whose acts would be planned, co-ordinated, and controlled under continuous expert direction. His system had some of the inevitableness and objectivity of science and technology. A Taylor plant became one of those places where an important segment of the American intelligentsia saw the future — and saw that it worked.

The mingling of Taylorites with progressive thinkers brought an adjustment of the doctrines of scientific management to modes of progressive thought. Significantly, the scientific management engineers found a view of democracy which did not threaten the prerogatives of the expert. This was a democracy which they could accept. When progressivism was at its height, the Taylorites stepped out of the factory and projected a role for scientific management in the nation at large. When progressivism declined, they returned to the factory but brought with them the after-effects of their alliance with progressivism. In the 1920's the Taylorites were in the vanguard of American business thought. They had found a social outlook for the accommodation of business, in which ultimate authority lies on top, to the environment of political democracy, in which ultimate authority lies below.

This very accomplishment tells us something about the progressivism that helped to make it possible. The progressive movement is often described as an attempt to revitalize government by the people, and there is much to be said for this view. It helps to explain the enthusiasm for such political devices as the direct primary, initiative, referendum, and recall during these years. However, alongside the attempt to bring government close to the people was an equally important attempt to keep government somewhat distant. Both these efforts can be seen not only within the same social movement but, at times, within the same political formula, and even among the same men. The second tendency was usually linked to efficiency and scientific management.

Scientific management, therefore, can serve as a tracer element to reveal some of the less familiar aspects of the vast movement for progressive reform. It draws attention to reformers who were trying to create a program of reform without an appeal to conscience, who called for experts and elites in the name of democracy, who asked for the elevation of the college-bred to positions of influence in the interest of social harmony. (These were the college-bred around whom Herbert Croly wished to build an interventionist state in which their creative self-realization and the advancement of the nation were to be mutual processes.) These reformers talked of social control, national guidance, and the end of laissez faire. They rejected the disorder of the uncontrolled market but often wished to preserve middle-class independence through expanding the realm of "professionalism." For this segment of progressivism, scientific management had an intrinsic appeal. It developed the notion of social control into a program of planning and placed the professional expert near the top. Its science seemed not only to rise above class interest but to bring the expert there as well.

At least since Andrew Jackson's day, American nationality has increasingly absorbed the ideas of equality and of rule by the people. Though many have found cause to be uncomfortable with these ideas, disavowal has often left one's patriotism open to question. Yet, if these ideas could not with ease be attacked frontally, they could be outflanked — and this most successfully when almost inadvertently. "Let the people rule" is, in part, a rhetorical phrase. Exactly how one lets the people rule is decisive. The progressives who greeted efficiency with enthusiasm were often those who proposed to let the people rule through a program in which the bulk of the people, most of the time, ruled hardly at all. Efficiency provided a standpoint from which those who had declared allegiance to democracy could resist the leveling tendencies of the principle of equality.

• CONTENTS

· CONTENTS ·

• CHAPTER I

Young Gentleman in the Steel Works

At the summer meeting of the American Society of Mechanical Engineers in 1895, a small, thin, pernickety engineer named Frederick Winslow Taylor read a paper entitled, "A Piece-Rate System, Being a Step toward a Partial Solution of the Labor Problem." [1] Most of those who heard it considered this paper but one more in the series of papers on the question of wage payments that had been presented to the Society over the years. Actually it was much more. It was the first inkling of a new order for the factory which Frederick W. Taylor was rearing at Midvale Steel Company in Nicetown, Pennsylvania.

Ostensibly, Taylor's paper dealt with incentive systems, and thereby fitted in with the growing interest in methods of wage payments which appeared in the last decades of the nineteenth century.[2] America was a country of high labor costs, in which almost any effort to save labor or use it more intensively was worth considering. The spread of cost accounting techniques and the reports of the growing strength of trade unions underscored the high cost of labor and gave the question of incentive wage payment added importance. Taylor's "differential piece rate" was more stringent than most incentive systems. It required that the shortest possible time for each job

[1] *Transactions of the American Society of Mechanical Engineers* (hereafter cited as *"Trans. ASME"*), XVI (1895), 856.

[2] Taylor's paper was reprinted by the American Economic Association as "The Adjustment of Wages to Efficiency," *Economic Studies*, I (June, 1896), along with those of F. A. Halsey and H. R. Towne which had been presented at earlier meetings of the ASME.

be computed and fixed. If the worker finished the job in this time he was given a good price per piece. If he failed, he was given a rate so low that the "lazy or inferior" worker could not hold the job. Taylor's piece rate was a carrot-and-stick device to make the laborer work harder and more quickly. The increased work speed rewarded the worker with a higher total wage, and the low cost per piece provided the employer with larger profits. Thus it made "each workman's interest the same as that of his employers."[3]

The differential piece rate, Taylor asserted, would root out the demoralizing effects which attended other wage systems. Other systems allowed or encouraged loafing and led to deceit between workers and employers. Fixing an honest day's work would put an end to all that.[4] Hard work, Taylor believed, built inner strength. From "A Piece-Rate System," the first public statement of his ideas on management, to the last statement of his program, twenty years later, Taylor always opened his lectures with a discussion of "soldiering" — the worker's loafing on the job. The factory, for Taylor, was not only an instrument for the production of goods and profits, it was also a moral gymnasium for the exercise of character.[5]

Yet morality worked hand in hand with science. Taylor proposed that an "honest day's work" be fixed scientifically, by methods free from human bias. This immediately set Taylor's piece rate system apart from all others. At first Taylor tried to calculate a day's heavy labor by "how many foot-pounds of work a man could do in a day."[6] But he discovered that there was no relation between work measured in foot-pounds and its tiring effects on the laborer. He then hit on the idea of breaking the job down into its "elementary operations" and timing each operation by use of a stop watch and a first-rate worker. He hoped to develop a handbook which would list the "elementary operations" from which the correct speed of any job could be reckoned. To get an "honest day's work" did not require the selection of only honest workers or urging the workers to honesty. "If a man won't do what is right," Taylor

[3] Taylor, in *Trans. ASME*, XVI (1895), 856, 864.
[4] Ibid., pp. 861–62.
[5] See, for example, Frederick W. Taylor, "Competitive Profit Sharing: Speech before the Boston Efficiency Club," *Greater Efficiency: Journal of the Efficiency Society*, III (March, 1914), 28.
[6] Frederick W. Taylor, *The Principles of Scientific Management* (New York: Harper, 1911), 55.

said, "*make* him." [7] The differential piece rate was an attempt to make the worker do what was right. It meant the transfer of the category of wages from economics to physics — from a realm (as then understood) beyond direct control to one where most things could be manipulated.

"Scientific rate-fixing" had ramifications throughout the factory. The speed at which the laborer worked was inextricably tied to the kind and the quality of his tools, the shop procedures, and even the over-all organization of the factory. If one were really to fix an honest day's work "scientifically," then the entire plant had to be brought under control. In retrospect, Taylor's reorganization of the factory can be seen as logically following from his notion of "scientific rate-fixing." Yet clearly, logic alone was not enough to draw him on. For this logic led through a long series of flops and frustrations that afforded much bitterness and derision. It led to exacting experiments on machine belting which extended over a period of nine years, and to between thirty and fifty thousand experiments on metal cutting over a period of twenty-six years. It led to schemes which often seemed unprofitable or beyond good sense. The logic is clear, but to understand the relentless drive behind that logic, the vehemence which sometimes made even Taylor's friends uncomfortable, we must take a closer look at Taylor the man. [8]

Frederick Winslow Taylor was born into Proper Philadelphia. The Winslows and the Taylors were important families in America as far back as the seventeenth and eighteenth centuries. The Philadelphia branches were Quaker, but even before Frederick was born Quakerism had become a faded and parochial creed to many of its followers. Frederick's mother, Emily Taylor, took up more ardent beliefs. She was interested in transcendentalism and active in the anti-slavery and women's suffrage movements. When she broke her ties to the Society of Friends she chose Unitarianism, the communion of the high-born and high-minded, as her religion. [9]

[7] Frank Barkley Copley, *Frederick Winslow Taylor: Father of Scientific Management* (New York: Harper, 1923), I, 183. Emphasis in the original.

[8] Copley, I, 243; Frederick W. Taylor, "On the Art of Cutting Metals," *Trans. ASME*, XXVIII (1907), 35.

[9] "Testimony of Frederick W. Taylor," *Hearings of the Commission on Industrial Relations (April 13, 1914)*, U.S., 64th Cong., 1st Sess., Senate Doc., 415 (Ser. Vol. 6929), p. 810; Copley, I, 40–41, 50.

Franklin Taylor, Frederick's father, was a lawyer who devoted himself to literature, languages, and the good works of charity rather than the practice of law. It is unexpected and yet suggestive that the father of the man who tried to revolutionize the world of work was a leisured gentleman. Emily Taylor was said to have had "the stronger personality." She was blunt and exacting; Franklin was sensitive and delicate. He loved poetry; she did not. Frederick wrote that his father had a "soft, mild manner and a gentleness which was almost that of a woman." And the son often showed concern with his own manliness. Though young Taylor was noted for his full-dress female impersonations in the skits at the Philadelphia Cricket Club, he wished that he were bigger and more brawny. He studiously developed the knack of cussing, and was terribly earnest in sports.[10]

Young Fred was an obedient son, likable but rigid and intense. One of his childhood friends remembered that Fred's quarrels with his playmates often stemmed from his insistence on subjecting their games to strict and elaborate rules. He was disturbed by oppressive dreams and decided that they were related to sleeping on his back. Taylor therefore made a harness of straps and wooden points which he wore to bed at night and which would wake him when he turned. This was but one of his nightmare-fighting machines. Throughout his life he used many devices to force himself to sleep in a sitting position.[11]

Many who knew Taylor commented on what his biographer called his "nervous disposition" and what his doctor described as his "extraordinary intense nature." Taylor's youthful pictures seem to show much feminine sweetness. Yet the man who looks out from the later photographs usually adopts an even more brisk and belligerent stance than was customary in the scowling pictures of that day. There is something anxious and obstructed-looking about the man. Taylor gave many signs of deep emotional turmoil. He would turn white at any talk of illness or death. He suffered from recurrent sleeplessness and indigestion, and even in sport found it hard to relax. He worked at play.[12] At one time he appealed to his

[10] Copley, I, 44–48, 89–91; II, 215–23.
[11] *Ibid.*, I, 56–59.
[12] At sports, where non-professionals find room for the spontaneous, impulsive, offhand way, Taylor created a domain of discipline, calcula-

doctor to help him stop thinking, to get rid of the thoughts that were oppressing him.[13]

Taylor's program for systematizing the factory should be seen in terms of his attempt to systematize most things, including himself. Order can serve to curb impulse and to limit hazards and perhaps pain. The machines and machine-like organizations with which Taylor busied himself resembled human beings in their capabilities, but were more malleable and predictable and were exempt from human feeling and hurt. Taylor's frenzy for order was the counterpart of the disorder within him.

Taylor's very entry into industry was linked to a psychological crisis. The family had planned that he should be a lawyer like his father. He was sent to Phillips Exeter to prepare for college, but toward the end of his studies developed unusual headaches and eye troubles. At this point, young Taylor wanted to give up law and study medicine at Yale or perhaps engineering at Rensselaer Polytechnic Institute. After a long family conference, however, he took the Harvard entrance examination and passed with honors. Yet his eyesight soon became so poor that he could not even complete the work at Exeter. After a few month's rest at home, Taylor went to work as an apprentice patternmaker, a job which called for the reading of complicated mechanical drawings. He persisted in this apprenticeship though his eye troubles soon disappeared. Clearly, this troublous period of impaired vision hinged as much upon problems of the mind as of the body.[14]

tion, and planning. Meticulous experiments produced a peculiar spoon-shaped racket to perfect his tennis game; a uniform synthetic soil to replace all natural earth for more dependable putting greens; a weird assortment of golf clubs and ungainly golf positions to better his golf scores. (Taylor's "highly unique" two-handled putter was banned from the links by the United States Golf Association long before the American Federation of Labor banned the stop watch from the arsenals.) Copley, I, 143; II, chaps. iv and v.

[13] Ibid., I, 59, 75, 79; II, 170, 399, 438.

[14] Emily Taylor to F. W. Taylor, Sept. 27, 1873; Emily Taylor to F. W. Taylor, [undated], 1873; Emily Taylor to F. W. Taylor, Thursday [no month given] 26, 1873; Franklin Taylor to F. W. Taylor, April 24, 1873; Franklin Taylor to F. W. Taylor, Sept. 19, 1873; Franklin Taylor to F. W. Taylor, Sept. 25, 1873; Frederick Winslow Taylor Collection, Stevens Institute of Technology, Hoboken, N.J. Copley, I, 69, 74–76. This story of his entry into industry was very important to Taylor. Although the clipped autobiographies that he wrote for Who's Who from 1906 to 1914 vary over these eight years in important particulars, the account of his

The decision not to become a lawyer might plausibly be linked to the psychological difficulties of following in his father's footsteps. However, the decision to enter industry as a laborer, once the legal career was abandoned, suggests the influence of his mother. Emily Taylor presided over his early education and the shaping of his first precepts and pursuits. His ascetic and use-minded temperament mirrored hers. Like his mother, Taylor identified himself with the Unitarian Church. Though in later years he assumed an agnostic position, he remained a member of that church until his death. Of the many attitudes and beliefs which passed from mother to son, by far the most important was the general tendency to demand much of oneself.[15]

Many children of the well-to-do found the work-centered morality of the second half of the nineteenth century menacing. Riches and ease, it was believed, arrested the development of character. The achievements of one generation seemed to threaten destruction of the next.[16] Henry Ward

leaving Phillips Exeter because of impaired eyesight is prominent throughout. Its very inclusion seems a little odd, since a simple catalogue of facts without whys and wherefores is the accepted form. Moreover, this public (and perhaps private) explanation of his career was not fixed before 1906. In the same year that his first self-portrait for *Who's Who* appeared, Taylor, in testimony before a congressional committee, repeatedly described himself as having entered his apprenticeship after coming out of college. The discrepancy is revealing, in light of Taylor's pervading literal-mindedness — a quality which even made it impossible for him to tell the conventional fictitious anecdotes so important to the public speaker. Frederick W. Taylor, "Testimony before the Congressional Committee Hearings on the Littauer Bill" (1906), pp. 4, 6, 16, manuscript in the Taylor Collection.

[15] Copley, I, 70–72. It would be tempting to trace this predilection back to modes of thought in Quakerism — secularized by the mid-nineteenth century. Max Weber in his classic study, *The Protestant Ethic and the Spirit of Capitalism* (trans. Talcott Parsons [New York: Charles Scribner's Sons, 1958], pp. 144 ff.), devotes a good deal of space to the Quakers in order to prove this point. Frederick B. Tolles, in *Meeting House and Counting House: The Quaker Merchants of Colonial Philadelphia, 1682–1773* (Chapel Hill: University of North Carolina Press, 1948), pp. 56 ff., seems to support Weber. However, a close examination of both books suggests that "worldly asceticism" developed alongside Quaker holiness rather than within it. In religion the Puritan demanded of himself, but the Quaker seems to have invited his soul.

[16] Kenneth S. Lynn, *The Dream of Success: A Study of the Modern American Imagination* (Boston: Little, Brown, 1955). Mr. Lynn deals extensively with the problem of the "second generation" in the novels of David Graham Phillips, Frank Norris, and Robert Herrick. See especially the discussion of Phillips' novel, *The Second Generation*, pp. 137 ff.

Beecher told his wealthy congregation that their business losses might be their children's gain. "How blessed, then, is the stroke of disaster which sets the children free, and gives them over to the hard but kind bosom of Poverty, who says to them 'Work!' and, working, makes them men."[17] Carnegie's proposal for returning the "surplus" wealth to society seemed too radical an answer. A professional career for the children of the rich was more acceptable. When Taylor's way to the legal profession was blocked, however, he was given over to a mock poverty with the understanding that he would work his way to the top.

Of course, Taylor did just that. He became an apprentice patternmaker at the age of eighteen and promptly raced up the familiar ladder of success. After his apprenticeship he went to work at Midvale Steel Company as a journeyman machinist and in six years was chief engineer. He went on to independent consulting work, the discovery of high-speed steel, and the presidency of the American Society of Mechanical Engineers. After he retired from active engineering, at forty-five, he often described his accomplishment in public lectures on success and education. He extolled "the real monotonous grind which trains character" and directed the young man to go out of his way, if necessary, to find it. He condemned the "kindergarten plan of interesting and amusing children," the lax college discipline, and the university elective system. Every student, whether intending to be a minister or a mechanical engineer, should leave college at the end of the freshman year and spend at least one year "in actual hard work . . . under careful and constant supervision." He preached the strenuous life of the workshop and foundry. The Midvale Steel Company was to Taylor what the Big Horn Mountains were to Theodore Roosevelt.[18]

[17] Quoted in Irvin G. Wyllie, *The Self-made Man in America: The Myth of Rags to Riches* (New Brunswick, N.J.: Rutgers University Press, 1954), p. 22.

[18] Frederick W. Taylor, "Why Manufacturers Dislike College Graduates," *Sibley Journal of Engineering*, XXIV (1909–10), 198–99, 202, "Success: A Lecture to Young Men Entering Business," *Bulletin of the Taylor Society* (hereafter cited as "*Bull. Taylor Soc.*"), XI (April, 1926), 76, "A Comparison of University and Industrial Discipline and Methods," *Stevens Institute Indicator*, XXIV (Jan. 1907), 41, and "Ich Dien," address before the Harvard Engineering Society of New York, February, 1908, manuscript in the Taylor Collection.

It must be noted that Taylor's rise did not strictly follow the rules of Ragged Dick. When young Taylor left the shop after a day's work he went home to Germantown, one of the most exclusive sections of Philadelphia. He was probably the only laborer in America with a membership in the local cricket club. Because he could work for little or no money, he moved quickly through his apprenticeships. During the early years of Taylor's rise at Midvale, one of the principal owners was a friend and neighbor. His social connections undoubtedly gave him entry to places otherwise inaccessible.[19]

Taylor brought to the factory the type of sustained and methodical thinking derived from the formal academic world he had left. In his early days at Midvale he felt the need of increasing his scientific education and took home-study courses in mathematics and physics. Through an arrangement with Stevens Institute of Technology, he planned a course of study which brought him a degree in Mechanical Engineering. Taylor became a member of the newly formed American Society of Mechanical Engineers and found his way into a milieu within which he developed his ideas. The impulse toward order came from within; the imperatives of hard work came from his education and upbringing; and the specific content of his work owed much to the profession in which Taylor found himself.[20]

Before the middle years of the nineteenth century, the direct influence of contemporary science on engineering practice was quite uneven. Some of America's most prominent mechanical engineers, even in the last decades of that century, were still men of little or no scientific training who had happened into apprenticeships at various engine works and evinced a knack for machine building. However, the scientific and mathematical achievements of such technologists as William Rankine and Rudolph Clausius soon gave the mechanical engineers with scientific and mathematical training such a decided advantage that they, in effect, blocked entry into the field for most engineers who were not graduates of the engineering colleges. This brought important changes in the social composition of the engineering fellowship. For a college education was often costly and required, even in the

---

[19] Copley, I, 88, 117.
[20] Frederick W. Taylor, "Letter to Morris L. Cooke," *Bull. Taylor Soc.*, II (December, 1916), 6.

state colleges which were nominally free, a sum of leisure which in itself was an expensive luxury. The elevation which science provided and the new sources of recruitment which it demanded converted mechanical engineering from what had been often considered a trade to what was now more often called a profession.[21]

The mechanical engineers of the late nineteenth century strained for the prestige of the traditional "learned professions" and took much of the pre-capitalist professional ethic as their own. In appraising motive, manner, and accomplishment in their new profession, they often looked to standards which stood outside the market place. Within their profession, the engineers frowned on advertising, urged *esprit de corps* rather than competition, insisted that prerogatives and prestige should derive from proven competence, and proclaimed responsibility to the social good as a solemn duty.[22]

This professionalism was invested with an aura of independence. The engineer apparently would not simply do his client's bidding. He saw himself as standing closer to the doctor who gave the patient what he needed than to the merchant who gave the customer what he wanted.[23] Those who

[21] On the cost of a college education in the last quarter of the nineteenth century see Charles F. Thwing, *American Colleges: Their Students and Work* (New York: G. P. Putnam's Sons, 1883), chap. ii, and *The American College in American Life* (New York: G. P. Putnam's Sons, 1897), chap. vii. An interesting study of high-school education in a later period which has important implications for college education in an earlier period is George Sylvester Counts, *The Selective Character of American Secondary Education* (Chicago: University of Chicago Press, 1922). For the contrast between the older shop-trained engineers and the new college-bred engineers see H. F. J. Porter, "How Can the Present Status of the Engineering Profession Be Improved?" in *Trans. ASME*, XIV (1892–93), 487–90, 501; Robert Allison, "The Old and the New," *ibid.*, XVI (1894–95), 742–61; Frederick W. Taylor, "Laws vs. Public Opinion as a Basis of Management," lecture delivered before the YMCA of Philadelphia, Oct. 12, 1914, Taylor Collection.

[22] Robert H. Thurston, "President's Inaugural Address," *Trans. ASME*, I (1880) 13, and "The Mechanical Engineer — His Work and His Policy," *ibid.*, IV (1882–83), p. 78; George H. Babcock, "The Engineer: His Commission and His Achievements," *ibid.*, IX (1887), p. 23; Oberlin Smith, "The Engineer as a Scholar and a Gentleman," *ibid.*, XII (1891), p. 42; Porter, *loc. cit.*, pp. 496, 499.

[23] William H. Bryan, "The Relation between the Purchaser, the Engineer, and the Manufacturer," *Trans. ASME*, XIX (1898), 686–99. The engineer who was an employee rather than a consultant was in a more difficult position. However, he did not figure prominently in the discussions of professionalism in the nineties.

enlarged upon the ideals of the engineering profession often designated the engineers as a new industrial intelligentsia, standing between capital and labor, and peculiarly fitted to resolve the nation's social conflicts.[24]

The lofty temperament of the professional ethic seems particularly to have appealed to many of the engineers who came to the field from established old-stock families like Taylor's. Men of this sort provided the American Society of Mechanical Engineers with much of its initial leadership.[25] They demanded that engineering be esteemed and influential. Of course, there were other, less exalted, aspects of the enthusiasm for professionalism. The fixing of minimum fees and the elimination of jurisdictional disputes among the various branches of engineering were also considered important steps toward improving the status of the profession.[26] Economic gain itself was never condemned; only grasp and greed. Acquisition was a just reward of hard work and character. The mechanical engineer of the late nineteenth century often spoke of his own reward as a "competence" — an adequacy of means for living comfortably, but without excess. The engineer's task was not "the piling of gold and silver in treasury vaults, and not the aggregation of fictitious values in Wall Street," wrote the first president of the American Society of Mechanical Engineers, but the production of "durable

[24] Thurston, "The Mechanical Engineer . . . ," p. 96; Porter, *loc. cit.*, p. 496.

[25] Although a comprehensive survey of the membership of the ASME was not possible, there were many scattered indications that the Society in the nineties served as a meeting place for a membership from the lower middle class and a leadership from well-to-do old families. See, for example, Smith, *loc. cit.*, p. 42. For more definite proof of the lower-middle-class origins of the majority of engineers in the decades that followed see Edwin T. Layton, "The American Engineering Profession and the Idea of Social Responsibility" (Ph.D. dissertation, University of California at Los Angeles, 1956), pp. 16–18. This is a helpful study covering the years 1900–1940.

[26] Porter, *loc. cit.*, pp. 494–96, 510. This aspect of professionalism became more conspicuous in the first decades of the twentieth century. See the discussion in Vol. LXIX of *Engineering News*: "The Status of the Engineer" (Jan. 2, 1913), pp. 34–35; L. B. Stillwell and Samuel Whinery, "The Status of the Engineering Profession" (Jan. 23, 1913), 155–58; "More Discussion of the Engineering Profession" (Jan. 30, 1913), pp. 221–22; "The Status of the Engineer" (April 24, 1913), pp. 878–79; "The Problem of Protecting the Younger Members of the Engineering Profession" (June 5, 1913), 1189–90.

materials" essential to the comforts of mankind.[27] The engineer was in the market place, but not completely of it. This was true of his day-to-day work as well as his broader social outlook.

Efficiency, the unifying concept of mechanical engineering, lives a double life — having one meaning in mechanics and another in commerce. Mechanical efficiency is an output-input ratio of matter or energy, whereas commercial efficiency is the relation between price and cost. Occasionally, these efficiencies are opposed. Taylor's first paper before the American Society of Mechanical Engineers concerned just such a conflict. Comparing the efficiency of two gases in the steel-making process, he found that the one which yielded the greatest heat per unit did not yield the greatest heat per dollar.[28] The solution was straightforward. In the event of such a divergency, profit obligations prevailed and the mechanically less efficient gas was used. But at times, this decision was made with some suggestion of discomfort.

The intellectual fascination of a scientifically trained mind with the skillful adaptation of material means to ends was quite a distinct and separate thing from the profit to be produced. Costs and prices varied with time and place and were dependent upon apparently accidental circumstances, while matter and energy could be dealt with in accordance with enduring scientific laws. Science had a luster all its own. For a generation in which most people believed that progress was written into the laws of the universe, true and good often seemed to be indistinguishable. Science, which was a more certain form of the true, could also appear as a more rigorous form of the good. The very fruitfulness of science seemed to substantiate this. Furthermore, for the engineers, science was the passkey into their new profession. It is not surprising, therefore, that the problems of mechanical efficiency and the skills employed in their solution afforded considerable prestige. "Economy may be taught even if the material costs nothing," declared a speaker at the same meeting where Tay-

[27] Robert H. Thurston, "Our Progress in Mechanical Engineering," *Trans. ASME*, II (1881), 451.

[28] Frederick W. Taylor, "The Relative Value of Water Gas and Gas from the Siemens Producer for Melting in the Open-Hearth Furnace," *Trans. ASME*, VII (1886) 669 ff.

lor delivered his first paper. "We can teach intrinsic values without meddling with market values. The former are permanent, the latter fluctuating. . . ."[29]

Nevertheless, in the day-to-day work of the engineer, more clearly than in the presidential addresses at conventions, the demands of the market place prevailed. If the better mousetrap which the engineer built was unprofitable, hardly a soul would beat a path to his door. The constant awareness of the commercial limitations of engineering was essential to success within the profession. And it was with a certain grimness that the engineers who seemed to believe that engineering could be practiced without regard to money values were condemned. "These men may be ingenious inventors or designers, they may be great mathematicians, they may even be eminent as scientists, but they are not engineers."[30] On at least two issues, this conflict between the scientific and business emphasis broke out into the open. These were the question of the adoption of the metric system and the problem of the engineer's attitude toward conservation.

The metric system had various attractions for the scientist. Its smaller unit was more useful for exact measurement and was well on the way toward being internationally accepted.[31] Equally attractive was the fact that the metric system mirrored in the realm of measurement the unified picture of the

[29] Calvin M. Woodward, "The Training of a Dynamic Engineer in Washington University, St. Louis," *Trans. ASME*, VII (1886), 754. The vigorous assertion of these "intrinsic values" was typical of those engineers interested in Ostwald's "energetics." This doctrine placed "the physical idea of energy" at the basis of things. It carried this analysis to the point where "the measure of culture is the efficiency of the transformation of raw materials to humanly valuable purposes." Henry Hess, "Energetics and Cultural History: A Chapter of Ostwald's Philosophy," *Scientific American Supplement*, LXXIII (May 11, 1912), 290–91. Ostwald was popular with some of the Taylorites, and F. W. Taylor claimed an extensive correspondence with the famous scientist.

[30] Alexander C. Humphreys, "The Engineer as a Citizen," *Stevens Institute Indicator*, XXIV (January, 1907), 7. Humphreys was a national leader in the cooking gas industry and president of Stevens Institute of Technology. Under his leadership Stevens shifted away from the academic emphasis of its previous president Dr. Henry A. Morton, a chemistry professor, toward a business-conscious orientation. John T. Cunningham, "Versatile Engineers: Stevens Institute of Technology," *Newark Sunday News*, Jan. 1956, p. 16.

[31] William Hallock and Herbert T. Wade, *Outlines of the Evolution of Weights and Measures and the Metric System* (New York: Macmillan, 1906), pp. 140, 161.

world that was presented by the physical sciences. Like science, the metric system presented simple and elegant relations between the different kinds of units and allowed the scientist to interconvert mass, length, and capacity. The unity of science seemed to make intelligible, and the metric system to reflect, the unity of reality itself.

At the very first meeting of the American Society of Mechanical Engineers, a prominent member delivered a paper attacking the metric system. He insisted that it was unwise to tamper with the English standard because of its central position in the system of interchangeable parts so important to American industry. The speaker personified American industry's huge investment in the inch: he was manager and later president of the machine works whose system of screw sizes prevailed in America. The Society endorsed his view.[32]

Metric reform, however, could not be turned aside so easily. It seemed to have a fascination for engineers. The issue was debated back and forth again in 1885, in 1902 and in 1906. The arguments and the results, however, remained much the same. The "scientific enthusiasts . . . captivated by the nicety of the thing," were amply denounced. And the picture which was drawn of catastrophic cost and confusion which would result from conversion to the meter was admonition enough to secure a rejection of metric reform proposals.

Conservation ideas found a more favorable reception at the meetings of the American Society of Mechanical Engineers. Conservation presented a problem quite similar to Taylor's juggling of material and economic efficiencies in his first paper. The process which yielded the maximum coal per mine, for example, often did not yield the greatest amount of coal per dollar. Conservation reformers, nevertheless, urged

[32] Coleman Sellers, "The Metric System — Is It Wise To Introduce It into Our Machine Shops?" *Trans. ASME*, I (1880), 45. One opponent of the metric system presented this view with yet broader sweep: "These [the English units] are so identified with all our measurements and the welfare and protection of society and property, that to disturb them seems to me to be as criminal as the burning of the great library at Alexandria." Frederick Fraley, "Mechanics and the Progress of Mechanical Science," *ibid.*, III (1892), p. 219. In a referendum ballot of the Society taken in 1881, approximately 20 per cent of those answering favored legislation which would promote the adoption of the metric system, *ibid.*, II (1881), p. 9. In a similar ballot taken in 1903, 20 per cent again favored such legislation. *Ibid.*, XXIV (1902–3), 855.

the elevation of physical values above market values.[33] The particular business ties of the mechanical engineers were not as directly challenged by the conservation programs as they had been by the proposals for conversion to the metric system.[34] Moreover, the social and moral interest which the conservationists aroused in their cause gave it a compelling force which metrics never had. The appeal to the social responsibility of the engineer (of which the advocates of professionalism spoke so much and so often) helped to lift conservation ideas out of the class of dangerous scientific distractions.

Official representatives of the American Society of Mechanical Engineers attended Roosevelt's conservation conference in 1908 and approved its resolutions. The Society devoted a meeting to the subject and listened patiently to exhortations that engineers must direct themselves to "the larger interests of humanity." The engineering societies must fall in with the conservation idea, the Society president declared. Perhaps the doctrine of government "appropriation and beneficial use" was needed as an antidote to "the uncontrolled greed for gain." However, the engineer had to build

[33] This was especially true of the technical men close to the leadership of the conservation movement. There were three distinct elements in the conservation movement: the technical men, the resource users, and the broad reform-minded public. When mechanical and commercial efficiency could be made to coincide, technical men and resource users could work together; when mechanical and commercial efficiency were in conflict, these two groups usually parted company. For the reform-minded public, conservation was frequently translated into a preachment of national thrift and an attack upon the plutocrats and commercialism. See Samuel P. Hays, *Conservation and the Gospel of Efficiency: The Progressive Conservation Movement, 1890–1920* (Cambridge, Mass.: Harvard University Press, 1959), pp. 30–35, 74–77, 141–46. For popular conservationism see J. Leonard Bates, "Fulfilling American Democracy: The Conservation Movement, 1907–1921," *Mississippi Valley Historical Review*, VLIV (June, 1957), 29; Arthur Henry Chamberlain, *Thrift and Conservation* (Philadelphia: J. B. Lippincott, 1919).

[34] The various engineering societies reacted differently to these issues. Civil engineers, led by the Boston Society of Civil Engineers, generally favored metric legislation. Among the engineers, the strongest opposition to conservation came from members of the American Institute of Mining Engineers. See R. W. Raymond, "The Conservation of Natural Resources By Legislation," *Conservation of Natural Resources: Meeting of Engineers Called Jointly by the A.S.C.E., A.I.M.E., A.S.M.E., A.I.E.E.* (New York: Published jointly by the societies, 1909), pp. 20 ff.

and operate works so as to compete with others in the same line. The crucial test remained in the cost per unit of output. Therefore "the real work of the engineer, in the field of conservation, will be measured by the ability of the works designed by him to compete in the markets of the world." The engineer supported conservation but with conspicuous qualifications and confusions.[35]

This was the situation of the mechanical engineer of this era — he could not feel completely at ease either as a scientist or as a businessman. Though the values of business prevailed, the values of science, especially in questions of broader scope, occasionally provided a counterforce which left the engineer off-balance.

At first glance it would appear that Taylor made common cause with those who stressed the exigencies of the commercial enterprise of which technical engineering was but a part. This is not at all surprising, for during those very important years at Midvale his close personal ties to its owners surely made him aware of the interests and needs of a business venture. At the time when the metric controversy was provoking tempers at the meetings of the ASME, he dutifully testified against a law which would have required metric units of all contractors for the government. He was particularly interested in the early papers on management problems and presented two management papers of his own. He cautioned young engineering students to "remember that the kind of engineering that is most wanted is that which saves money; that your employer is first of all in business to make money and not to do great and brilliant things."[36]

Yet he did not arrive at this outlook without struggle, and, once attained, it was not easily held. The occasional tug-of-war within engineering between science and business found its counterpart within Taylor. Though he testified against the metric-system bill he admitted that he had earlier favored it, now thought it should be introduced voluntarily, and used

[35] M. L. Holman, "The Conservation Idea as Applied to the American Society of Mechanical Engineers," *Trans. ASME*, XXX, (1908), 25, 616.

[36] "Statement of Mr. Fred W. Taylor in Congressional Committee Hearings on the Littau[e]r Bill," 1906, pp. 5, 33, Taylor Collection; Frederick W. Taylor, "Success," *Bull. Taylor Soc.*, XI (February, 1926), 74.

metrics himself. He also showed sympathy for conservation principles.[37] When he lectured the engineering students about their employers being in business to make money and not to do great things, he was probably lecturing to himself as well. After he left Midvale, Taylor frequently got into difficulty with his employers because of his habit of "making money fly." [38] In a letter to a friend he confessed that if he had followed his personal inclinations he would have given a greater part of his time to invention and scientific investigation. Taylor loved the quiet of the laboratory and the study and often became worried by the diverse and clashing activities of the shop. His biographer tells us that "he seemed always in danger of reverting to the pure engineer." Yet Taylor is important to us precisely because he did not revert; rather, he thrust the laboratory and the study directly into the realm of the factory. But there was always something ambiguous about this intrusion.[39]

This ambiguity was implicit in Taylor's first presentation of his ideas on management. The discussion which followed his paper, "A Piece-Rate System," was lively and generally sympathetic; yet Taylor was disappointed. The method of "scientific rate-fixing," which he considered its most important feature, was almost completely ignored.[40] This was a portent for the future. What Taylor thought to be the crux of the matter, his ever widening audience often felt to be simply a tendency to carry things to crazy extremes.

The very notion of a completely integrated, scientific system for the factory was a distraction. The truly "scientific" standard for "an honest day's work" (the point of maximum mechanical efficiency of the human machine) could not be

[37] For Taylor's views on metrics and for the similarly equivocal opinions of the previous president of the ASME see Taylor's "Statement on the Littau[e]r Bill," pp. 4, 5; and John R. Freeman to F. W. Taylor, March 20, 1906, Taylor Collection. Taylor's views on conservation may be gleaned from Copley, I, 380; and *Trans. ASME*, XXVIII (1906), 545.

[38] Copley, I, 380. It is interesting to note that Taylor's facts-of-life speech which insisted upon the employer's desire to make money and not to do great things ends on a different note: "But back of this each engineer should have, at all times, the hope, the ambition, the determination to do great things. . . ." Taylor, "Success," p. 75.

[39] Frederick W. Taylor to Morris L. Cooke, Dec. 2, 1910, in *Bull. Taylor Soc.*, II (December, 1916), 6; Copley, I, 149.

[40] *Trans. ASME*, XVI (1894–95), 902–3.

established and maintained unless the entire factory was systematized. Yet most business firms, as Taylor himself once noted, need only be more efficient than their competitors.[41] This was one of the reasons that businessmen preferred efficiency stunts, devices, and mechanisms to a complete system of scientific management. The adoption of a complete system was often not the most profitable use of investment capital. Here, unlike the discussion of which gas to use in steelmaking, commercial efficiency did not automatically come first. The system should be adopted, Taylor's most orthodox disciple asserted, even when it might not be a paying investment.[42]

Though Taylor and his followers directed their attention toward business, they seemed to be looking beyond it. Their occupation was management, but their preoccuption often was "science."

The sources and supports of Taylor's program for the factory were manifold. His own personality furnished the initial thrust. The morality of hard work, in which Taylor had been sedulously schooled, played an important role. And of course, the new profession of engineering, with its occasional dissonance between the modes of science and business, provided a persistent influence. This dissonance was responsible, in part, for the limited appeal that Taylor's system had for businessmen, as well as some of its particular attractiveness for many progressive reformers.

[41] Frederick W. Taylor, *Shop Management* (New York: Harper, 1911), p. 19.
[42] Carl G. Barth, "Discussion," *Bull. Taylor Soc.*, II (January, 1917), 25.

• CHAPTER II

Taylor's Factory World

In applying "science" to what had been considered strictly business problems, Taylor overstepped the interest of many of his fellow engineers — both those of technical and those of commercial bent. In 1910 the ASME shelved a paper on management by Taylor on the grounds that the membership was not interested in papers of this sort and that there was nothing new in it.[1] This work subsequently became world-famous under the title, *The Principles of Scientific Management.*[2]

Of course, Taylor was not alone in the study of management. In fact, the placing of Taylor's program against the background of contemporary ideas in this field helps to emphasize his special accomplishment. There were at least two usually distinct groups that devoted themselves to these matters: the "systemizers" and the proponents of "industrial betterment." "Industrial betterment" or "industrial welfare" was an uneven and varying mixture of philanthropy, humanitarianism, and commercial shrewdness. Some of its outstanding exponents were ministers seeking redemptive agencies supplementary to the Word of God. Pullman's model town of the 1880's was an early industrial betterment venture in America, but the "practical religion" of John H. Patterson's National Cash Register Company soon dominated the field and became the archetype of almost all the programs that

[1] Frederick W. Taylor to Alexander C. Humphreys, Oct. 22, 1910, Frederick Winslow Taylor Collection, Stevens Institute of Technology Library, Hoboken, N.J.

[2] There are translations of *The Principles of Scientific Management* (New York: Harper, 1911) in Chinese, Dutch, French, German, Italian, Japanese, Russian, Spanish, and Swedish in the Taylor Collection.

followed. One of the important aims of these schemes was to prevent "labor troubles" and get better work from the workman. This was to be accomplished by providing lunchrooms, bathhouses, hospital clinics, safety training, recreational facilities, thrift clubs, benefit funds, profit-sharing plans, and Ruskinesque garden cities. Industrial betterment proclaimed that human happiness was a business asset.[3]

The "systemizers" were a diverse group of accountants, engineers, and works managers who rose to some prominence in the last decades of the nineteenth century, along with the growing size of American factories and business enterprises. The systemizers attacked improvisation in business and taught the profitability of orderly arrangements. "The object of modern administrative organization," wrote one of the leaders in the field, "is to readjust the balance of responsibilities disturbed by the expansion of industrial operations, and to enable central control to be restored in its essential features." [4] The literature of system leaned heavily upon analogies to the human body, the machine, and the military. The body and the machine usually illustrated the need for close integration within the factory while military organization exemplified hierarchy and discipline. At times, these illustrations passed beyond analogy and appeared as instances of natural laws of organization which justified the hierarchy and discipline of the factory as well as described it. But for the most part the

[3] Some of the better contemporary accounts of the industrial betterment movement are Edwin L. Shuey, *Factory People and Their Employers: How Their Relations Are Made Pleasant and Profitable* (New York: Lentilhon, 1900); E. Wake Cooke, *Betterment* (New York: Frederick A. Stokes, 1906); *Employers' Welfare Work* by Elizabeth Lewis Otey (U.S. Bureau of Labor Bulletin No. 123, "Miscellaneous Series," No. 4 [Washington: U.S. Government Printing Office, 1913]). Among the useful periodical articles are Richard T. Ely, "Industrial Betterment." *Harper's Magazine*, CV (September, 1902), 548; H. F. J. Porter, "The Rationale of the Industrial Betterment Movement," *Cassirer's Magazine*, XXX (August, 1906), 343; F. W. Taylor, "Holbrook Fitz John Porter," *ibid.*, (May, 1906), p. 94. The role of social gospel ministers can be seen in William Howe Tolman, *Industrial Betterment* (New York: Social Service Press, 1900), and Edwin Lee Earp, *The Social Engineer* (New York: Eaton & Mains, 1911). See also Samuel Crowther, *John H. Patterson, Pioneer in Industrial Welfare* (Garden City, N.Y.; Doubleday, Page, 1923), and Henry Eilbirt, "Twentieth-Century Beginnings in Employee Counseling," *Business History Review*, XXXI (Autumn, 1957), 310.

[4] Alexander Hamilton Church, "The Meaning of Commercial Organization," *Engineering Magazine*, XX (December, 1900), 395.

systemizers had no explicit theory, and system usually took the form of a series of maxims based on recent shop practice and business arrangements.[5] Like the industrial betterment advocates, Taylor tied productiveness to morality and well-being. But Taylor stressed one side of the equation (hard work yields morality and well-being), while the advocates of industrial betterment insisted upon the other (morality and well-being yield hard work).[6] Taylor concentrated on the worker in the factory and the industrial betterment advocates on the worker after work. This was more than a difference in interest. It stemmed from contrasting views of the human being and differing moral outlooks. The literature of industrial betterment made much of the goodness which would flower if man were nurtured in a benevolent environment. Against this, Taylor emphasized the weakness in man which must be curbed by the "habit of doing what is right." "Too great liberty," Taylor wrote, "results in a large number of people going wrong who would be right if they had been forced into good habits."[7] Out of this differ-

[5] The first important examples of this kind of systematic thinking about business organization in America appeared in connection with the railroads. See Leland H. Jenks, "Early History of a Railway Organization," *Business History Review*, XXXV (Summer, 1961), 153–79, and "Multiple-Level Organization of a Great Railroad," *ibid.* (Autumn, 1961), pp. 336–43. For the development of "system" in the metalworking industries see Leland H. Jenks, "Early Phases of the Management Movement," *Administrative Science Quarterly*, V (December, 1960), 421–47, and Joseph A. Litterer, "Systematic Management: The Search for Order and Integration," *Business History Review*, XXXV (Winter, 1961), 461–76; the latter has interesting excerpts from the early writings on "system." For the development of "system" at DuPont see Ernest Dale and Charles Meloy, "Hamilton McFarland Barksdale and the Du Pont contributions to Scientific Management," *Business History Review*, XXXVI (Summer, 1962), 127–52. Typical of the manuals on system were J. Slater Lewis, *The Commercial Organization of Factories* (New York: Spon & Chamberlain, 1896); Clinton E. Woods, *Woods' Reports on Industrial Organization, Systemization, and Accounting* (Brooklyn, N.Y.: Clinton E. Woods, 1908); Russell Robb, *Lectures on Organization* (Cambridge, Mass.: Privately printed, 1910). Minna C. Smith, "Reorganizing Industries: A Novel Profession," *World's Work*, V (Dec. 2, 1902), 2872, is suggestive of the public reception given the systemizers. The magazine *System* (later *Magazine of Business*), founded in 1900, devoted its pages to "system" with emphasis on the office.
[6] Taylor, "Shop Management," *Trans. ASME*, XXIV (1902–3), 1454, 1363, 1346–47, and *Principles of Scientific Management*, pp. 71–72.
[7] Frederick W. Taylor to Charles W. Eliot, April 25, 1907, Taylor Collection.

ence came arguments, perplexing to both sides, in which the spokesmen of industrial betterment pursued Taylor and his followers with accusations of "ignoring the human element," while the Taylorites declared that they alone actually paid attention to it.[8]

There was less open controversy with the systemizers. In fact, Taylor often described his own work as "systemizing." He fully accepted the imperatives derived from the division of labor and the expansion of industry — co-ordination, hierarchy, and discipline. Like many of the systemizers, Taylor favored the analogy between the organization and the machine. Taylor was not satisfied, however, simply with an orderly arrangement of parts. He wanted to know how well each component performed its task, and he intended to bring each component "to its highest state of excellence." The usual standard for judging an innovation of the systemizers was whether it paid off in dollars and cents. Though profit was important, Taylor decided that the adequacy of a shop's management frequently was not reflected in the dividends it paid. Science, he thought, could supply a more precise and well-founded standard. First, by way of calculations in footpounds, and later with the aid of his techniques of time and motion studies, Taylor went in search of scientific laws of work to answer the closely related questions of how a job could best be done and how much could be produced. He derived a "science" of shoveling, pig-iron lifting, lathe work, etc., through a controlled variation of the isolated elements in each task.[9] This usually meant the conversion of the task into its physical quantities. Taylor thus passed from commercial to mechanical efficiency.

Taylor's work was more comprehensive and complex than that of most systemizers [10] and writers on industrial better-

[8] For example, see the discussion of scientific management in *Congress of Human Engineering, October 26–28, 1916* ("Ohio State University Bulletins," Vol. XXI, No. 12 [January, 1917]), and the reaction of the members of the Taylor Society to Horace B. Drury's paper which was delivered there, in the *Bulletin of the Taylor Society*, II (November, 1916), 7 ff.

[9] Taylor, "Notes for a Talk on Management Given to Leading Officials of the Bethlehem Steel Co. in the Fall of 1899," Taylor Collection, and "Shop Management," pp. 1341–42, 1424–45.

[10] Perhaps Alexander Hamilton Church, an early writer on "system" and a critic of Taylor's work, is something of an exception here. Church's "functional" classification of business organization was surely comprehen-

ment. He posed questions, explicitly and by implication, which were beyond the bounds of their inquiries. He developed a system of factory polity with an image of the worker and a shop hierarchy which referred directly to his science of work.

Taylor's image of the worker had within it a personal as well as a more generalized component. Copley tells us that he deliberately adopted "much of the culture of working people" in protest against the overrefinement and effeminacy of polite society. When Harvard invited him to lecture on scientific management he shocked his audience by sprinkling his talk with a good number of cusswords from the shop. He would bring a steelworker as his dinner guest to Philadelphia's plush Hotel Bellevue-Stratford and also warn college students that there were first-class mechanics who were their mental equals. But if he rattled the genteel by proclaiming the virtues and virility of workers, when he confronted the working man, it was usually as a boss.[11]

The worker was like everyone else but also quite different. His motives were the ordinary motives of men (that is, middle-class motives), but his abilities were usually of a more limited order. When Taylor discussed the incentives which brought special effort from the worker, he drew upon

---

sive. In fact, it was exhaustive, though its categories overlapped and were probably fruitless. Like a number of other systemizers, Church aimed at a system of classification which was not "arbitrary or accidental" but "really fundamental." With this system he proposed to diagnose and cure business ailments by isolating and treating the particular business "functions" which were unsound. Church took his comprehensive view of business organization from the position of topmost official, while Taylor usually looked out on the organization from the "tool point" in the process of production. A. Hamilton Church, "Has 'Scientific Management' Science?" *American Machinist*, XXXV (July 20, 1911), 108–12; A. Hamilton Church and L. P. Alford, "The Principles of Management," *ibid.*, XXXVI (May 30, 1912), 857–61; A. Hamilton Church, "Practical Principles of Rational Management," *Engineering Magazine*, XLIV (January, 1912), 487–94, and *The Science and Practice of Management* (New York: Engineering Magazine Co., 1914) ; Joseph A. Litterer, "Alexander Hamilton Church and the Development of Modern Management," *Business History Review*, XXXV (Summer, 1961), 211–25.

[11] Frank Barkley Copley, *Frederick W. Taylor: Father of Scientific Management* (New York: Harper, 1923), I, 90–92, 158–64, 174–76, 323–24, II, 297; H. B. Drury, "Scientific Management and Progress," *Bull. Taylor Soc.*, II (November, 1916), 7; Taylor, "Why Manufacturers Dislike College Graduates," *Sibley Journal of Engineering*, XXIV (1909–10), 199, and *Principles of Scientific Management*, pp. 43 ff.

these middle-class motives, such as the desires to excel, to rise, and to increase one's income. Even "Schmidt," Taylor's famous pig-iron handler, whom he calls "a man of the type of the ox," is depicted as buying a plot of land and building a house on it.[12] Incentives were important because man was naturally lazy and the worker had learned under most previous systems of management that it was not in his interest to work hard. In addition, the work of the factory was often tiresome and uninteresting and might become even more so. For one of the aspects of applying "science" to work was elimination of the elements of play that are intermingled with it.[13]

When discussing the place of each worker in the factory, Taylor turned to Platonic metaphors of racehorses and dray horses, songbirds and sparrows. He saw the factory hierarchy as one of abilities. The division of labor did not constrict the worker excessively, because he might rise to that level of competence of which he was capable. Taylor insisted that workers be treated individually and not *en masse*. Each was to be rewarded and punished for his particular deeds.[14] In this way Taylor introduced individualism into the factory, but individualism in a diminished form. It could not measure up to the model of the entrepreneur in the market. The worker

[12] "The Principles of Scientific Management: Address before Cleveland Advertising Club, March 3, 1915," *Bull. Taylor Soc.*, II (December, 1916), 15; Frederick W. Taylor to George Elbert Taylor, Aug. 22, 1912, *ibid.*, p. 3; Copley, I, 188; "Testimony of Frederick W. Taylor," *Hearings of the U.S. Commission on Industrial Relations*, 64th Cong., 1st Sess., Senate Doc. 26 (Ser. Vol. 6929), pp. 774–75; Taylor, "Shop Management," pp. 1353, 1389, "A Piece Rate System," *Trans. ASME*, XVI (1894–95), 895, and *Principles of Scientific Management*, p. 44. Like many of his contemporaries, Taylor may not have granted middle-class virtues to large segments of the "new immigration." Significantly, he calls his good workers "Schmidt and Patrick." When the day laborer rises from digging dirt to making shoes, "the dirt handling is done by Italians or Hungarians." Also, like many of his contemporaries, Taylor believed that Negroes were of an inferior race. "Shop Management," pp. 1451, 1422; F. W. Taylor, "Laws vs. Public Opinion as a Basis of Management," Taylor Collection.

[13] Taylor, "Shop Management," p. 1349; *Principles of Scientific Management*, pp. 19, 87; "Testimony before the Special House Committee," in *Scientific Management: Comprising Shop Management, the Principles of Scientific Management, Testimony before the Special House Committee* (New York: Harper, 1947), p. 129; "Why Manufacturers Dislike College Graduates," p. 199.

[14] Taylor, "Testimony before the Special House Committee," pp. 63, 172, "Shop Management," pp. 1360–61, 1410, 1422, *Principles of Scientific Management*, p. 127, and "A Piece-Rate System," p. 857.

was granted an individuality of incentive but not of discretion; the intricate interrelation of parts in the factory did not allow for that. There was no "invisible hand" in the factory to bring order out of complexity. This order was to be discovered and realized by the systemizer. The workers must "do what they are told promptly and without asking questions or making suggestions. . . . it is absolutely necessary for every man in an organization to become one of a train of gear wheels." [15]

The worker's power of free decision was further limited by the necessities of the "science" of work. For one of the most important general principles of Taylor's system was that the man who did the work could not derive or fully understand its science.[16] The result was a radical separation of thinking from doing. Those who understood were to plan the work and set the procedures; the workmen were simply to carry them into effect. This separation might have been reinforced by the need of Taylor's system for exact measurement. The stop watch, an instrument for timing overt action, could gauge only the most routine mental processes. Therefore, to the extent that Taylor's science strained at strict precision, to that degree it had to externalize work and remove the thinking from it.[17]

The Taylor System placed restrictions upon the entrepreneur and the manager in the factory as well as the worker. Taylor attacked the cult of personality in management. Methods were primary, not particular men. The discovery of a science of work meant a transfer of skill from the worker

[15] Taylor, "Why Manufacturers Dislike College Graduates," p. 202, "Shop Management," p. 1413, and, *Principles of Scientific Management*, pp. 86, 140–41. This contrasts interestingly with Carnegie's earlier and opposite maxim, "Always break orders to save owners . . . smash the routine regulations and make new ones. . . ." Andrew Carnegie, *The Empire of Business* (New York: Doubleday, Page, 1902), p. 12.

[16] Some years earlier Lenin had formulated a similar principle for the "science" of socialism. The worker could achieve "trade union consciousness" (realize his income incentives) but not "socialist consciousness." It was the job of the professional revolutionaries, the Bolsheviks, to lead the way to socialism, just as it was the job of the management experts, the Taylorites, to lead the way to increased productivity in the factory. For Lenin's acceptance of the Taylor System after the Bolsheviks seized power, see chapter viii, below.

[17] Taylor, *Principles of Scientific Management*, pp. 25–26, "Testimony before the Special House Committee," p. 49, "Testimony of Frederick W. Taylor" *Hearings of the U.S. Commission on Industrial Relations*, p. 777, and "Shop Management," pp. 1405, 1442.

to management and with it some transfer of power. Yet this power was fixed not directly at the top but in the new center of the factory, the planning department. Taylor asserted:

The shop (indeed the whole works) should be managed, not by the manager, superintendent, or foreman, but by the planning department. The daily routine of running the entire works should be carried on by the various functional elements of this department, so that, in theory at least, the works could run smoothly even if the manager, superintendent, and their assistants outside the planning room were all to be away for a month at a time.[18]

The planning department was to be the repository of the science of production and therefore to possess a new kind of authority which stemmed from the unveiling of scientific law rather than the expression of arbitrary will. Taylor warned that scientific law should not be tampered with by either worker or employer. "Nine-tenths of our troubles," Taylor said, "come in trying to make men on the management side do what they ought to do. . . ."[19]

The "military system" of factory organization, with ranks built of the successive levels of worker, foreman, assistant manager, manager, and a chain of command which allowed for much undirected choice at all levels, was no longer adequate. Under Taylor's program the foreman, for example, could no longer hire and fire or assign tasks. These functions were to be performed in the planning department by the "disciplinarian" and the "instruction card clerk." Much of the traditional hierarchy of the factory was to be maintained for the surveillance of the work, but some of its authority on all levels would be drained into the planning department.[20]

The new demands on management would necessarily raise the proportion of auxiliary employees to those directly involved in production. In this sense Taylorism was in step with

[18] "Shop Management," p. 1398, *Principles of Scientific Management*, p. 7, and "A Piece-Rate System," p. 860. The installation of the Taylor System, moreover, "should only be undertaken under direct control [not advice but CONTROL] of men who had years of experience and training in introducing this system." Frederick W. Taylor, "On the Art of Cutting Metals," *Trans. ASME*, XXIII (1907), 28.

[19] Taylor, "The Principles of Scientific Management; Address before Cleveland Advertising Club, March 3, 1915," *Bull. Taylor Soc.*, II (December, 1916), 18, "Shop Management," p. 1449, *Principles of Scientific Management*, p. 143, and "Testimony before the Special House Committee," pp. 31, 149, 199; Copley, I, 175.

[20] Taylor, "Shop Management," pp. 1386–1406.

the overall trends in American industry. But the popular notion which equates Taylor's system with the outstanding features of modern industrial order, with exaggerated forms of division of labor, mass production, and mechanization and technological innovation, is inaccurate on all three counts. Taylor did not disapprove of these developments, but they were not a significant part of his particular program. Converting each job into a "science" often made possible routinization and the accompanying increase of dexterity in each task without further dividing it among different workmen. Taylor's system had its first complete developments and its typical subsequent applications in small and medium-sized plants which made diverse items. This placed severe limits to the further division of labor.[21] Also, Taylor could not be considered a fervent advocate of technological innovation and mechanization. In fact, he was suspicious of new and radical inventions in machinery and instead laid emphasis upon perfecting the tools at hand to a point of high efficiency. In order to press the broadest application of his stop-watch studies, he did insist upon extensive standardization and synchronization of machines. Yet while he would eliminate any obviously antiquated tools, his inclination was toward getting the most out of existing equipment.[22]

Taylor's system not only applied to the factory but reached out to society as a whole. He tried to broaden the scope of his

[21] However, Taylor made some attempt to keep the well-paid, highly skilled worker at those tasks which required his skill. The unskilled tasks which by custom had been part of the skilled worker's job were given to unskilled workers who did them at lower pay. (Taylor's disciple, F. B. Gilbreth, was especially fond of this device.) Furthermore, Taylor did make a special point of dividing the work of "management" so that "each man in management should be confined to the performance of a single function." Not only was much of the foreman's authority placed in the planning department, but his supervisory tasks were fractionalized. One foreman looked after the worker's speed, another the techniques used, another the quality of the work, and another the repair of machines. Taylor, "Shop Management," pp. 1391 ff., 1045–46; H. S. Person, "Scientific Management," *Bull. Taylor Soc.* XIII (October, 1928), 201–2; F. W. Taylor to Carl G. Barth, Dec. 30, 1909, Taylor Collection.

[22] Frederick W. Taylor, "Scientific Management: Address to the First National Efficiency Exposition and Conference, April 7, 1914," *Greater Efficiency: Journal of the Efficiency Society, Inc.*, III (September, 1914), 19–20; Copley, I, 199; "Testimony of H. K. Hathaway" *Evidence Taken by the Interstate Commerce Commission in the Matter of Proposed Advances in Freight Rates (1910–11)*, 61st Cong., 3d Sess., Senate Doc. no. 725 (Ser. Vol. 5905), p. 2675; Taylor, "Shop Management," p. 1407.

proposals to an extent unimagined by most systemizers and by a method more definite and internally consistent than that of the industrial betterment advocates. He proposed to make each workman's interest the same as his employer's. The differential piece rate was to give the worker a high daily wage and the employer a low labor cost per piece. For society as a whole, the increased production would lower prices and raise the general standard of living. Especially in Taylor's later writings, increased productivity became a salient point of his social program. He asserted that "the one element more than any other which differentiates civilized countries from uncivilized countries — prosperous from poverty-stricken peoples — is that the average man in one is five or six times as productive as in the other." [23] When critics contended that scientific management might be helpful in the realm of production but ignored the problems of distribution, Taylor replied that this was precisely its great accomplishment. Scientific management brought about a "mental revolution" which set the employer and worker pulling together rather than apart. For "both sides take their eyes off the division of the surplus until this surplus becomes so large that it is unnecessary to quarrel over how it shall be divided." [24]

At first sight, this was a twentieth-century Whiggism. The commonplaces about the harmony of interest among all groups in the American social order were given a current appropriateness and a "scientific" cogency. In the Whiggism of former generations, the tariff had served as the economic bond between employer and worker. In Taylor's program, increased productivity was to play that role. It was from the standpoint of this credo of production that he criticized the profit-sharing schemes which were so dear to advocates of industrial betterment. Profit-sharing, he said, did not lend itself to increased production, and even if all profits were divided among the working people, the addition to wages would be slight. Furthermore, this belief in the primacy of production also led Taylor to condemn the entrepreneur's

[23] *Principles of Scientific Management*, p. 142.
[24] "Testimony before the Special House Committee," p. 30; Taylor, "Reply," *American Magazine*, LXXII (June, 1911), 244–45, "Scientific Management: Address to the First National Efficiency Exposition . . . ," p. 25, and "The Principles of Scientific Management: Address before the Cleveland Advertising Club," p. 16.

restriction of output to maintain prices, just as he had disapproved of the worker's "soldiering." On occasion, he contrasted the engineer as hero to the "financier" as villain; the one constantly in the presence of the production process and sensitive to its needs, and the other distant from production but with the power to control it.[25]

Because scientific management allowed for operation at low cost, Taylor thought that it would be thrust upon entrepreneurs through competition. However, it became apparent that in important sectors of the economy, competition was no longer an effective force [26] and, therefore, could not be relied on exclusively. When the Eastern Rate Case splashed scientific management before a large public audience, Taylor came upon a new way to spread his program. He appealed to the "whole people" to repudiate "the type of employer who has his eye on dividends alone," or the laborer who demands more pay and shorter hours but resists efficiency. The "whole people" would be the agents of his system.[27] The role of the consulting scientific management engineer, upholding "science" in the factory against the narrow vision and vested interests of worker and employer, bore some resemblance to that of the middle-class reformer in society upholding the public interest against the pressures of both capital and labor. When Taylor invoked the public interest, scientific management was drawn toward that growing company of progressives who set the tone for the era.

Though Taylor appealed to public opinion for support, he did not look to public opinion for any sort of guidance. All the guidance, so far as scientific management was concerned, would come from experts. The application of science to business, Taylor thought, would have effects much like those which had followed the application of science to engineering

[25] F. W. Taylor to G. E. Taylor, Aug. 22, 1912, *Bull. Taylor Soc.*, II (December, 1916), 4; "Testimony before the Special House Committee," pp. 18–19; "Discussion," *Trans. ASME*, XXXVI (1814), 627; Copley, II, 387–88; F. W. Taylor to Carl G. Barth, Dec. 29, 1910, Taylor Collection.

[26] F. W. Taylor to Ernest Hamlin Abbott, Nov. 18, 1911, Taylor Collection.

[27] Taylor, *Principles of Scientific Management*, pp. 136, 138, 139, 144. Taylor also saw his system in broad terms as an instrument of progress and, like progress itself, inevitable. He compared his opponents to the machine wreckers of a hundred years earlier and confidently predicted that opposition to his work would be equally fruitless. "Testimony before the Special House Committee," pp. 14–16.

a half a century earlier. There would be handbooks of "elementary operations," codifying the laws of work, similar to those engineering handbooks which codified the laws of machines. But, most important, authority would be placed in the hands of those who followed the rules of science rather than the "rule of thumb." The scientific management expert would replace arbitrary command with the dictates of science. And science, Taylor thought, was an oracle free from human bias and selfishness which would point the way to an elevating moral purpose. It would bring a professional attitude. "It is inconceivable," Taylor declared, "that a man should devote his time and life to this sort of thing for the sake of making money for a whole lot of manufacturers." [28]

Many of the shifts in emphasis in Taylor's program over the years were tied to its widening audience. Taylor's first paper, "A Piece-Rate System," was addressed to a small group of engineers and manufacturers and printed in the *Transactions of the American Society of Mechanical Engineers*; his last paper, "The Principles of Scientific Management," was serialized in the *American Magazine*, which spoke the vernacular of reform to a large segment of America. "Early" Taylor cast his proposals primarily in the form of a business service, while "late" Taylor stressed their more widely beneficial aspects. His picture of his own work was changing. Those close to Taylor toward the end of his life tell of "his dreams of the ultimate applicability of Scientific Management principles and ideas, not only to every industrial activity but to every conceivable human activity." [29]

Paradoxically, Taylor's stress on the broader relevance of his system was accompanied by a lessening in his specifically moral tone. This, at first, is even more perplexing, since his new audience was deeply imbued with moral sentiment. Yet

[28] "Testimony of Frederick W. Taylor," *Hearings of the U.S. Commission on Industrial Relations*, p. 766; "Laws vs. Public Opinion as a Basis of Management: Lecture Delivered before the YMCA of Philadelphia, October 12, 1914," Taylor Collection. See also "Testimony of Charles W. Mixter" *Hearings of the U.S. Commission on Industrial Relations* 64th Cong., 1st Sess., Senate Doc. 26. (Ser. Vol. 6929), pp. 851–52.

[29] *Bull. Taylor Soc.*, VII (August, 1922), p. 168; Taylor, *Principles of Scientific Management*, pp. 7, 8. Not only did Taylor begin to describe his system in the idiom of uplift and democracy, but he was drawn into projects of social betterment. He served as consulting expert to the Department of Public Works of Philadelphia, which Morris L. Cooke was reorganizing on principles of scientific management, and helped Cooke

Taylor's code differed from theirs. His underscored man's weakness and placed punishment at its center, while theirs usually dealt with man's potential and emphasized precepts of permissiveness. While Taylor, for the most part, did not bring himself to accept the moral outlook which prevailed among most of his new audience, he gradually muffled his own. In the "science" of work, the problem of how work was to be done began to overshadow the determination of the time in which work ought to be done. The differential piece rate, which embodied a dedication to hard work and some fear of its material products (if men have too much they become "shiftless, extravagant and dissipated"), almost disappeared. While in 1895 the Taylor System always meant hard work, by 1911 it sometimes meant easy work.[30]

Taylor could make this transition because scientific management had become almost an end in itself for him. "Indeed, so intense was his will to get there, so grim was his resolution not to let anything stand in his way, that sometimes he resorted to stratagems and subterfuges so far from guileless as rather to puzzle and pain some of his most devoted followers."[31] The toning down of the "old fashioned" moralism of his system gave it the appearance of a neutral device. Because scientific management became almost an end in itself for Taylor, it could become simply a means for others.

Yet the continuity within scientific management must not be overlooked. Taylor's system, from his first public statement of it in 1895 to his last, twenty years later, encompassed three things: it was a method of business therapy; it was a "science"; and it was a social program. During Taylor's lifetime these were three aspects of one outlook. In the generation of his disciples they were separated and each set in its own direction.

---

expose crimes of the boodlers who had just been thrown out of office. He also became a member of the board of trustees (along with Charles R. Van Hise, Felix Frankfurter, and other prominent reformers) of a Public Utilities Bureau which furnished expert advice for cities in their rate controversies with utility companies. Morris L. Cooke to Louis D. Brandeis, July 9, 1914, Taylor Collection. Copley, II, 394–97.

[30] Compare Taylor, "Shop Management," p. 1346, with Taylor, "Testimony before the Special House Committee," p. 16. "Testimony of Frederick W. Taylor," *Hearings of the U.S. Commission on Industrial Relations*, p. 768.

[31] Copley, II, 156.

• CHAPTER III

The Little Band of Taylorites

The principal gathering place of Taylor's followers was the Taylor Society, an informal but exclusive club of Taylor disciples founded in 1911. The purposes of the Society, as described by Frank Gilbreth at the first meeting, were to maintain and make known Taylor's work, to provide for the cooperation of his followers, and to set up a central body which would serve as an authority on all questions of management. Taylor objected to the formation of the Society, believing that it would isolate the advocates of scientific management from possible converts in the American Society of Mechanical Engineers. He became reconciled to its existence, however, and consented to address one of its meetings shortly before he died. The power of Taylor's personality was a cohesive force in the Society long after his death. All accepted his greatness almost without question. "Invariably when I have thought of Mr. Taylor and attempted to value his services to mankind," confessed one admirer, "an impelling desire to compare him with Darwin has seized me." [1]

[1] H. S. Person, "F. W. Taylor as a Seeker of Truth," *Journal of the Efficiency Society*, IV (April, 1915), 8. For a random sample of similarly exalted estimates from prominent members of the Taylor Society see: H. K. Hathaway, "Mr. Taylor As I Knew Him," *Journal of the Efficiency Society*, IV (April, 1915), 7–8; Richard A. Feiss, "Discussion," *Bull. Taylor Soc.*, III (March, 1917), 16; Wilfred Lewis, "Discussion," *ibid.*, VI (December, 1921), 230–31. Originally, the Taylor Society was called the Society To Promote the Science of Management, but after Taylor's death it was renamed in his honor. *Bull. Taylor Soc.*, II (January, 1916), 1. For the early history of the Taylor Society see Milton J. Nadworny, "The Society for the Promotion of the Science of Management," *Explorations in Entrepreneurial History*, V (May, 1953) 245–47, and Robert T. Kent, "The Taylor Society Twenty Years Ago," *Bull. Taylor Soc.*, XVII (February, 1932), 39–40.

Whereas in its first years the Taylor Society restricted its membership mainly to engineers and its concerns to technical matters, the election of H. S. Person as president in 1913 (he succeeded himself annually until 1919) marked a broadening of the Society's membership and interests. Person was the dean of the Amos Tuck School of Administration and Finance. He viewed his work in business education from a wide social perspective [2] and, once having joined the Taylor Society, was inclined to look at scientific management in broad terms as well.

The membership of the Taylor Society centered in Philadelphia and the area north and east of it and soon included management engineers, businessmen and an assortment of notables of academic and professional background. The businessmen were of an uncommon sort. They often had avid technological interests or elaborate opinions on public issues, or both. James Mapes Dodge pioneered in the development of the link-belt conveyor, which was the basis of the belt line system, and also worked fervently for Philadelphia civic betterment. Wilfred Lewis was a well-known authority on gearing and a friend of metric reform. Richard Feiss and Henry Dennison were employers devoted to advanced ideas of personnel management. While most of these businessmen deferred to considerations of profit, it was a rare occasion when one would raise his voice at Taylor Society meetings in the stockholders' interest.[3]

The management engineers were the preservers of Taylorite orthodoxy. They were willing to broaden the Society's membership but only to the extent of admitting those who "unqualifiedly stand for the principles set forth by Frederick W. Taylor." The complaints that the Society was not giving suitable attention to the techniques and devices of scientific

[2] H. S. Person, *Industrial Education: A System of Training for Men Entering upon Trade and Commerce* (Boston: Houghton Mifflin, 1907).
[3] "James Mapes Dodge," *Trans. ASME*, XXXVII (1915), 1505; George P. Torrence, *James Mapes Dodge* (New York: Newcomen Society of North America, 1950); H. K. Hathaway, "Wilfred Lewis," *Bull. Taylor Soc.*, XV (February, 1930), 45–46; "Wilfred Lewis," *Record and Index: American Society of Mechanical Engineers*, III (1929), 329; F. A. Halsey, in *Trans. ASME*, XXIV (1902–3), 397; Mary Barnett Gilson, *What's Past Is Prologue* (New York: Harper, 1940), pp. 51 ff.; *The Golden Book of Management*, ed. L. Urwick (London: Newman Neame Ltd., 1956), pp. 196–200.

management came from the management engineers.[4] Some of them (Morris L. Cooke, Robert B. Wolfe, and Walter N. Polakov, for example), however, were quite at home with far-ranging issues. These issues were usually raised by the members of academic and professional background who helped maintain the contact with the progressive community. In this they were aided by the many non-members who came to the meetings as visitors. The Society members listened to the views of such visitors as Felix Frankfurter, then a Harvard law professor, John A. Fitch, an editor of *Survey*, and Ida Tarbell, the remarkable free-lance muckraker.

One of the points at which Taylorite orthodoxy snagged prevailing progressive attitudes was the role of labor unions. The progressive movement, in its Democratic phase, had come to accept the trade union as a proper agency for the advance of the worker. Yet it was difficult to find a place for unions in Taylor's scheme of things. Under scientific management, wages, hours, and working conditions were subjects for scientific determination rather than for bargaining. Many Taylorites believed that unions were addicted to the limitation of production. The most that Taylor would grant was that, "If Unions will compel their members to do a full day's work and compel every man in the union to learn his trade, then we will be with them."[5] But few progressives could envisage the unions as mere instruments of labor discipline.

Robert G. Valentine was the most dedicated of the "social scientists" seeking agreement between Taylorism and trade unionism, and in his approach he resembled many of the progressive sympathizers of scientific management. For Valentine, both scientific management and trade unionism were but preliminaries to all-encompassing economic reform. He believed that the old unionism, based on craft skills, was being destroyed by technological progress. The new unionism would finds its strength in "consumers' organizations with a primarily educational interest." Industrial democracy, which

[4] *Bull. Taylor Soc.*, II (January, 1916), 2; H. K. Hathaway, "Field of Activity of the Society," *ibid.*, p. 3; Arthur B. Green, "Scientific Methods Applied to the Beating of Paper Stock," *ibid.*, II (October, 1916), 6; Robert T. Kent, "Discussion," *ibid.*, III (May, 1917), 12.

[5] Frederick W. Taylor, "Scientific Management and Labor Unions," *Bulletin of the Society To Promote the Science of Management* (hereafter cited as *"Bull. SPSM"*), I December, 1914), 3.

for Valentine meant a polite form of consumer-minded syndicalism, lay in the future. Existing unionism, despite all its imperfections and its "monstrous economical fallacies," should be accepted as a first step in this line of development. Once scientific management engineers began to co-operate with the unions, Valentine maintained, the unions could "be counted on to consent to all that makes for efficiency." [6]

Most of the Taylorites were not convinced. Though the Society heard provocative discussions which challenged Taylor's teachings at several points, the principles and practices of scientific management remained curiously unchanged. The unofficial veto power of the management engineers over what could be accepted as Taylorite doctrine was one of the factors preventing modification. This power derived from the exalted place of the engineer in Taylor's hierarchy as well as from Taylor's belief that scientific management could be understood best through its practice — through experience in a plant organized on its precepts. In addition, the Society was warned by a leading management engineer, Carl G. Barth, that Taylor had not set his entire message in writing and therefore only his "direct disciples," those who had worked closely with him, fully understood the system. [7]

The most direct of the "direct disciples" proved to be Barth himself. A few years before Taylor's death, Barth's pre-eminence would have been considered unlikely, for Henry Gantt had been with Taylor earlier and Frank Gilbreth was far better known as an exponent of his cause. Both Gantt and Gilbreth, however, had introduced additions and revisions into scientific management which Taylor had found unacceptable, and both were cast out of the church. Barth, in contrast, was content to work strictly within Taylor's prescriptions. He

[6] Robert G. Valentine, "The Progressive Relation between Efficiency and Consent," *Bull. SPSM*, I (November, 1915), 28, and "Scientific Management and Organized Labor," *ibid.* (January, 1915), p. 3. For biographical information on Valentine see: Felix Frankfurter, "Robert Grosvenor Valentine," *Dictionary of American Biography* (New York: Charles Scribner's Sons, 1936), XIX, 142–43; "Robert Grosvenor Valentine," *National Cyclopedia of American Biography* (New York: James T. White, 1927), XVII, 276; "Robert Grosvenor Valentine," in *Golden Book of Management*.

[7] Frank Barkley Copley, *Frederick W. Taylor: Father of Scientific Management* (New York: Harper, 1923), II, 290, 295; Carl G. Barth, "Discussion," *Bull. Taylor Soc.* (September, 1920), 149.

was "exceedingly proud of being accused of being Mr. Taylor's most orthodox disciple."[8]

Barth came from Norway as a young man trained in mechanics and advanced mathematics. He was short and slender, distinguished by an absence of smiles and a crusty no-nonsense manner. He was an admirer of "Bob" Ingersoll, and it was his outspoken ridicule of conventional religion, even more than what appeared to be his anti-union views, that angered the devout labor members of the Commission on Industrial Relations investigating scientific management.[9]

Taylor brought Barth to the Bethlehem Steel Company to help in the metal-cutting experiments which were part of the reorganization of the plant. Barth successfully analyzed Taylor's immense accumulation of experimental data and developed formulas and special slide rules which became basic mechanisms for machine shop systemization. The reorganization of Bethlehem, however, which at first seemed the high point in Taylor's career, ended in failure. Taylor's interference with the customary pattern of authority raised opposition from the management staff which he met head-on. When the tensions broke, Taylor was fired and his system emphatically disowned.[10] Barth left Bethlehem and soon became a management consultant under Taylor's guidance. He took part in the first complete installations of scientific management.[11]

The turn of mind which made Barth a worthy follower made him a poor leader. His loyalty to Taylor's work and hostility

[8] Carl G. Barth, "Discussion," *Trans. ASME*, XXXIV (1912), 1204.

[9] "Carl G. Barth," in *Golden Book of Management*; "Testimony of Carl G. Barth," *Hearings of the U.S. Commission on Industrial Relations*, 64th Cong., 1st Sess., Senate Doc. 26 (Ser. Vol. 6929), April, 1914, pp. 892, 897.

[10] Copley, II, chap. xi, contains a detailed discussion of the overthrow of the Taylor System at Bethlehem. This incident suggests an explanation for the unexpected fact that the factories in which the Taylor System was successfully applied were typically small or medium-sized. In a large firm, where the owner or manager had to rely more heavily upon the knowledge and co-operation of his subordinates, members of the staff were in a better position to block Taylor's reorganization, which would have drained much of their authority.

[11] These were at the Link Belt Company and the Tabor Manufacturing Company. Scientific management entered both firms through a side door. James Mapes Dodge of Link Belt was chiefly interested in using Taylor's invention of high-speed steel, and Wilfred Lewis of Tabor accepted scientific management as one of Taylor's conditions for investing in the company. Both companies became model installations of the Taylor System.

toward any "tampering" with it contributed to the hardening of the doctrines and devices of scientific management. He demanded that there be no alterations except on the suggestion of those who had actually adopted the Taylor System and on the approval of a "competent judge." Even in the field of machine technology, where Taylor had given him considerable freedom, Barth tried to hold on to the methods of the original Taylor shops. "Indiscriminate" electrification of machine shops was condemned. Electrically driven machines were subject to more speed variation than steam-engine belt-driven machines, thereby introducing uncertainties beyond the control of the management engineer. Of course, Barth came to accept electrification but regretted the high allowances it forced upon his calculations.[12]

As disabling as this intransigence was Barth's tendency to present scientific management in terms of the field he knew best. His attention was fixed principally upon the factory, and even more specifically upon the machines. Probably the closest Barth ever came to poetry was when he told the Commission on Industrial Relations:

My dream is that the time will come when every drill press will be speeded just so, and every planer, every lathe the world over will be harmonized just like musical pitches are the same all over the world . . . so that we can standardize and say that for drilling a 1-inch hole the world over will be done with the same speed [sic]. . . . That dream will come true, some time.[13]

Barth seemed to take the social order as he found it; it was not his job to meddle in broad social issues. When he presented an "engineer's analysis" of the income tax, Barth carefully put aside the economic and political problems to discuss the mathematical difficulties in computation. The topic of labor turnover, which led others to questions of the psychology of work and social mobility, led Barth exclusively to the question of reliable statistics. On those rare occasions when he did

[12] Carl G. Barth, "Discussion," *Bull. Taylor Soc.*, V (September, 1920), 149, and "The Transmission of Power by Leather Belting," *Trans. ASME*, XXX (1909), 100–101; "Discussion," *ibid.*, XXXII (1910), 262–63; "Discussion," *Bull. Taylor Soc.*, VI (June, 1921), 109.
[13] "Testimony of Carl G. Barth," *Hearings of the U.S. Commission on Industrial Relations*, p. 889.

openly deal with broader issues as such, it was usually behind a paraphrase or quotation of Taylor.[14]

Barth invested his orthodoxy with an air of hard-headed
practicality. "While you fellows are writing about it, and
talking about it," he told the Taylor Society, "I am doing
it."[15] But his was a practicality too narrow to help the Taylor
Society to its powers and opportunities. In Barth's hands,
Taylorism came to resemble simply a business service.

This helped to bring about the divergence within scientific
management which developed after the founder's death. In
the possession of his three outstanding followers, specialization developed, with each follower emphasizing a particular
aspect of the master's system. Barth looked to the factory;
Frank Gilbreth concentrated on the "scientific" nub of Taylorism; and Henry Gantt emphasized its social implications.
While Barth's influence centered in the Taylor Society, Gilbreth and Gantt developed their ideas, for the most part, beyond its bounds.

Before coming under the influence of scientific management, Frank Bunker Gilbreth had been a successful building
contractor, with a national reputation in his field. He was a
businessman with a flair for invention and new ideas and was
probably one of the first to apply the notions of system to construction work. In the first decade of the century, Gilbreth set
down his management techniques in a series of manuals
which pictured his organization as a machine built on the
interchangeable-part plan and specializing in speed work. By

[14] Carl G. Barth, "The Income Tax: An Engineer's Analysis with Suggestions," *Mechanical Engineering*, XL (October, 1918), 839, and "Labor
Turnover: A Mathematical Discussion," *Industrial Management*, LIX
(April, 1920), 315. Although what Barth said and did publicly was governed by this limited field of vision, in the privacy of his family circle
and in the last years of his retirement Barth occasionally permitted himself more general speculations. In politics, Barth always registered as a
non-partisan, but he told his family that socialism lay in the future, the
distant future, and even voted for the Socialist party ticket. Barth's socialism probably owed much to his early socialist background in Norway. It
was what Barth said and did publicly, however, rather than what he con-
fided to his family or divulged in the last years of his retirement, that was
important for the history of scientific management. Carl G. Barth to Mr.
Louis Adamic, July 28, 1939, in the possession of J. Christian Barth, J.
Christian Barth to author, July 31, 1962.

[15] Quoted by Kent, "The Taylor Society Twenty Years Ago," p. 41.

the time that the last of these manuals was written, Gilbreth had discovered Taylor's work and was greatly impressed by it. He soon came to believe that Taylor was the greatest man he had met and that the advent of scientific management was the most important thing that had happened in his lifetime.[16]

However, Gilbreth was always uneasy in the role of a disciple. From his early meetings with Taylor, it was not only the methods of scientific management which took hold of Gilbreth but also the magnitude of Taylor's aspirations. Gilbreth showed a good-natured and respectful envy of the accomplishments of Taylor and others and became eager to make his own mark as well. He developed a unique emphasis on the elimination of the worker's unnecessary motions and the selection of the best motions for the job.[17]

Gilbreth left the construction industry in 1912 for the booming field of management consulting. He put aside Taylor's simple stop watch and introduced the motion-picture camera to get more exact measurements. Gilbreth grew increasingly excited about his success in this work. Consequently, when Taylor treated motion study as but an aspect of scientific management, "undoubtedly good where one was investigating the minutiae of motion," Gilbreth was disappointed. Taylor, he complained, "did not recognize its meaning." Earlier, Taylor had approved of Gilbreth's experiments and had drawn examples from Gilbreth's bricklaying work to illustrate the principles of scientific management. Now Taylor began to suspect Gilbreth's grandiose ambitions and his concentration on motion study to the neglect of scientific management as a whole. He finally became convinced that Gilbreth did not understand scientific management or its implications. The break came when, in response to a complaint of one of Gilbreth's clients, Taylor sent a more dependable follower to take over Gilbreth's job.[18]

[16] Frank B. Gilbreth, *Field System* (New York: Myron Clark, 1908), p. 13. His other manuals were *Concrete System* (New York: Engineering News, 1908), and *Bricklaying System* (New York: Myron Clark, 1907); Edna Yost, *Frank and Lillian Gilbreth: Partners for Life* (New Brunswick, N.J.: Rutgers University Press, 1949), pp. 155, 204.

[17] Frank B. Gilbreth to F. W. Taylor, Oct. 7, 1912, Taylor Collection; Frank B. Gilbreth, *Motion Study* (New York: D. Van Nostrand, 1911), 94; Yost, *op. cit.*, p. 240; Gilbreth, *Bricklaying System*, p. 140.

[18] Taylor to Gantt, Aug. 7, 1914, Taylor Collection; Yost, *Gilbreth*, p. 225; Milton J. Nadworny, "Frederick Taylor and Frank Gilbreth: Com-

Soon Gilbreth came to see his own methods as surpassing some of Taylor's rather than supplementing them. Even before the clash, Gilbreth thought that motion study could be used not only in scientific management installations but in any factories and with almost anything that moved.[19]

The movement for shorter work hours for women put the question of fatigue in the factory in the spotlight, and the Gilbreths (Frank and his wife, Lillian, worked as a team) responded with a demonstration that elimination of fatigue was a matter of eliminating waste motions. They addressed themselves to mental fatigue as well. Lillian Gilbreth's *The Psychology of Management* was one of the first studies in this new field.[20] The Gilbreths seized upon the suggestion that mental states have physical correlates and predicted that their study of motion might even pry into the mind. They began to talk about "happiness minutes" as if these were as measurable as turns of the wrist. When the United States entered the war, Gilbreth enlisted in the Army and used his motion-picture technique for machine-gun assembly training and for the introduction of "films with hate-rousing atrocities" into soldier education.[21]

petition in Scientific Management," *Business History Review*, XXXI (Spring, 1957), 28–29.

[19] Frank B. Gilbreth and Lillian M. Gilbreth, "Motion Study and Time Study Instruments of Precision," *Transactions of the International Engineering Congress at the Panama-Pacific Exposition*, XI (September, 1915), 475; Gilbreth, *Motion Study*, p. 84. Gilbreth took motion study beyond the factory and applied it exuberantly to the work of musicians, baseball players, fencers, and oyster-openers. Once Gilbreth had hoped to be a surgeon and now he was especially relentless in his motion studies of surgery and hospitals. While some of his applied motion study may have been frivolous, his aid to the handicapped, by contrast, was of lasting importance. Frank B. Gilbreth and Lillian M. Gilbreth, *Applied Motion Study* (New York: Sturgis & Walton, 1917), p. 39, and *Motion Study for The Handicapped* (London: George Routledge, 1920), pp. 16, 18 ff.; Yost, *Gilbreth*, p. 245; Albert Jay Nock, "Efficiency and the High-Brow," *American Magazine*, LXXV (March, 1913), 50.

[20] Frank B. Gilbreth and Lillian M. Gilbreth, *Fatigue Study* (New York: Sturgis & Walton, 1916); "The Waste of Getting Tired," *Independent*, XCI (Sept. 10, 1917), 427; "Are You Working Too Hard?" *ibid.*, XCII (Nov. 17, 1917), 336. This last article condemns etiquette as waste motion. L. M. Gilbreth, *The Psychology of Management* (New York: Sturgis & Walton, 1914), said nothing new about psychology or management but merely asserted that the laws of psychology supported rather than conflicted with the laws of scientific management.

[21] Frank B. Gilbreth and Lillian M. Gilbreth, "Closure," *Bull. Taylor Soc.*, VI (June, 1921), 134, and *Fatigue Study*, p. 149; Frank B. Gilbreth,

The multifarious applications of motion study did not distract the Gilbreths from the further development of the underlying logic of their technique. The "scientific" nub of Taylor's program was the reduction of work to component elements or "elementary operations" which were to be fixed, timed with stop watch, and reassembled when needed to provide the method and measurements of any new task. It was to this aspect of scientific management that the Gilbreth energies were devoted.

His motion study techniques, Gilbreth claimed, provided new accuracy, objectivity, and generality. The stopwatch gave only approximate results, while the motion-picture camera was accurate to the thousandth of a minute. The calculations which were necessary to stop-watch timing and so liable to bias were to be eliminated through the use of the camera. The increased precision also made possible his isolation of sixteen fundamental elements of hand motion, called Therbligs,[22] which purportedly were *true elements* not merely . . . subdivisions that are arbitrarily called 'elements.' "[23] Taylor's elementary operations were specific to each trade, but the Therbligs were the same whether the hand held a scalpel, a trowel, or a monkey wrench. Where Taylor predicted the compilation of a handbook of elementary operations in each trade, Gilbreth, because of the greater generality in which he cast his units, expected to derive basic data from his motion study laboratories that would be transferable to a great many different kinds of work.

Rather than try to put the existing trades on a scientific basis, Gilbreth called for their complete reorganization. All the industrial skills were to be studied and their required motions standardized in terms of Therbligs. Then they were

---

"Science in Management for the One Best Way To Do Work," *Compterendu de la IIIème Conférence Internationale de Psychotechnique Appliquée à l'Orientation Professionelle*, Milan, October 2–4, 1922, pp. 6, 7; Yost, *Gilbreth*, p. 274. Earlier, Gilbreth had been pro-German. Though swept into support of the preparedness campaign, he cautioned against arming for a definite enemy. Frank B. Gilbreth, "Discussion," *Trans. ASME*, XXXVIII (June, 1916), 437.

[22] An approximation of "Gilbreth" backwards. Originally there were sixteen Therbligs, but gradually others were added.

[23] Frank B. Gilbreth and Lillian M. Gilbreth, "Classifying the Elements of Work," *Management and Administration*, VIII (August, 1924), 151. Emphasis in the original.

to be reclassified according to necessary motion skills instead of traditional tasks. This revolution seems to be the extreme development of Taylor's separation of planning and doing. It was to be accomplished through a United States Government Bureau of Standardization of Trades.[24]

Floating above the development of the principles of motion study and its diverse application was the Gilbreth all-embracing, inexhaustible concept of "The One Best Way To Do Work." This idea was similar to the notion of the survival of the fittest, and just as ambiguous. However, the One Best Way had supposedly survived the process of careful alternation of variables in the Gilbreth laboratory rather than the haphazard circumstances of the outside world. Of course, the Gilbreths admitted that factory conditions differed from laboratory conditions, but they insisted that the "conditions of the shop should be changed until they duplicate the most desirable conditions of the laboratory."[25]

The one Best Way became idiomatic in the writing and thinking of the Gilbreths. They would quickly fall into the discussion of the one best everything and anything. Furthermore, they came to believe their methods to be the One Best Way to find the One Best Way. Frank Gilbreth carried the message with an earnest, contentious, overbearing manner. "I think that Gilbreth should be a good Christian and turn the other cheek" quipped an observer; "only he hasn't gotten around to apply motion study in these lines."[26]

Frank Gilbreth did not attend meetings of the Taylor Society in the period following his break with Taylor. However, after an absence of over five years, he agreed to appear and confront the orthodox Taylorites with an indictment of stopwatch time study. Gilbreth, in his paper, quoted Taylor on the fundamental importance of the scientific study of elementary operations for the entire system of scientific management and condemned Taylor's self-proclaimed orthodox followers for accepting perfunctory and inexact stop-watch methods. Barth, delivering the authoritative reply, countered that one should

[24] Frank B. Gilbreth, "Broader Aspects of Motion Study," *100%: The Practical Magazine of Efficient Management*, V (September, 1915), 80.

[25] Frank B. Gilbreth and Lillian M. Gilbreth, "Applications of Motion Study," *Management and Administration*, VIII (September, 1924), 296.

[26] Nock, "Efficiency and the High-Brow," p. 49.

"make allowances for Taylor's enthusiasm, and not take him as seriously as all that." The work could not be exact, Barth said, and the stop watch was good enough for finding a fair time to allow for a particular task. He appealed to the moderating influences of "past general experience and the common sense that goes with it." To Gilbreth this savored "of the 'rule of thumb' that Dr. Taylor so strenuously tried to supersede. True Taylor philosophy," he said, "has suffered in the hands of Mr. Barth and many other loyal friends of Dr. Taylor." In a letter written to a prominent Taylorite soon after the debate, Gilbreth declared, "We shall continue to stand for Science in Management, even if we stand alone." [27]

While Gilbreth fastened upon the "scientific" nub in Taylor's system, Gantt, the third of Taylor's outstanding disciples, developed its social reform implications. Henry Laurence Gantt was the only prominent Taylorite whose roots lay in the post-Civil War South.[28] He received a degree in mechanical engineering from Stevens Institute of Technology and had worked with Taylor at Midvale and Bethlehem. Like Barth, he became a consultant in management after the failure at Bethlehem and maintained close ties with Taylor for many years. But Gantt drifted from Taylor's strict precepts. Taylor

[27] Frank B. Gilbreth and Lillian M. Gilbreth, "An Indictment of Stop-Watch Time Study," *Bull. Taylor Soc.*, VI (June, 1921), 97; Carl G. Barth, "Discussion," *ibid.*, pp. 108–110; Frank B. Gilbreth and Lillian M. Gilbreth, "Closure," *ibid.*, pp. 121–22; Frank B. Gilbreth to Morris L. Cooke, quoted in Nadworny, "Frederick Taylor and Frank Gilbreth," *Business History Review*, XXXI (Spring, 1957), 32. Gilbreth died in 1924, and it was not long before some of his own direct disciples were abandoning his pretensions to science. The Therbligs were kept, but they were considered convenient rather than "true" elements. By the early thirties the accommodation of the Gilbreth to the Barth school was almost complete. See Allan H. Mogensen, *Common Sense Applied to Motion and Time Study* (New York: McGraw-Hill, 1932).

[28] Gantt's father, who had been a warm supporter of the Confederacy, was unequal to the new conditions in the South after Appomattox. When Henry was ten the family lost the plantation and moved to Baltimore, where his mother set up a boarding house and took the burden of the support of the family into her own capable hands. There are interesting family resemblances among the early leaders of the scientific management movement, Taylor, Gantt, and Gilbreth. All had strong mothers, to whom they were close and devoted. Taylor's and Gantt's fathers were soft and somewhat ineffectual. Gilbreth's father died when he was very young. Most of my biographical data on Gantt come from L. P. Alford, *Henry Laurence Gantt: Leader in Industry* (New York: American Society of Mechanical Engineers, 1934).

was unbending in his requirements for a systemized plant and demanded complete authority before he would accept a client. Gantt, by contrast, was more flexible. He introduced as many improvements as the client would accept and asked for little authority to accomplish this. His easygoing way with Taylor's methods led Taylor to doubt, as he had with Gilbreth, whether Gantt fully grasped the underlying philosophy of scientific management. Curiously, Gantt, who in his day-to-day work deferred to the boss's authority more than Taylor thought proper, in the realm of theory challenged that authority in a more far-reaching manner than his mentor.[29]

What were merely suggestions of social criticism in Taylor's system became developed principles in Gantt's writings. Three of Taylor's themes — the substitution of "facts" for "opinion," the new hegemony of the engineer, and the credo of production, provided the starting points for Gantt's reform program.

Among the often repeated slogans of Taylorism was "the substitution of science for rule of thumb." While to Gilbreth this meant the establishment of laboratories in factories, the precise measurement of tasks, and the isolation of the fundamental elements of work, to Gantt it simply conveyed a general disposition to replace present usage with practices based on critical knowledge. This critical knowledge lay in "facts" rather than "theories" or "opinions," in information rather than speculation. Prevalent customs, Gantt thought, were based solely on opinion; therefore, he adopted the general maxim that "the usual way of doing a thing is always the wrong way." The engineer was the man of few opinions and many facts. He would achieve industrial leadership because he promoted production, the nation's source of wealth and strength, in contrast to the financier and the labor leader who tended to impede production.[30]

[29] Horace Bookwalter Drury, *Scientific Management: A History and Criticism* (New York: Columbia University Press, 1915), p. 95; Copley, II, 23.

[30] Copley, I, 112; Gantt to Taylor, Jan. 2, 1910, Taylor Collection; H. L. Gantt, *Work, Wages and Profits: Their Influence on the Cost of Living* (New York: Engineering Magazine, 1910), p. 194, and *Industrial Leadership: Page Lectures, 1915, before the Sheffield Scientific School, Yale University* (New Haven: Yale University Press, 1916), pp. 22–24, 63.

Not only did Gantt give special emphasis to these ideas but, more important, he pointed them in a new direction. The bulk of Taylor's work in the factory centered upon the problems of setting the worker's tasks. Reflecting this approach, his discussion of scientific management usually centered upon the problem of "soldiering." Gantt came to believe that the best place to strike at inefficiency was not in the work methods of the laborer, but in those of management. "For years, with lack of efficiency at the top staring me in the face and hampering me at every turn," Gantt declared, "I have labored to find a means of measuring that efficiency." Most of Gantt's technical innovations in management, his cost system, and his long series of production charts, arose from his search for a device to set standards for management analogous to the stopwatch standards for the worker.[31]

Gantt's criticism of "the lack of efficiency on top" was applied first to the factory and then to society as a whole. Idleness of man or machine in the factory (disclosed in detail by the use of Gantt charts) was seen as a sign of malfeasance at the top. This should be punished with lessened profits. The expense of maintaining part of the factory in idleness, under Gantt's cost system, was not added to the product of men and machines that were working. It was deducted directly from profits rather than passed on to the consumer as a higher price.[32]

Gantt's dramatic step from the planning room of the factory to the world at large came in December, 1916, with the formation of the New Machine. This was an organization of engineers and sympathetic reformers under Gantt's leadership which announced its intention to acquire political as well as economic power. The forming of the New Machine was prompted by Gantt's reading of the works of Thorstein Veblen and the lesser-known Charles Ferguson. It is easy to see the affinity of Gantt for Veblen. Veblen's account of the workings of American society probably struck Gantt as just what he had been saying all along. But if Gantt asked, "What

[31] Gantt, in *Trans. ASME*, XXXVIII (December, 1916), 1318, 1227, and *Industrial Leadership*, p. 39.

[32] Gantt, "The Relation between Production and Costs," *Trans. ASME*, XXVII (June, 1915), 109–28; Alford, *Gantt*, pp. 178–82.

then?" Veblen, as of 1916, gave no answers. Charles Ferguson, on the other hand, gave many answers.[33]

Ferguson had been a lawyer, a minister, an editorial writer for the Hearst papers, a government agent, and an idea man for Colonel Edward M. House, President Wilson's adviser. Ferguson's first books, written at the turn of the century, presented discussions of religious and political problems in a popular manner. He preached a joyous and robust mysticism. He advocated a "religion of democracy" which disdained politics, politicians, and majorities and summoned an aristocracy of the capable to put down the rule of the mob and destroy privilege. Ferguson was a derivative thinker. His early books are like poorer pages plucked from Carlyle's and Ruskin's critiques of modern society, while his later books adopt the anti-state doctrines fashionable among some of the English political pluralists.[34] Yet where Carlyle and Ruskin condemned industrialism, Ferguson made a distinction, common among Americans, between industry and commerce and reserved his censure for the latter. And while accepting the political pluralists' emphasis on society rather than state, Ferguson ignored their concern for group co-operation and stressed, instead, the need for the leadership of an elite. Ferguson's writings spurned the middle ground of everyday

[33] Alford, *Gantt*, p. 264.

[34] These political pluralists, led by the Reverend J. N. Figgis, were exploding the "myth" of state sovereignty and maintaining that certain associations within the state had interests and "personality" independent of it and inviolable by its authority. These views were in vogue in many circles and had a distinct influence on Harold J. Laski and guild socialism in England and on R. G. Valentine (see n. 6). They were an Anglo-Saxon counterpart of continental syndicalist ideas. Though hostile to politics in theory, Ferguson actually was an adept wire-puller. In 1912, he arranged an interview between Frank P. Walsh, an influential Kansas City attorney, and Woodrow Wilson, which brought Walsh into the Wilson camp and, allegedly, many other Midwest city reformers with him. Walsh was rewarded by appointments as chairman of the Federal Commission on Industrial Relations and co-chairman of the War Labor Board. Ferguson was similarly rewarded with appointments as special commissioner of the U. S. government investigating methods of corporate organization, 1913–14, special representative of the Secretary of Commerce, 1914–15, and later agent of the State Department in the Far East. Although Ferguson wrote scornfully that the psychology of party politics was identical with that of sectarian religion, for a long time he leaned toward and lived off the Democratic party.

politics and tossed back and forth between utopianism and putschism.[35]

Ferguson's political or anti-political thinking easily lent itself to an exposition on the order of Bellamy's *Looking Backward*. And it was in this form, as a fictional piece in *Forum Magazine*, that his ideas found their widest audience. The "story," purporting to be an engineer's recollections set down in 1967, described the bringing of America by "artists and engineers" to an "Augustan age of Democracy." [36] Gantt picked up Ferguson's proposal for an elite organization of the capable to carry forward this transformation. He put Ferguson on his payroll and gave him the job of chief theorist and general manager of the New Machine. Ferguson brought journalists and social-reforming clergymen to the organization, and Gantt brought engineers and factory managers of Taylorite persuasion. They declared themselves "a conspiracy of men of science, engineers, chemists, land and sea tamers and general masters of arts and of materials — a fellowship at deadly enmity with all parasites and pretenders," and called upon members to be "a little ruthless and unscrupulous on the side of civilization." Meetings were held, manifestoes were issued, and a long expository letter was sent to President Wilson asking for his approval and support.

The program of the New Machine was a jumbled assortment of Ferguson's and Gantt's ideas. Matter-of-fact proposals were side by side with others that were inflated and ambiguous. The New Machine declared for an increase in the purchasing power of a day's work in New York City, the elimination of plutocracy, technical surveys of cities, transfer of "control of the huge and delicate apparatus of industry into

[35] Rev. Charles Ferguson, "The Economics of Devotion," *Publications of the Church Social Union*, No. 33 (Jan. 15, 1897), *The Religion of Democracy: A Memorandum of Modern Principles* (New York: Funk & Wagnalls, 1900), and *The Affirmative Intellect: An Account of the Origin and Mission of the American Spirit* (New York: Funk & Wagnalls, 1901).

[36] Charles Ferguson, "The Men of 1916," *Forum Magazine* (February, 1916). This theme, the man of science cleaving the Gordian knot of politics with one swift blow, was not unusual in this period. Jack London had published a bloodthirsty version (equally disdainful of the mob) in his short story "Goliath," and Hollis Godfrey, Taylor's friend, had written a book, *The Man Who Ended War* (Boston: Little, Brown, 1908), with a similar plot.

the hands of those who understand its operation," employment bureaus for the better placement of men according to
their abilities, and "public service banks" to extend credit
on assets of personality and capability rather than property.
In the letter to President Wilson, the leaders of the New
Machine called for "an all-correlating moral adventure." [37]

The "all-correlating moral adventure" came, but it was not
what the writers of the letter had expected. Soon after the
United States entered World War I, many of the members of
the New Machine found their way into government service, and
the organization dissolved. Yet the influence of this venture
upon Gantt was lasting and important. Once he had addressed
himself to national issues, Gantt was never again content
simply with factory matters. During the war period and the
months immediately following the Armistice, he pushed his
line of reasoning to yet more audacious conclusions. He
attacked the profit system itself.

Private industry, Gantt asserted, was not using more than
a small percentage of its capacity in the war effort, for it was
in the interest of profits that there be a shortage of goods.
Furthermore, the profit system dissipated much of the energy
of the community by internal friction. The only solution,
therefore, was the subordination of profit to production. The
new singleness of purpose which America had discovered
through its war effort was not a temporary device but a fundamental truth. Traditional politics was sterile, and, if anything
worthwhile were to be accomplished, economic and social
groupings had to be relied upon. Gantt's reproof of politics
was the reverse side of his belief in the primacy of production, reinforced by Ferguson's anti-state teachings. From this
angle, Gantt admired the Russian Soviets ("an attempt to
make the business and industrial system serve the community
as a whole, and in doing so to take over the function of and
entirely supplant the political system") but disliked the Bolsheviks who controlled them. [38]

[37] *The Public Ledger* [Philadelphia], Dec. 10, 1916, pp. 7, 8; Charles
Ferguson, "Letter to the Editor," *ibid.*, p. 9; Alford, *Gantt*, pp. 264,
269–77; Charles Ferguson, *The Revolution Absolute* (New York: Dodd,
Mead, 1918), pp. vii–ix, 272–79, 301–11.

[38] "Efficiency Expert's View of National Outlook," *New York Evening Post*, June 4, 1917, p. 4; Gantt, *Organizing for Work* (New York:
Harcourt, Brace & Howe, 1919), pp. iii–iv, 6–7, 24, 108, and "Efficiency
and Democracy," *Trans. ASME*, XL (December, 1918), 800.

When politics was disparaged, however, political democracy also suffered. Gantt scorned the "debating society theory of government," for "true democracy" was to be ruled by "facts" and not "opinion."

True democracy is attained only when men are endowed with authority in proportion to their ability to use it efficiently and their willingness to promote the public good. Such men are natural leaders whom all will follow.[39]

For Gantt, democracy had nothing to do with the control of policy by those affected by it, but rather concerned the method and purpose of managing men.

His damning of the system of production guided by profits did not mean approval of socialism. Gantt thought that the matter of ownership would be mere detail if production and distribution were scientifically managed. This was to be accomplished through the transformation of industries into "real public service corporations." Committees were to be set up with representatives of producers, distributors, and consumers. These would set prices based on accurate knowledge of supply and demand, bringing maximum production and reducing cost. Of course "the engineer, who is a man of few opinions and many facts and many deeds, should be accorded the economic leadership which is his proper place in our economic system."[40]

Gantt's wartime social program may seem naïve in retrospect. Yet to many of his contemporaries, he was a penetrating thinker and a man of vision. His inflated hopes and theirs were supported in the atmosphere of the "all-correlating moral adventure." In those war years one could point to Hoover the "Food Dictator," man of the hour, as evidence of the likelihood of the hegemony of the engineer. The much

[39] "War for Democracy," *Philadelphia Evening Mail*, April 24, 1917, quoted in Alford, *Gantt*, pp. 196, 259–60.
[40] *New York Sunday World*, Oct. 12, 1919, quoted in Alford, *Gantt*, p. 296; see also Alford, *Gantt*, pp. 261, 262, 298; Gantt, *Organizing for Work*, pp. 20, 101, and "Industrial Leadership and Its Relation to Production and Scientific Distribution," *Journal of the American Bankers Association*, X (November, 1917), 365. A concise summary of Gantt's views can be found in Charles W. Wood, *The Great Change: New America As Seen by Leaders in American Government, Industry and Education Who Are Remaking Our Civilization* (New York: Boni & Liveright, 1919), chap. iv.

publicized dollar-a-year men who descended upon Washington, leaving their businesses behind, gave promise of a future in which profits would come second to service. And even Gantt's public service corporations for production, which would make questions of ownership unimportant, seemed less improbable when the government was taking over the railroads, the country's biggest industry, without working out the details of what sort of rent to pay until months later. We now see all these measures as wartime expedients. But to many onlookers, America seemed to be going through a rapid and fundamental change, and before the fall of 1919 few were willing to set its limits.

Gantt died in November, 1919, just as his hopes were being made absurd. Most of his social schemes were abandoned by his disciples. He had matured his attack on the profit system while in the employ of a non-profit concern, the United States Government. It would have required a special kind of sophistication for his followers to carry his message into the era of normalcy, consciously undermining the authority of the group that was to provide their livelihood.[41] Right after the war there had been some hints at an alliance between Gantt and Veblen.[42] For Veblen and those who thought like him, however, it was not so much Gantt's ideas that were attractive as the existence of Gantt himself, an engineer on the outs with the social order. Few progressives needed to come to Gantt for ideas on society. They had their own. What some of them wanted was a reform program for the factory, and for that they usually went to the better-known writings of Taylor.

The scientific management movement, after Taylor's death, was in some ways a comedown from the movement of the era that had preceded it. None of Taylor's disciples had the founder's commanding presence and ferocious devotion to the cause. Taylor had sketched his program in quick strokes and the disciples developed and elaborated upon his suggestions.

[41] Only Walter N. Polakov managed that. He mixed his Ganttism with his own version of Marxism and added some Korzybski. In the late twenties he went to Russia to help map Stalin's First Five-Year Plan on Gantt charts, returning to America in time to take part in the technocracy craze.

[42] Joseph Dorfman, *Thorstein Veblen and His America* (New York: Viking Press, 1941), pp. 454, 459–60.

They were often more flexible than their master but also more specialized. Each of his three prominent followers, Barth, Gilbreth, and Gantt developed an aspect of Taylor's system which seemed to swallow the system itself. In the eyes of the Taylorites, however, this was not in any way an era of decline but one filled with a sense of things opening up. Scientific management seemed to be growing in power and influence.

• CHAPTER IV

A Normal American Madness

In the decade preceding American entry into World War I, the high cost of living was one of the most talked-about economic issues. The persistent rise in prices was international and provoked an international discussion. Participants ranged from John Bates Clark, the dean of American economists, to the veteran Marxist theoretician Karl Kautsky. In the United States, a Senate committee investigating the matter was joined by a throng of journalists and ministers asking who or what was to blame for the rising prices. Some asserted that the high cost of living was but the cost of high living, while others pointed to "the middlemen," the trusts, the tariff, the exhaustion of natural resources, Alaskan gold, or housewives who had been distracted from their domestic duties.[1]

Middle-class and professional families were most sensitive to these rising costs, for their incomes were least responsive to general price changes. This group provided the most vocal segment of "the public" and produced the spirited support of reform in these years. The Eastern Rate Case of 1910–11, which arose out of the railroads' demands for an increase in freight rates in the northeastern states, became one of the contests into which middle-class opinion entered, hoping to see the general rise in prices held. While this explains some of the excitement of the case, it still leaves its outcome un-

[1] John Bates Clark, "Prices and Income," *The Independent*, LXVIII (March 10, 1910), 514–18; Karl Kautsky, *The High Cost of Living*, tr. AustinLewis (Chicago: C. H. Kerr [1913]) ; "Lodge Cost of Living Committee," *Journal of Political Economy*, XVIII (October, 1910), 637–38; "Symposium on the Cost of Living," *Independent*, LXVIII (April 14, 1910), 794–803.

expected. For with this case, an efficiency craze hit America. It hit like a flash flood, at first covering almost the entire landscape but soon collecting in various places to be absorbed slowly and to enrich the immediate surroundings. At its height the efficiency craze exhibited many forms. Efficiency appeared as a refurbishment of the commonplace exhortations to virtue and duty, as a means for the transference of personal morality to society, and as a means for the control of society without specific reference to morality. In one or more of these forms it appealed to a huge public. Champions of specific reform measures turned toward it. Church leaders, educators, home economists, a bewildering variety of people found uses for it. Of course, efficiency had its opponents and detractors. Organized labor was foremost among these. But this opposition was balanced by support from businessmen's organizations; some finding in efficiency simply an anti-union issue, but a much larger group viewing it as a destroyer of selfishness as well as a producer of bigger and better profits.

When the shippers disputed the proposed advance in railroad rates before the Interstate Commerce Commission, they were immediately portrayed as representatives of the public in many of the popular journals. This, despite the fact that prominent among the shippers were the Chambers of Commerce of Boston and Philadelphia, the Merchants' Association of New York, and other powerful business organizations. The railroads, not insensitive to popular sentiment, based their petition on a wage raise they had granted their workers as well as the general increase in costs. The early hearings, aside from some moments of clever and intricate cross-examination, moved slowly and produced a maze of unassimilable statistics into which it seemed that the railroads might lead the shippers and lose them.[2]

Clifford Thorne, counsel for the shippers of the Midwest, presented an argument along traditional lines which emphasized the hardships that a rate increase would create for the

[2] J. D. Stevens, "Soaring Cost of Living and the Railroad Crisis," *Harper's Weekly*, LIII (Dec. 25, 1909), 8; C. E. Russell, "Paying of the Bill," *Hampton's Magazine*, XXV (October, 1910), 507–26; C. M. Keys, "Shippers Fight for Life," *World's Work*, XX (October, 1910), 13555–64; H. S. Smalley, "Should Railway Rates Be Increased?" *Independent*, LXIX (Oct. 13, 1910), 806–11; "Shall Railway Rates Be Raised?" *Outlook*, XCVI (Dec. 10, 1910), 809–11.

Iowa farmer. However, 1910 was not a particularly good year for this sort of argument. Iowa farmers had never had it so good.[3] Louis D. Brandeis, representing eastern business associations, was more resourceful. His argument began with the contention that the railroads had not proved their need for additional revenue, and then unexpectedly he shifted to the offensive. Even if the railroads had proved their case, Brandeis asserted, the solution did not lie in granting higher rates but rather in introducing the new science of management into railroading. In fact, he promised to show how the railroads could save a million dollars a day.[4]

This argument lifted the Rate Case from inside the daily papers to the front page. It overflowed into the Sunday supplements and was caught up by the weekly magazines. A lawyer for the railroads countered with the argument that the Interstate Commerce Commission had no right to tell the owners how to handle their business. The railroads were economically run,

though their efforts to solve the problem of coal economy had been wrought out rather by use of logarithms than under the basic principles of mechanics as expounded by Blackstone, and the coke they have relied on has been physical rather than philosophical. . . . Much weary toil and wearing anxiety could have been saved had they known what an easy and offhand process it is to save a million a day — on the railways — from the law library in Boston.[5]

Brandeis met this sarcasm with a sober sincerity which won the applause of most onlookers. The day was gone when the critics of "the interests" could be passed off as impractical; reformers were nothing if not practical. The new science of management, Brandeis said, did not come from the law library in Boston but from factories all over the United States. He paraded engineers and businessmen before the Commission to show that scientific management had been applied to diverse industries and to describe how it raised wages and cut costs. After calling ten such witness, Brandeis capped this testimony with Harrington Emerson, a systemizer

[3] *Evidence Taken by the Interstate Commerce Commission in the Matter of Proposed Advances in Freight Rates by Carriers*, 61st Cong., 3d Sess., 1910 (Ser. Vol. 5906), pp. 1152 ff.
[4] "Argument by Louis D. Brandeis," *ibid.*, p. 2620.
[5] "Argument by William Ellis," *ibid.*, pp. 3723–24.

who had actually used time study techniques for the Santa Fe Railroads. Emerson endorsed Brandeis' claim that the railroads could save a million dollars a day.[6]

The railway unions, fearing for their newly won wage increases, came out in support of the railroads. While the hearings were still in session, railway workers held a mass meeting to declare that "whoever opposes fair returns for railroad investments tampers not only with the railroads but with their employees." They submitted a statement condemning Brandeis' argument as unprecedented interference in the running of the railroads and derided scientific management as oppressive and impractical.[7]

The Eastern Rate Case was transformed into a morality play for up-to-date middle-class reformers. On the one side stood the railroads demanding an increase in rates. On the other side stood the unions backing the railroads in their demand. And squeezed between them was the "public," which would have to bear the cost in yet higher prices. Brandeis' solution was impeccable. It would not injure the railroad system whose growth, after all, was associated with the industrial growth of the country. Nor would it wound labor, which more often than not was an exploited segment of the population. Scientific management would guide and restrain both for their own good and for the "public" good.[8]

This was in keeping with the sophisticated style of some of the younger reformers. This sophistication began with the understanding that the battle was not simply between good and evil. Reform was less a matter of rooting up and destroying than of management, control, and regulation. It was not

[6] "Testimony of Harrington Emerson," *ibid.*, pp. 2846–47. The rapid rise of popular interest in the Eastern Rate Case after Brandeis introduced scientific management arguments is clearly seen in the clippings in the Brandeis scrapbooks. See "Advance Rate Case" books Nos. 2, 3, and 4, Louis Dembitz Brandeis Collection, University of Louisville Law School, Louisville, Ky.

[7] *The Commercial and Financial Chronicle*, XCI (Oct. 1, 1910), 830; Mr. P. H. Morrisey, on behalf of a committee representing railway employees, *Evidence Taken by the I.C.C.*, pp. 4358 ff.

[8] Clifford Thorne, reflecting an older style of reform outlook, protested the assertions that there should be no hostility between the parties to the investigation. It was to the interest of the railroads to have high rates and was to the interest of the shippers to have low rates. "Argument of Clifford Thorne, Esq. on behalf of the Corn Belt Meat Producers Association, American National Livestock Association, and Farmers' Cooperative Grain Dealers' Association," *ibid.*, p. 4465.

that good and evil did not exist, but rather that, to maximize good and diminish evil, some sort of "method of intelligence" must be used. Evil, in this complex view, was tied to ignorance and error, while good implied intelligence and fact. Seen from this light, reform became a technical question in which considerations of efficiency were important.

"Efficiency" and "scientific management" were the two catchwords of the popular excitement which followed the Eastern Rate Case, and each caught the imagination of a somewhat distinct audience. Earlier, Taylor's methods had often been called by such names as "functional management" and "the Taylor System." Only infrequently had the term "scientific management" been used. But when Brandeis, in an informal meeting with some of Taylor's followers, asked for an attractive label with which to refer to Taylor's methods at the hearings, the more commonly used names were rejected and "scientific management" was chosen.[9]

This fitted the temperament of many of the new recruits to reform. The word "management" could stand alongside "control," "regulation," and, later, Walter Lippmann's "mastery," in the vocabulary of those whose first principle was the inadequacy of laissez faire. Like the other terms, management implied guidance and constraint, both of which were thought necessary to achieve social harmony. The adjective "scientific" strengthened its appeal further by suggesting disinterestedness, rigor, and a method employing the power of laws of nature which would make the appeal to conscience of the old-style uplifters unnecessary.

The slogan of the largest segment of those excited by the Eastern Rate Case, however, was simply "efficiency." The significance of this particular slogan was that it could embody explicit moral meaning. Efficiency expressed the familiar idea of effectiveness which the popular journals translated into hard work, will power, and thrift. The efficiency movement, like conservation and to a lesser extent even metric reform, had both its explicitly moral and its apparently technical aspects.

The most important link between scientific management

[9] Horace Bookwalter Drury, *Scientific Management: A History and Criticism* (3d ed., rev. and enlarged; New York: Columbia University Press, 1922), pp. 36–38; Frank Barkley Copley, *Frederick W. Taylor: Father of Scientific Management* (New York: Harper, 1923), II, 372.

and efficiency was Harrington Emerson. Emerson's diversified career had included teaching, banking, railroading, speculation in real estate, and "systemizing." Although he had come upon Taylor's work and had been influenced by it, he was not a member of the Taylor group. Strict doctrines were unsuited to him. With sentiment by the bucketful and exhaustless tact, Emerson's charm contrasted sharply with Taylor's nervous intensity and taut ambition.[10]

The Emerson System was a blend of management mechanisms and moral exhortation. Emerson brought no new science. He claimed only to apply maxims that were as old as man. With a penchant for selecting words with moral connotations, he defined efficiency as "the right thing . . . done in the right manner. . . ." Among his twelve principles of efficiency were ideals, common sense, discipline, and the fair deal. Added to these were such favorite words as character, competence, energy, and initiative. Unlike Taylor, Emerson made his living selling efficiency to business. The Emerson Company claimed a hundred employees and offices in six cities. It had no orthodoxy. Emerson was willing to embrace almost any available management device that "worked." He adopted the stop watch but supplemented it with his own more generous bonus plan. (A bonus system was the easiest kind of business nostrum to concoct, and there was rarely a systemizer without his own brand.) When Gilbreth began attracting attention with his motion study techniques, Emerson put away the stop watch and took up the camera. Rather than disrupt the customary line of command in the factory as Taylor had done, Emerson more affably supplemented traditional authority with staff advisers. Because of Emerson's flexibility, his "efficiency engineering" was easier to combine with new ideas than Taylor's system. Sometimes this flexibility bordered on fad-mongering. Emerson offered a twenty-four–lesson home study course in efficiency which was to provide "the short-cut to business success." He added to his staff a "character analyst," Katherine M. H. Blackford, who held a medical degree from Keokuk Medical College and who used a form of phrenology for "scientific" selection of workmen. Emerson boasted

[10] "Harrington Emerson," *National Cyclopedia of American Biography* (New York: James T. White, 1916), XV, 81–82; Harrington Emerson, "Discussion," *Trans. ASME*, XXV (1904), 73.

that Mrs. Blackford never allowed a labor agitator to get past her into the shop.[11]

Overshadowing in importance any of Emerson's techniques was his insistent translation of those techniques into the language of moralism. This gave him a popularity much broader than Taylor's but also more shallow and short-lived. When an efficiency society opened in Kalamazoo, Harrington Emerson was its first speaker. When William Jennings Bryan gave an "efficiency reception" to members of the diplomatic corps, it was Harrington Emerson who lectured.[12]

It could have been predicted that some enthusiasts would establish Benjamin Franklin as "The Father of Efficiency" and adopt No. 6 in his famous list of virtues as the essential principle. "Lose no time; be always employed in something useful; cut off all unnecessary action." The selection of William James as the philosopher of efficiency was less obvious. His name, however, was so bandied about in the popular journals that Josiah Royce felt it necessary to declare that James was not "the dupe of the cruder forms of our now popular efficiency doctrines." It was not so much the William James who tested ideas by their consequences who was celebrated as the James who opposed sloth, warned against the divided self, and emphasized courage. This was the James of "The Will to Believe" and the James that was close to Royce himself. The most frequently quoted essay was "The Energies of Man," in which James wrote, "Compared with what we ought to be we are only half awake. . . . We are making

[11] Harrington Emerson, *Efficiency as a Basis for Operation and Wages* (New York: Engineering Magazine, 1911), p. 224, *The Twelve Principles of Efficiency* (New York: Engineering Magazine, 1912), p. 423, and "Growth of the Efficiency Movement," *Efficiency: The Magazine of Efficient Management*, I (September, 1913), 8 ff.; "The Emerson Company," *Efficiency Magazine*, II (June, 1912), 16; Harrington Emerson, "Testimony before the Commission on Industrial Relations," *U.S. Senate Documents* (Ser. Vol. 6929), p. 1432, and "Principles upon Which Industrial Leadership Rests," *Proceedings of the Society of Industrial Engineers*, April, 1921, pp. 23–24; "Let Emerson Train You," *Scientific American*, CIX (October 11, 1913), 295; Katherine M. H. Blackford and Arthur Newcomb, *The Job, the Man, the Boss* (Garden City, N.Y.: Doubleday, Page, 1915), and *Analyzing Character* (New York: H. Allen, 1917); Katherine Blackford, *Employers' Manual* (New York: Emerson, 1912); Robert Franklin Hoxie, *Scientific Management and Labor* (New York: D. Appleton, 1915), p. 157.

[12] *100%: The Practical Magazine of Efficient Management*, III (December, 1914), 36; *ibid.*, IV (April, 1915), 90.

use of only a small part of our possible mental and physical resources."[13]

Most of the preachers of personal efficiency simply elaborated upon this theme. Their message was of the hope and duty of hard work, thrift, and will power. They called for the development of an efficiency conscience as an obligation to oneself and to society. Most of the literature is crude and comical, but some of the humor and tragedy lies in the simple optimism it shared with the more profound James and Royce. The dominance of personal efficiency was obvious in the symposium held in the *Independent* magazine. Of all the distinguished personages who participated, Brandeis alone discussed industrial production. For the most part, efficiency was preached to bolster old ideas rather than to invite new ones. Herbert Kaufman's *The Efficient Age*, one of the most successful of the many ephemeral books on the subject, followed his equally successful volume, *The Man Who Sneered at Santa Claus.*[14]

Alongside the simpler message of personal efficiency was the complex but often equally hopeful discussion of social efficiency. The advocates of social efficiency related their message more directly to Taylor's system, or one of its derivatives, which usually provided both model and mechanism. Still, the advocates of social efficiency were a mixed group.

[13] "The Father of Efficiency," *Efficiency Mag.*, II (July, 1912), 9; "About Scientific Management," *Springfield Republican*, April 30, 1911; "A New Science of Business Management," *American Magazine*, LXXI (February, 1911), 479–80; "William James," *Executive Economist*, I (March, 1911), 9; *100%*, IV (January, 1915), 80; Josiah Royce, *William James and Other Essays on the Philosophy of Life* (New York: Macmillan, 1911), p. 35.

[14] "What Efficiency Means to Ten Efficient Men: Symposium," *Independent*, LXXX (Nov. 30, 1914), 326–36. The literature of personal efficiency is enormous. Among its best-known writers were ex-ministers and sons of ministers. A random sample: Herbert N. Casson, "Efficiency in Intellectual Life," *Independent*, LXX (May 11, 1911), 999–1001; "Personal Efficiency," *Journal of the Efficiency Society*, III (January, 1919), 73; "Can Efficiency Be Applied to Individuals," *Efficiency Magazine and Sales Manager*, V (July, 1915), 6; Herbert Kaufman, *The Efficient Age* (New York: George H. Doran, 1913); Edward Earle Purinton, *Efficient Living* (New York: R. M. McBride, 1915); Thomas Dyson West, *The Efficient Man* (Cleveland: Gardner Prtg., 1914); Robert Grimshaw, *Personal Efficiency* (New York: Macmillan, 1918). These were sometimes joined by the writers of the earlier success literature: Elbert Hubbard, Orison Swett Marden, and Horatio Willis Dresser.

To one segment, what seemed most important was the projection of the Christian moral code onto society as a whole, while to another social efficiency was tied to social control, which was somewhat harder to reduce to moral terms. A letter to the editor of the *American Magazine* in response to the first installment of "The Principles of Scientific Management" epitomized the views of the moralist advocates of social efficiency. Taylor's scheme, the reader asserted, was the answer to the revelations of the muckrakers:

After wading through the recital of these conditions — the outcome of selfishness and greed — one feels contaminated with filth and would never be clean again, for there seems to be so much the matter with our country. . . . Mr. Taylor's article especially appeals to me because it is creative. It gives more than facts — it teaches. Best of all, it shows the man in control of affairs that further progress is practically impossible unless he adopts the course that will secure the interest of the employee in his business.[15]

Here, the diverse connotations are revealed which made moralistic social efficiency so attractive to so many. First of all, this social efficiency promised a moral clean-up. The high wages and low costs provided by the efficiency systems would check the greed of the employer and the laziness of the employee. One writer described the Taylor System as striking the balance between the impossible selflessness of Tolstoy and the impossible selfishness of Nietzsche. Second, moralistic social efficiency directed its message to "the man in control of affairs." Third, it showed the interests of the employer and the employee to be identical and the wastes of class conflict unnecessary. (Ida Tarbell called this the Golden Rule in Business.) And finally, moralistic social efficiency declared the spread of efficiency systems throughout society to be inevitable.[16]

[15] Y. W. Jacques, "Letter to the Editor," *American Magazine*, LXII (May, 1911), 139.

[16] Typical specimens of this type of social efficiency are: E. D. H. Klyce, "Scientific Management and Moral Law," *Outlook*, XCIX (Nov. 18, 1911), 659–63. Ida M. Tarbell, "Golden Rule in Business," *American Magazine*, LXXVIII (October–December, 1914), LXXIX (January–September, 1915); "The Larger Efficiency," *Independent*, LXXII (June 6, 1912), 1282. Members of the Taylor Society often spoke in this vein, but with less emphasis on an appeal to "the man in control of affairs." M. L. Cooke, "Spirit and Social Significance of Scientific Management,"

Those who spoke of social efficiency in terms of social control rarely mentioned moral purification. They usually looked to neither capital nor labor but to some force outside both, most often the state, to bring the needed social efficiency. They often agreed with the social moralists that the efficiency systems had uncovered the underlying harmony of society and that their spread was inevitable. To the moralists, the efficiency systems were inevitable because they were in line with the economic self-interest of all groups and in accord with moral law. To the advocates of social control, scientific management was inevitable because it was a further development of the industrial revolution, a product of the advance of science. Both groups had nuclei but no clear boundaries. The *Independent*, which stayed with the efficiency craze longer than most popular magazines, was somewhere between them. It predicted "an organization of human relations and activities with reference to economy of energies, efficiency . . ." but insisted that "social control will be moral and plastic." [17]

Through its various forms, efficiency provided something to almost everyone's taste. Scientific management and the efficiency systems, given this new advertising, found their market brisk, and so did the host of charlatans who peddled their own concoctions. Efficiency societies with curious memberships came and went rapidly in most of the major cities of the

Journal of Political Economy, XXI (June, 1913), 481–93, and "Scientific Management, Collective and Individual," *100%*, December, 1913, p. 6. James M. Dodge, "Scientific Management — Progressive and Irresistible," *100%*, January, 1914, p. 5.

[17] "Social Control Presently," *Independent*, LXXXII (April 26, 1915), 132; "Social Efficiency," *ibid.*, LXXI (Nov. 16, 1911), 1103–4. The up-and-coming young sociologist, L. L. Bernard, saw scientific management as an integral part of an all-encompassing system of social efficiency and control. For Bernard, it was the "objective standard" of group survival and growth rather than subjective morality which made social efficiency necessary. As civilization advanced, Bernard believed, the need for social efficiency and control, scientific ruling elites, and compulsion increased. Luther Lee Bernard, "The Transition to an Objective Standard of Social Control," *American Journal of Sociology*, XVI (January, 1911), 519, and "The Application of Psychology to Social Problems," *The Mind at Work: A Handbook of Applied Psychology*, ed. Geoffrey Rhodes (London: Thomas Merby, 1914), p. 208 ff. See also Frank Johnson Goodnow, *The American Conception of Liberty and the American Conception of Government: The Colver Lectures, 1916* (Providence, R.I.: Standard Printing Co., 1916), pp. 11, 21, 61–62; Franklin Henry Giddings, *The Responsible State: The Colver Lectures, 1918* (Boston: Houghton Mifflin, 1918), pp. 98–108.

United States. In April, 1914, in the midst of the popular furor, an efficiency exposition was held at the Grand Central Palace in New York, with Frederick W. Taylor as the main speaker. Before it closed, 69,000 people had attended and its success prompted a similar exposition in the Midwest. Lecture courses in efficiency became familiar offerings in YMCA's all over the country.[18]

The spread of the glad tidings was hastened through their easy acceptance by professional reform leaders who were already committed to specific measures of their own. Miss Edith Wyatt of the National Consumers' League, in her quest for answers to the problems of the woman worker, turned from legislation (because of the enormous difficulties of enforcement) and from unionization (because she thought it diverted trade orders to non-unionized shops) to scientific management.[19] In most cases, however, it was spread not through conversion but through something more akin to syncretism. Scientific management was in the public eye, and leaders of other causes dependent upon popular attention began to translate their appeal in its terms. This was most apparent in the conservation campaign which preceded and the Americanization movement which followed the efficiency craze. Brandeis came to the Eastern Rate Case directly from his work as counsel in the Ballinger-Pinchot conservation investigation and brought the headlines with him. Early explanations of scientific management often described it as a form of conservation. But within a year the conservation congresses were talking the very popular language of efficiency. Americanization, a program for nation-building through a deliberate formative process, made its first appearance in national politics on the Progressive party platform of 1912. Yet when, in 1915, it actually became a dramatic public crusade, one of its foremost slogans was "Efficiency." In fact, "100 per cent Americanism," which became its most famous slogan, may

[18] *Journal of the Efficiency Society*, III (November, 1914), 12; *ibid.* (April, 1914), p. 5; *Efficiency Magazine and Sales Manager*, IV (May, 1914), 1; "Efficiency Exposition in Cleveland," *ibid.* (October, 1914), p. 15; *ibid.* II (April, 1912), 8; *ibid.* (September, 1912), p. 10; *100%*, II (February, 1914), 24.

[19] Sue Ainslie Clark and Edith Wyatt, *Making Both Ends Meet: The Income and Outlay of New York Working Girls* (New York: Macmillan, 1911), pp. xi–xii, chap. vii.

have been derived from Harrington Emerson's very popular phrase, "100 per cent Efficiency."[20]

Undoubtedly, reform syncretism was more than a matter of publicity and slogans. Conservation, scientific management, and Americanization expressed cognate sentiments. The ideologists of the first two thought in terms of physical efficiency, and, more important, the leaders of all three suggested measures which involved a rejection of laissez faire and the acceptance of social guidance and constraint.

Scientific management and efficiency sometimes appeared in unexpected places. Some feminists began to apply scientific management to the home. "Our hope is to bring the masculine and feminine mind more closely together in the industry of home-making by raising housework to the plane of Scientific Engineering," wrote one authority on domestic management. The extreme proposal of dissolving the private home and living in hotels was examined but usually put aside for the sake of morality. The home, however, was to be mechanized, systemized, provided with time-and-motion studies — made free "from mere tradition and social custom." With drudgery banished from the household, the woman would be capable of assuming her equal role in society. Housekeeping Experiment Stations were set up to discover the "principles of domestic engineering." When a series of articles appeared in the *Ladies' Home Journal* applying efficiency science to the household, the response was extraordinary. In one month 1,600 women wrote in for information. Elsewhere, the middle-class mother was told to stop "soldiering" on her job, for the home was "part of a great factory for the production of citizens."[21]

[20] *Proceedings of the Fourth National Conservation Congress,* Indianapolis, October 1-4, 1915. Of course, some of the leaders of the conservation movement thought in the logic of efficiency long before they began to use its terms in their propaganda. See Samuel P. Hays, *Conservation and the Gospel of Efficiency* (Cambridge, Mass.; Harvard University Press, 1960); "The National Americanization Committee," *Journal of the Efficiency Society,* IV (November, 1915), 14; Frances A. Kellor, "Welfare or Manpower Engineering?" *National Efficiency Quarterly,* I (November, 1918), 27; John Higham, *Strangers in the Land: Patterns of American Nativism, 1860–1925* (New Brunswick, N.J.: Rutgers University Press, 1955), p. 238. The best interpretive account of the Americanization movement is to be found in chap. ix. It contains a brief biography of Frances Kellor, who provided an important bridge between efficiency and Americanization.

[21] Mrs. Mary Pattison, *The Business of Home Management: The Principles of Domestic Engineering* (New York: Robert M. McBride,

Many Protestant churches were also open to suggestions. Discussions of declining church membership, which led some church leaders to painful self-scrutiny, sent others in search of expedients. Scientific management and efficiency were way-stations in this search. Rev. Charles Stelzle, who had written on *The Principles of Successful Church Advertising* a few years earlier, now joined the Efficiency Society in New York and became the chairman of its Church Efficiency Committee. Dean Shailer Mathews advised the adoption of the organizational techniques of the factory, while another minister favored efficiency tests and charts. "People," he said, "like to be tied up to progressive, wide awake and going concerns." A prominent layman, who believed in Billy Sunday because Sunday succeeded where others failed, recommended functional management in the church, with experts heading each department for more lasting results. From the vantage point of these new revelations, one minister could look back on the Crusades as "only a mob impulse and a terribly wasteful undertaking in life and time." Scientific management and efficiency became a talisman for both the modernists and the fundamentalists in the church. While the latter talked of adopting "business methods of efficiency," the former unabashedly called for the use of scientific methods in the work of the church.[22]

1915), p. 1; Charlotte Perkins Gilman, "The Waste of Private House-keeping," *Annals of the American Academy of Political and Social Science*, XLVIII (July, 1913), 91–95; Mrs. Christine Frederick, *Household Engineering: Scientific Management in the Home* (Chicago: American School of Home Economics, 1915), p. 16, and *The New Housekeeping: Efficiency Studies in Home Management* (New York: Doubleday, Page, 1914); "A Brandeis for the Kitchen," *Boston Evening Transcript*, Jan. 23, 1911; Belle Case La Follette and Caroline L. Hunt, "Home and Education," *La Follette's Weekly Magazine*, April 29, 1911; Francis E. Leupp, "Scientific Management in the Family," *Outlook*, XCVIII (August, 1911), 832; Martha B. Bruere and Robert W. Bruere, *Increasing Home Efficiency* (New York: Macmillan, 1912), pp. 290–91.

[22] Rev. Charles Stelzle, "Efficiency in Church Work," *Journal of the Efficiency Society*, III (March, 1913), 61, 64; Shailer Mathews, *Scientific Management in the Churches* (Chicago: University of Chicago Press, 1912), "How To Apply Efficiency Tests to a Church," *Current Literature*, LIII (December, 1912), 675; Eugene M. Camp, "Better Church Methods," *Journal of the Efficiency Society*, IV (April, 1915), 25; Rev. Frederick B. Greul, D.D., "Organizing the Church for Efficient Economic Service: A Present Day Necessity," *ibid.*, III (March, 1913), 65; Carroll E. Harrington, "The Fundamentalist Movement in America, 1870–1920" (Ph.D. dissertation, University of California, 1959), p. 54;

If American homes and churches were willing to open their doors to efficiency, American schools seemed ready to welcome it with abandon. The schools, like many other public institutions, had come in for their share of investigations, exposures, controversies, and reforms. Americans were told repeatedly that their schools were old-fashioned, ineffective, and impractical. As if to prove these accusations false, school administrators seized upon the principles and techniques of scientific management which the Eastern Rate Case had brought to the public view. Here was a "science" that could give their work a professional rationale. "The burden of finding the best methods," explained a lecturer on educational administration, "is too large and too complicated to be laid on the shoulders of the teachers." Scientific management prescribed the centralization of authority and the close supervision of all tasks. As applied to the schools, it increased the authority of the administrator and limited the freedom of the teacher. In the midst of the efficiency craze, the new profession of public school administrator took form.[23]

The history of scientific management was influenced by its opponents as well as by its advocates. Even at the height of its popularity some spoke out in sharp disagreement. The leaders of the industrial betterment movement, which after all was a rival reform program for the factory, were among scientific management's first critics. Although, of all the writers on industrial problems, they adopted the crudest mechanical analogies — they were among the first to use such terms as human engineering — when confronted with Taylor's system they decried its neglect of the "human element." Sometimes this referred to Taylor's elimination of exhortation in his program, but more often it expressed their belief that Taylor laid stress on those aspects of industrialism which least deserved reinforcement. They accused scientific management of exaggerating the division of labor and of making man into a machine. The uncompromising critique of industrialism developed in the writings of Carlyle, Arnold, and

George Arthur Andrews, *Efficient Religion* (New York: George H. Doran, 1912); *Making Religion Efficient*, ed. Clarence Augustus Barbour (New York: Association Press, 1912); Paul Moore Strayer, *Reconstruction of the Church* (New York: Macmillan, 1915).

[23] Raymond E. Callahan, *Education and the Cult of Efficiency* (Chicago: University of Chicago Press, 1962), p. 87, chaps. iii, iv, v, and viii.

Ruskin was applied specifically to Taylor's system by those advocates of industrial betterment who believed that factory life could be tempered by humanitarianism and made Christian.[24]

The socialists played both sides of the street. While they condemned Taylorism as a refined form of exploitation, "objectively" it was a further step toward the inevitable coming of socialism. To some of the socialists the Taylor system, with its central planning department and its orderly regulation of production, had an intrinsic attractiveness. Some called for an "Americanized Socialism" which would argue in terms of efficiency, and others showed up at Taylor Society meetings to take part in discussions. Even Morris Hillquit, reflecting these leanings, began to emphasize waste rather than exploitation as capitalism's outstanding evil.[25]

At the other end of the social scale, the upholders of the Genteel Tradition in American found much that was objectionable in the efficiency craze. Many saw it as an attack on spirituality and culture. Henry Cabot Lodge, presenting his attack from the floor of the Senate, cast his argument in the form of a brief lecture on Italian art. He championed quality in preference to mere quantity, and deliberation against speed. Criticism similar in tone often appeared in the *Unpopular Review*, the quarterly in which the eccentric publisher Henry Holt provided a platform for Irving Babbitt. The issue became acute when efficiency invaded such inviolable places as the university and the church. Morris L. Cooke, one of Taylor's closest disciples, had been selected by the Carnegie Foundation for the Advancement of Teaching to investigate university organization. His report, which treated

[24] Ohio State University, "Congress of Human Engineering, October 26, 27, 28, 1916," *Bull. Taylor Soc.*, XXI (January, 1917), 5, 6 ff.

[25] Louis Duchey, "Scientific Business Management: What Is It? What Effect Will It Have on the Revolutionary Movement?" *International Socialist Review*, XI (April, 1911), 628; William English Walling, *Progressivism — And After* (New York: Macmillan, 1914), chap. iii; Rufus W. Weeks, "The Socialized Efficiency Expert To Be," *Masses*, III (May, 1912), 16; Maud Thompson, "Scientific Management," *New York Call*, May 6, 1911; J. B. Mac Farland to F. W. Taylor, March 8, 1911, in the Taylor Collection; Frank B. Gilbreth to F. W. Taylor, May 27, 1913, Taylor Collection; James MacKaye, *Americanized Socialism* (New York: Boni & Liveright, 1918); Charles P. Steinmetz, *America and the New Epoch* (New York: Harper, 1916); Harry W. Laidler, *Socialism in Thought and Action* (New York: Macmillan, 1920), chap. i.

the college teacher as a producer and recommended standardized lecture notes and the adoption of the "student-hour" as
a unit of measurement of administrative efficiency, shocked
many educators. "Reads as if the author received his training
in a soap factory," said one. The *Nation*, which had given scientific management a lukewarm reception at the time of the
Eastern Rate Case, now declared that this had gone too far.
It was absurd to measure college professors and pastors whose
work was "too deep for the mechanical probe to reach. . . .
There are some things off which it [efficiency] must keep its
hands; and the spirit that bloweth where it listeth is one of
them." [26]

The most sustained and effective opposition came from organized labor.[27] The efficiency craze posed a threat both in
the form of antagonistic public sentiment and in the form of
specific factory techniques. The middle-class reformers who
became enthusiastic about guidance and control usually saw
themselves as the controllers, while the workers saw themselves as the controlled. Even the preachments of hard work
had ominous overtones. The worker was urged to the traditional virtues of hard work, but his work experience was
deprived of the traditional rewards of craftsmanship or entre-

[26] Henry Cabot Lodge, in *The Congressional Record*, 63d Cong., 3d
Sess., LII (Feb. 23, 1915), 4352; *H.R. Report No. 698* 64th Cong., 1st
Sess., (Ser. Vol. 6904), p. 13; William Chase Greene, " 'Efficiency' and
Efficiency," *Unpopular Review*, V (April, 1916), 281; Emily R. Boole,
"The Crime of Efficiency," *ibid.*, VI (July, 1916), 157; George B. Dut-
ton, "System versus Slippers," *ibid.*, III (April, 1915), 367; Morris L.
Cooke, *Academic and Industrial Efficiency* (Carnegie Foundation Bulle-
tin No. 5 [New York: Carnegie Foundation, 1910]); Kenneth E.
Trombley, *The Life and Times of a Happy Liberal: A Biography of
Morris Llewellyn Cooke* (New York: Harper, 1954), p. 11. Among the
many similar appraisals were Professor A. G. Webster, "Scientific Man-
agement and Academic Efficiency," *Nation*, XCIII (Nov. 2, 1911), 416;
A. L. Lowell, "Measurements of Efficiency in College," *Education*,
XXXIV (December, 1913), 217; "Efficiency Nostrum at Harvard," *Nation*, XCVI (Jan. 16, 1913), 49; "Efficiency Tests for Clergymen," *ibid.*,
XCV (Oct. 31, 1912), 403. The clash between the advocates of efficiency
and the upholders of the genteel tradition and the implications of this
clash for American society are discussed with discernment by Henry F.
May, in *The End of American Innocence: A Study of the First Years
of Our Own Time, 1912–1917* (New York: Alfred A. Knopf, 1959), pp.
132–36.

[27] Milton J. Nadworny, *Scientific Management and the Unions: 1900–
1932* (Cambridge, Mass.: Harvard University Press, 1955), is the standard work on the subject.

prencurial independence. Labor was that peculiar entity which was treated as both a commodity and a moral act, and often suffered the difficulties of each. It could never completely enter the realm of buy-cheap–sell-dear in which other commodities moved. While organized labor was using its growing strength to assert its rights, the right to take it easy was rarely among them.

Basic to Taylor's program was the view that laborers did not work as hard as they should. This was partly out of laziness but more significantly (as he emphasized in his later writings) out of a mistaken understanding of their interests and in reaction to outmoded management systems and wage policies. This latter explanation did not remove the moral reproach of "soldiering," and the unions were put on the defensive. They were quick to announce that they did not approve of a man lying down on the job. "We give the best that is in us," Gompers insisted. One of his first rebuttals of the Taylor System was a categorical denial of the existence of "soldiering," the disease which Taylor was out to cure.[28]

As Taylor's proposals for reorganization of the factory were better understood, organized labor's opposition hardened. At many points the arguments of the railroad brotherhoods during the Eastern Rate Case resembled those of the railroads, even to the point of praising J. P. Morgan's entrepreneurial abilities. John Mitchell, in an expression of labor solidarity, backed the brotherhoods. He protested against the anti-union views of some of the proponents of the efficiency systems and added objections which had already been made by non-labor critics. Labor leaders were later to quote Henry Cabot Lodge to good advantage. In the early days of the efficiency campaign some of the leaders of the AFL seemed somewhat uncertain of their grounds for opposition, but the metal trades unions were not in the least in doubt. In a circular letter of April 26, 1911, James O'Connell, president of the International Association of Machinists, declared that

[28] "Testimony of Samuel Gompers," *Investigation of Taylor System of Shop Management*, 62d Cong., 1st Sess., Hearings on H.R. 90 (Washington, D.C., 1911), p. 27. See also "Testimony of John R. O'Leary," *Investigation of the Taylor System and Other Systems of Management*, 62d Cong., 2d Sess., Hearings, House Special Committee (Washington, D.C., 1912), I, 95. Samuel Gompers, "Miracles of Efficiency," *American Federationist*, XVIII (April, 1911), 273.

scientific management would deprive the machinist of his exclusive skills and would overturn his union. "Either the machinists will succeed in destroying the usefulness of this System through resistance, or it will mean the wiping out of our trade and organization. . . ." The metal trades unions took the lead in the fight against Taylorism.[29]

The most important clash between the unions and the Taylorites arose over the attempted introduction of scientific management into the government arsenals. For the Taylorites, the arsenals provided a strategic spot for the application of their system. Military discipline eliminated the problem of obstruction at the top. Also, the success of the system in the arsenals, which had a reputation for the most enlightened conditions of work, would have provided excellent advertising. The arsenals, however, presented an even more favorable field of battle for the unions. Not only were a large proportion of the workers union members, but the unions, through their influence in Congress, also had a voice in the management. The unions used both their weapons; they struck and they lobbied.[30]

The thrusting of the Taylor System before Congress resulted in a series of inconclusive hearings which gave Taylor the opportunity to present a classic case for his system and the unions a chance to sharpen their arguments against it. Bills were introduced into both houses of Congress forbidding the use of the stop watch and the payment of bonuses on government work. The debate in the Senate indicated that most senators didn't understand the Taylor System and voted in accordance with their sympathy or lack of sympathy toward

[29] Warren S. Stone, Grand Chief International Brotherhood of Locomotive Engineers, "Railway Engineer Opposed to Efficiency," *Eleventh Annual Meeting of the National Civic Federation* (Jan. 12, 1911), p. 110; John Mitchell, "Efficiency Not Acceptable to Wage Earners," *ibid.*, p. 113; 64th Cong., 1st Sess., *Directing the Work of Government Employees,* (Ser. Vol. 6904), 13; Philip Taft, *The AF of L in the Time of Gompers* (New York: Harper, 1957), p. 299; James O'Connell, International President of International Association of Machinists, "Official Circular," reprinted in *Investigation of the Taylor System and Other Systems of Management,* 62d Cong., 2d Sess., House Special Committee, Hearings (Washington, D.C.: 1912), p. 1222.

[30] Nadworny, pp. 31–33, 55–65. Sterling D. Spero, *Government as Employer* (New York: Remsen Press, 1948), pp. 449–63; Hugh G. J. Aitkin, *Taylorism at Watertown Arsenal* (Cambridge, Mass.: Harvard University Press, 1960).

organized labor. Lodge, of course, voted for quality and deliberation as against quantity and speed. Elihu Root, who, as Secretary of War, had introduced the German General Staff idea into the Army and reorganized the arsenals, demonstrated the clearest understanding of Taylorism and found it to his liking. Now he led the floor fight to permit its introduction. Yet the unions succeeded in getting riders outlawing the stop watch attached to the naval and war appropriation bills. These riders were successfully renewed each year, and they were extended to the entire federal establishment in 1917 and 1918.[31]

It was the unorganized and unskilled workers who bore the brunt of scientific management's advance in the factory. The new regime demanded greater work speeds and increased subordination. These workers, often new immigrants and women, did not organize to announce their happiness or unhappiness in their work. Investigators who visited these factories usually found what they wanted to find.[32] Whether the workers thrived under this new system, as the Taylorites claimed, or whether it broke something within them, as some contended, we do not know.

The debate over scientific management in Congress and the success of the trade unions in driving the stop watch from the arsenals brought new friends to the movement whose chief interest was in its anti-union implications rather than the advocacy of the principles of scientific management. A "Committee of Ten" was set up, headed by leading businessmen of the Taylor Society, to counter the unions' legislative offensive. Although the committee was granted a meeting with President Wilson, and won the endorsement of Secretary of War Baker and such notables as Thomas Edison, its principal

[31] *Congressional Record,* 63d Cong., 3d Sess., LII (February 23, 1915), 4343–90; Bureau of the Budget, Division of Administrative Management, *Legislative Restriction on Time Studies in the Federal Government* (Washington, D.C., 1945), p. 2; Nadworny, p. 84; Spero, pp. 458–63.

[32] John Golden, president of the United Textile Workers of America and Edith Wyatt, recent convert to Taylorism, visited the Brighton Mills at Passaic, N.J., where Gantt had installed the Taylor System. Their findings differ at almost every point. "Testimony of Edith Franklin Wyatt," *Hearings,* 62d Cong., 2d Sess., House Special Committee, pp. 592–605; "Testimony of John Golden," *Commission on Industrial Relations* (Ser. Vol. 6929), pp. 1018–19.

support in the congressional infighting came from James A. Emery, the chief lobbyist for the National Association of Manufacturers.[33]

During the Eastern Rate Case, *American Industries*, the journal of the NAM, had tactfully presented both sides of the controversy. Although the editor showed an interest in Taylor's ideas, this interest cooled when Taylor declined a request for an article explaining his system. Taylor had little use for NAM, or any organization whose primary purpose was fighting the trade unions. He disclaimed any intention of fighting the unions; rather, as he saw it, his reforms in the factory would simply eliminate much of the need for them. He usually advised businessmen bringing their factories under scientific management to quit the NAM. Taylor's reluctance to tie up with the NAM was understandable, moreover, in view of the extreme and isolated position of the organization and its comparatively small membership. The NAM was a predominantly midwestern body of medium-sized businesses. In sharp contrast to the prevailing hopefulness of the period, the NAM took a pessimistic view. Early in 1912, President Kirby declared both the Republican and Democratic parties overwhelmed by radicalism and called for the formation of a third party around which conservatives could rally. America talked of John Q. Public and aiding the oppressed, but the NAM frankly expressed the views of a class. The only oppressed the NAM recognized were those of foreign lands. And they could be uplifted only if the pressures of unionism were resisted and unfortunate foreigners allowed free entry into this country.[34]

[33] J. R. Dunlap, "Dangerous Labor Legislation Now before Congress: A Call for Prompt Action," *Engineering Magazine*, LI (April, 1916), 1–11; "The Defence of Premiums," *100%*, II (December, 1915), 16. Some businessmen used the slogans of the efficiency craze to urge their employees to harder work. The Hudson Motor Company posted a sign: "Don't you fight against Efficiency. If you do you are fighting your own best interests." *Efficiency Magazine and Sales Manager*, V (May, 1915), 4. The Ford Motor Company formed an efficiency club for their employees. *100%*, IV (April, 1915), 60.

[34] Correspondence between Frederick W. Taylor and H. H. Lewis (Dec. 16, 1910–May 22, 1911), Taylor Collection; Copley, II, 407; O. H. L. Wernicke, "Remarks," *Proceedings of the 17th Annual Convention of the National Association of Manufacturers, May 20–22, 1912*, p. 40; George S. Bondinot, "Secretary's Report," *ibid.*, p. 60; *Proc. 18th Ann. Conv. NAM*, p. 34; *Proc. 19th Ann. Conv. NAM*, p. 21; *Proc. 20th*

The NAM supported scientific management, but chiefly as a weapon against trade unions. "Of what avails your system of scientific management," complained President Kirby, "when in union shops it is a case of saving at the spigot and spending at the bung." This was not simply a question of avoiding distractions from the all-important struggle against unionism, for the NAM did busy itself with such questions as factory safety, workmen's compensation, and industrial education. But, there was something particularly uncongenial about scientific management. *The Scarlet Empire*, an anti-Utopian novel of violence and sentimentality by ex-president David M. Parry, which was serialized in *American Industries*, warns of the drying-up of knowledge and ability through system. Efficiency, a prominent NAM official explained, was really a matter of common sense and experience, qualities which most businessmen had in good store. But scientific management, with its science, its experts, and its placing of system above personality, undermined the traditional justifications of self-made men.[35]

Closer to the center of the progressive outlook was the National Civic Federation, an object of scorn to NAM officials, who preferred even the socialists. This was an organization which provided a meeting ground for organized labor and big business, with the purpose of promoting conciliation. The driving force of the organization came from neither capital nor labor, but from such men as Ralph Easely, an ex-journalist and its director, and prominent professional men like Seth Low and Benjamin Ide Wheeler. The National Civic Federation pounced upon scientific management and efficiency almost as soon as the Eastern Rate Case publicly announced their existence. It scheduled the first public meeting in which union officials and management engineers spoke from the same platform. The hope of accord, however, was quashed at this meeting, when the AFL came out in strong condemnation of Taylorism. Much enthusiasm for efficiency and scientific management persisted within the Civic Federation.

Ann. Conv. NAM, p. 7; John Kirby, Jr., "President's Address," *Proc. 17th Ann. Conv. NAM*, p. 84; "Resolutions," *ibid.*, p. 282.

[35] Kirby, *loc. cit.*, p. 97; David M. Parry, "The Scarlet Empire," *American Industries*, XIV (August, 1913), 37; F. C. Schwedtman, "What Co-operation Will Do," *100%*, III (August, 1914), 7; "The System Fanatics," *American Industries*, XIV (November, 1913), 20.

But as trade union opposition stiffened, the Federation's official interest declined. Easely always tried to avoid areas of discord and to concentrate upon problems in which agreement seemed possible.[36]

Efficiency and co-operation were bywords of business in the progressive era, and both of these interlaced considerations of morality and profit. The spirit of business co-operation was embodied in the newly organized Rotary Clubs and the flourishing trade associations, the former stressing uplift and the latter, dollar benefits.[37] The spirit of business efficiency was embodied in the various efficiency societies which tried simultaneously to eliminate selfishness, boost hard work and clean living, and seek devices for bigger and better profits. Those aims were further complicated by the diverse composition of the efficiency societies, which were not strictly businessmen's organizations.

Some of the efficiency societies were of such mixed membership that they could not find a common purpose and disappeared soon after efficiency dropped from the front pages. The three centers of the efficiency movement in New York before American entry into the war were the Taylor Society, the Efficiency Society [of New York], and *Efficiency Magazine*. The first was dominated by engineers devoted to the advancement of the science of management, and the last was a publishing venture by a seller of efficiency systems and labor-saving office machines, who was concerned unashamedly with questions of profit.

For the Efficiency Society [of New York] the issues were less clear. It was formed in the summer of 1911 with aspira-

[36] Kirby, *loc. cit.*, p. 93; Marguerite Green, *The National Civic Federation and the American Labor Movement, 1900–25* (Washington, D.C.: Catholic University of America Press, 1956), pp. 37–41, 286–87. "Scientific Management — Efficiency," *11th Annual Meeting of the National Civic Federation, January 12–14, 1911*, pp. 74–117.

[37] Of course, this differentiation was never complete. The early Rotary Clubs were organizations of small and middle-sized businesses which took in each other's trade and tried to freeze out other competitors. *Rotary? A University Group Looks at the Rotary Club of Chicago* (Chicago: University of Chicago Press, 1934), pp. 4–51. On the other hand, Arthur Jerome Eddy, "the father of the open price trade association," often championed co-operation and, using moral epithets, condemned competition. He also wanted to bring Culture to the businessman. *The New Competition* (New York: D. Appleton, 1911) ; *Ganton and Company* (Chicago: A. C. McClurg, 1908).

tions of becoming a national organization. The organizing committee included prominent business leaders, publicists, educators, economists, and "professional advisers" (engineers and management engineers).[38] The society soon gave up its national design as well as other ambitions. Some business members complained that the meetings were too academic and theoretical and asked that the "high-brow stuff" be eliminated. The engineers, they said, put the other members on the defensive. The businessman's wing soon took control, and the organization moved from the Engineering Societies Building to Park Row, the newspaper and advertising section of town. Yet once the organization was in the businessmen's hands they could not lead. They could live off the efficiency movement but they could not run it.[39]

A non-business group of lower caliber, some of them cranks, took over the leadership. One of the better-known presidents of the Society at this stage was Melville Dewey (Melville Lewis Kossuth Dewey, which he often spelled Melvil Dui for efficiency's sake). He was the inventor of the Dewey Decimal System, which classified all human knowledge into ten major categories. Dewey's erratic and contentious career led through library reform, metric reform, simplified spelling, and efficiency, with resignations from Columbia University, New York State Board of Regents, and the New York State Library. Even with its narrowed membership, the Efficiency Society [of New York], under his administration, did not reach a consensus as to what exactly it was all about. The usual article in the journal started by asking, "What Is Efficiency?" and ended with some simple maxim. Even from a

[38] On this organizing committee were T. C. du Pont, A. Barton Hepburn, Robert Fulton Cutting, Edward T. Devine, Irving Fisher, Edwin F. Gay, Jeremiah W. Jenks, Edward Alsworth Ross, E. R. A. Seligman, Albert J. Beveridge, Norman Hapgood, Ben B. Lindsey, S. S. McClure, Adolph S. Ochs, Walter H. Page, Oswald G. Villard, John Hays Hammond, Harrington Emerson, and others.

[39] "Action Needed Instead of Apologies," *Efficiency Magazine*, III (July, 1913), 10; H. S. McCormack, "Efficiency Society Redeeming Itself," *ibid.* (May, 1913), 9; Boyd Fisher, "A Plan of Reorganization," *Journal of the Efficiency Society*, III (July, 1913), 21; "Harmony Needed in Efficiency Society," *Efficiency Mag.*, III (September, 1913), 4; "Plans of the Efficiency Society," *ibid.*, (October, 1913), p. 4; "Changes in the Efficiency Society," *ibid.* (November, 1913), p. 4; Planning Efficiency Society Betterment," *Efficiency Magazine and Sales Manager*, IV (May, 1914), 10.

strictly business point of view, the Society meetings became less useful. There were talks on Dust and Efficiency, Pensions and Efficiency, Salesmanship and Efficiency, even Cheerfulness and Efficiency. Soon the "and Efficiency" disappeared, and then the organization itself.[40]

The efficiency craze, which began with the Eastern Rate Case in 1910, receded by 1915 and disappeared with America's entry into the war. Efficiency as morality, the most widespread and easily acceptable form, was quickest to evaporate. Efficiency as a series of profit-making stunts was soon discredited. Efficiency as a technique of industrial management and as a form of social control found a small but steadfast following and had more lasting effects.

[40] Grosvenor Dawe, *Melvil Dewey: Seer, Inspirer, Doer* (Essex Co., N.Y.: Lake Placid Club, 1932); Fremont Rider, *Melvil Dewey* (Chicago: American Library Association, 1944); "Melvil Dewey," *National Cyclopedia of American Biography*, IV, 492. The Melville Dewey Collection in the Butler Library at Columbia University reveals the sad plight of the Efficiency Society in its declining days.

• CHAPTER V

Three Reformers of Reform

Louis D. Brandeis, Herbert Croly, and Walter Lippmann picked up scientific management at the time of the efficiency craze but did not put it down quite as easily as many others did. Though all three men were prominent intellectual leaders of the progressive movement, they were actually of different generations. Brandeis came of age politically when Rutherford B. Hayes was in the White House, and Civil Service versus "the Stalwart ruffians" was the new issue of the day. When Croly came to politics, the Sherman Act had just been placed on the statute books, and business wildcatting was nearing its end. Lippmann cast his first vote amid the excitement of the insurgent Republican revolt, when many bright young men were predicting that socialism was the coming thing. Each reached intellectual maturity and made his first commitments (commitments which were never completely left behind) in very different times. Considered together, these three men reveal some of the different layers of experience that were reflected in the progressive thought of the years before 1917. All three were affected by scientific management. Their interpretation of its doctrines was important not only for scientific management but for their own social outlook as well.

Louis D. Brandeis was the son of Jewish refugees from the defeated European liberal revolution of 1848. His family settled and prospered in Louisville, Kentucky, where Brandeis was born. After starting his education in local private schools, he went on to study at a German *Gymnasium* and finally at the Harvard Law School.[1] Apparently Brandeis met with no anti-Jewish prejudice, and his brilliance admitted him to the circles of the Back Bay cultural elite. He heard Ralph Waldo Emerson at a private reading of his "Education" and later knew and visited with such important and representative figures as William Dean Howells and Barrett Wendell. "Those years were among the happiest of my life," he remembered. "For me, the world's center was Cambridge."[2]

Brandeis accepted New England ideals, and his speech even borrowed the regional twang. His law partner, Samuel D. Warren, wrote that in many ways Brandeis was a better example of New England virtues than the natives. And few were surprised when this son of immigrants (but member of the exclusive Dedham Polo Club as well) advised Bostonians to protect "the great heritage of an honorable, glorious past, handed down to us by our fathers."[3]

Brandeis' politics, at first, were also New England. A Republican until the Cleveland-Blaine election, he became a mugwump in 1884. Once having stepped out of the fold, however, Brandeis moved closer to the Democrats than most New Englanders, and gave his support to the Olney wing of the party. This was still considered quite reputable and conservative. When the rumblings of Populism reached Boston, Brandeis was recommending the establishment of law courses for laymen, since "the conservatism which the study of law engenders would be invaluable."[4]

By the time of the Eastern Rate Case, however, Brandeis had earned a national reputation as a proponent and defender

[1] Alpheus Thomas Mason, *Brandeis: A Free Man's Life* (New York: Viking Press, 1946), chaps. i, ii, and iii.

[2] Elizabeth Glendower Evans, "Mr. Justice Brandeis: The People's Tribune," *Survey*, LXVII (Nov. 1, 1931), 141; Mason, pp. 42–43, 76; Ernest Poole, "Brandeis, a Remarkable Record of Unselfish Work Done in the Public Interest," *American Magazine*, LXXI (February, 1911), 482.

[3] Louis D. Brandeis, *The Curse of Bigness: Miscellaneous Papers of Justice Brandeis*, ed. Osmond K. Frankel (New York: Viking Press, 1934), p. 263; Mason, pp. 329, 389.

[4] Louis D. Brandeis to Charles W. Eliot, March 20, 1893, quoted in *The Brandeis Guide to the Modern World*, ed. Alfred Lief (Boston: Little, Brown, 1941), p. 75; Alfred Lief, *Brandeis: The Personal History of an American Ideal* (Harrisburg, Pa.: Stackpole Sons, 1936), p. 30.

of social legislation; he had found one of the currents of reform which moved from mugwumpery to progressivism. This
current was formed by the admonitions and achievements of
the social workers, muckrakers, and social gospel sociologists.
The public health, safety, and morals, they asserted, were
not adequately protected by moral teaching and liberty of
contract in a competitive market economy. Brandeis started
from a limited concept of "police power," and gradually
found increasing need for government control. "The Government must keep order not only physically but socially."[5] The
mugwump ideal social order of moderate-sized enterprise,
personal independence, and social responsibility was to be
preserved not by opposing government power but by using it.

In addition to a growing acceptance of active government,
there was a change in Brandeis' social perspective. He came
to look upon the working classes through the eyes of the social
worker rather than the political economist. Labor appeared
more as a category of humanitarianism and even philanthropy and less as a category of economics and politics.
Stronger trade unions were necessary to protect the worker
from the greed of the employer and to provide a training
ground in the spirit of brotherhood and altruism. Occasionally Brandeis expounded the doctrine of the middle ground —
that society must be protected from the excesses of both capital and labor — but it is apparent that he found less to fear
from below than from above.[6]

His opposition to "plutocracy" took two forms. He condemned the power of the trusts, proposing a regime of pub-

[5] Ernest Poole, *loc. cit.*, p. 492. Moving into progressive currents, he
supported Theodore Roosevelt in 1904, Taft in 1908, Wilson in 1912,
and 1916, and was "100% for Hoover" in 1920. Alpheus Thomas Mason,
"Variations on the Liberal Theme," *Publications of the Brandeis
Lawyers Society*, I (1947), 2.
[6] Louis D. Brandeis, *Business — a Profession* (Boston: Small, Maynard, 1914), pp. 18–21, 83–84, 152–53, 321; Mason, *Brandeis: A Free
Man's Life*, chap. x; Louis D. Brandeis to Paul U. Kellogg, Dec. 19,
1911, in *Brandeis Guide*, p. 129; Mason, *Brandeis: Lawyer and Judge
in the Modern State*, (Princeton, N.J.: Princeton University Press,
1933) p. 75. Yet when the economic results of the growth of unionism
were thrust upon him, Brandeis could not discard his early-formed belief
in economic individualism. He favored strong unions but opposed the
closed shop. Louis D. Brandeis to Ray Stannard Baker, Feb. 26, 1912, in
Brandeis Guide, pp. 139–40; Mason, *Brandeis: A Free Man's Life*, pp.
294–301.

licly regulated and sustained competition as substitute; and he scorned "commercialism," offering the professional ethic in its place. Brandeis shared the characteristic mugwump disdain for "mere money making" and "the vulgar satisfaction which is experienced in the acquisition of money." Yet the longing for old ways and old families, often an important component in the mugwump response to a rapidly changing America, was not readily available to Brandeis. His family was not old and his way to prominence had been through the legal profession.[7]

It is understandable, therefore, that Brandeis came to place a special emphasis upon the virtues of professionalism. Moreover, where most engineers would have been happy to establish (and most lawyers happy to re-establish) the influence of professional ideals within their own occupation, Brandeis carried the teachings of professionalism to business itself. His efforts paralleled Taylor's. Brandeis' proposal for transforming business into a profession meant the rejection of financial return as the primary measure of success and the development of a technical knowledge, training, and discipline which would eliminate the charlatans and establish the leadership of the competent. The new graduate schools of business were to play an important part. The university would subdue and civilize the market place.[8]

Brandeis' belief in the leadership of the competent extended to the realm of politics as well. When the movement to "give government back to the people" was already well under way, Brandeis was still calling for a leadership of those with "greatest ability and intelligence" to act as a brake

[7] Brandeis, *The Curse of Bigness*, pp. 104–36; Mason, *Brandeis: A Free Man's Life*, chap. xxii; Brandeis, *Business — a Profession*, pp. 1–12; John C. Van Dyke, *The Money God* (New York: Charles Scribner's Sons, 1908). This book provides a synoptic example of mugwump attacks upon commercialism. It traces the disease through the American social organism and incidentally points to the Jew as a principal carrier. Van Dyke was a professor of art history at Rutgers University and the author of *Art for Art's Sake* (1893) and even *Nature for Its Own Sake* (1898). He was from an old family and did recommend the return to old ways (the Ten Commandments) as an antidote.

[8] Brandeis' view of the role of business colleges was often shared by their deans. Harlow Stafford Person, *Industrial Education* (Boston: Houghton Mifflin, 1907), pp. 22–26, 27. Herbert Heaton, *A Scholar in Action: Edwin F. Gay* (Cambridge, Mass.: Harvard University Press, 1952), p. 76.

upon democracy. He accepted neither Robert M. LaFollette's program of direct government nor Theodore Roosevelt's "recall of judicial decisions."[9] Nevertheless, as Brandeis himself rose to a position of political influence, his confidence in the people's ability to select capable guides increased. Leadership was important, but now Brandeis stressed that it must be leadership by consent. He became optimistic about the fruitful interaction of expert and public opinion.[10]

Brandeis prescribed the "logic of facts" to pry open outmoded precedents and theories and to provide a social understanding free from bias.[11] In this era of naturalism in the arts and new inductive techniques in the social sciences, there seemed to be much to support his belief that many large issues could be reduced to matters of fact. On a more sophisticated level, this belief was paralleled by John Dewey's attempt to provide an ethical outlook based on the methods of the descriptive sciences. And if Dewey's ethical pronounce-

[9] Brandeis, *Curse of Bigness*, p. 41; Mason, *Brandeis: A Free Man's Life*, pp. 94, 124, 368; Brandeis, *Business — a Profession*, pp. 341–42; Louis D. Brandeis to Roger Sherman Hoar [no date given], 1911, File Box NMF45, Louis D. Brandeis Collection, University of Louisville Law School, Louisville, Ky.; Louis D. Brandeis and others, *Preliminary Report on Efficiency in Administration of Justice* (Boston: National Economic League [1914]), pp. 6, 11, 15, 29. There were three principal reactions of those who accepted the progressive discovery that the courts made political decisions: (1) recall of judicial decisions (Theodore Roosevelt); (2) judicial reticence (Holmes and later Frankfurter); (3) sociological jurisprudence (Roscoe Pound and Brandeis). Brandeis' endorsement of sociological jurisprudence did not involve diminishing the position of the judiciary, but rather broadening its training. Brandeis, *Business — a Profession* (rev. ed., 1933), pp. 358–63, liv. Roscoe Pound liked to quote Sir Edward Coke on this issue — that judges are responsible only to God. Morris Cohen, "A Critical Sketch of Legal Philosophy in America," *Law: A Century of Progress* (New York: New York University Press, 1937), II, 299.

[10] Louis D. Brandeis to Morris L. Cooke, July 24, 1916, in *Brandeis Guide*, p. 71; Mason, *Brandeis: A Free Man's Life*, p. 602. In January, 1913, Felix Frankfurter, then an important link joining Brandeis, Croly, and Lippmann, asked for Brandeis' comment on a proposed organization of a small group of experts to draw up plans for the remodeling of the social system. Brandeis answered that such a group would be "of great assistance to the forward movement," but reliance could not be placed in any one small group. *Brandeis Guide*, p. 281. Often, in these later years, Brandeis seemed to echo Jefferson's belief in a natural aristocracy. The crucial difference was that Jefferson held his view when many believed in an aristocracy of property, and Brandeis held his amid cries for direct democracy.

[11] *Brandeis Guide*, pp. 121, 160, 209–10.

ments often turned out to be those of liberal Christianity, one should not be surprised that in the Brandeis brief, as in Frank Norris' *The Octopus* and the Pittsburgh Survey, the "facts" turned out to be on the side of the underdog.[12]

Related to this invocation of "the facts" was an eagerness to deal with conditions rather than motives. This was a reform without an appeal to conscience and without the usual struggle between the forces of good and evil. To stand at Armageddon was proof of failure. The reformer, rather than siding with any of the contending forces as he found them, was to discover harmonizing devices which would be to the interests of the antagonists and to the benefit of the general public. Reform was primarily an act of "social invention."[13]

Scientific management was just such a "social invention." At the time of the Eastern Rate Case it promised to preserve the shippers' current rates, the railroads' profits, and the union's wage increase and also hold down the cost of living for the public. Brandeis need not blame any of the parties. The railroad managers were not incompetent, for, as Brandeis pointed out, scientific management was so new that one could hardly have expected them to have adopted it earlier.[14]

Brandeis' fervor for scientific management persisted long after the Eastern Rate Case. Scientific management spoke to Brandeis' mugwump belief in the virtue of hard work and the strength of character which hard work fostered. Scientific management converted haphazard and unskilled jobs into precise and methodical tasks that permitted the worker to appraise his individual achievement and compete against a

[12] The major exception was the famous Report of the Immigration Commission which required 47 volumes to recommend a literacy test. After World War I, beginning with the Army intelligence tests and their findings that the average American was a moron, "the facts" were usually on the other side. After the war, the technique of the Brandeis brief was used to strike down social legislation. Mason, *Brandeis: Lawyer and Judge*, pp. 117–22.

[13] For Brandeis' most direct statement of this approach see "Testimony of Louis D. Brandeis," *U.S. Commission on Industrial Relations*, 64th Cong., 1st Sess., Sen. Doc. 415 (Ser. Vol. 6936), Jan. 23, 1915, p. 7669; Brandeis, *Curse of Bigness*, p. 40; Poole, *loc. cit.*, p. 492; *Brandeis Guide*, pp. 210, 280–85.

[14] Louis D. Brandeis, "Brief Submitted to the Interstate Commerce Commission," *Evidence in Matter of Proposed Advances in Freight Rates*, U.S., 61st Cong. 3d Sess., Sen. Doc. 725 (Ser. Vol. 5911), pp. 4752, 4759, 5262.

standard. Hard work need not be devitalizing work, Brandeis assured his social worker friends. In fact, he stressed the connection between reduced fatigue and increased production. The industrious were rewarded by rapid promotion, and the less able workers were shown the way to improvement through the intensified supervision provided under Taylor's system of functional foremen. These functional foremen, and the planning department to which they were responsible, provided a new type of leadership for the factory. It was a leadership based on knowledge and could provide means toward the professionalization of business. This technical knowledge was not elicited from abstract or *a priori* principles but from hundreds of thousands of industrial trial-and-error experiments. Taylor, like Brandeis, based his law on facts.[15]

Scientific management offered extraordinary proof for Brandeis' prediction of the professionalization of business. Before the Eastern Rate Case, he had discussed this idea only parenthetically, but afterward he extended and elaborated upon it. Scientific management also led Brandeis to shift his emphasis from questions of the distribution of wealth to those of its production. Furthermore, it added to his stock of "social inventions," thereby providing for more varied and flexible reform campaigns.[16]

Brandeis agreed with the Bull Moosers that bigness should be handled as a condition and not a crime. However, his insistence that the trusts were inefficient and that efficiency must prevail turned their own type of argument against them. The

[15] Louis D. Brandeis, *Scientific Management and the Railroads* (New York: Engineering Magazine, 1911), pp. 11–14, 25–29, 37–42; "Testimony of Louis D. Brandeis," *U.S. Commission on Industrial Relations*, 64th Cong. 1st Sess., Sen. Docs. Vol. 26 (Ser. Vol. 6929), pp. 1003–4; Brandeis, *Business–A Profession*, pp. 48–9; *Curse of Bigness*, p. 56; Josephine Goldmark, *Fatigue and Efficiency: A Study in Industry* (New York: Charities Publication Committee, 1912), chap. vii; *Business — A Profession* (rev. ed., 1933), p. 317; Louis D. Brandeis, "What Is the Relation between Efficiency and Modern Trusts?" *Efficiency Magazine*, II (November, 1912), 6, 16; Louis D. Brandeis to A. J. Portenar, Jan. 22, 1917, File Box NMF8, Brandeis Collection.

[16] "Testimony of Louis D. Brandeis," *U.S. Commission on Industrial Relations*, 64th Cong. 1st Sess., Sen. Doc. Vol. 19 (Ser. Vol. 6929), pp. 991, 1008–9; Vol. 26 (Ser. Vol. 6936), p. 7666; *Curse of Bigness*, p. 51. When Brandeis did support some redistribution of income, it was in terms of increased incentives to production. Louis D. Brandeis to Arthur T. Morey, Feb. 14, 1912, *Brandeis Guide*, pp. 230–31.

plants in which scientific management had been applied most thoroughly, Brandeis pointed out, were medium-sized. Too great a distance from the diversity of fact which made up the actual operation of a plant was destructive of sound judgment. The huge profits of the trusts, Brandeis insisted, owed more to control of the market than to efficiency in production. He admitted that free and unrestricted competition was a failure; but he did not accept the trusts as the inevitable alternative. Brandeis gave his support to resale price maintenance, co-operatives and the trade associations which could preserve medium-sized enterprises and (with the aid of scientific management) efficiency as well.[17]

Brandeis was that special type of progressive whose chief ideals remained those of a New England mugwump but whose manner became that of a social engineer. This manner seemed devious to many of his early allies in reform. In the tangled battle over Brandeis' appointment to the Supreme Court, some of his fellow reformers testified to what they thought was his fickleness to principles. For New Dealers, his failing was often precisely the opposite. "Brandeis was a wolf in sheep's clothing — more accurately a doctrinaire parading as an instrumentalist," thought Rexford Tugwell; and David Reisman, Brandeis' law clerk in the thirties, was of a similar opinion. Yet out of his dual outlook, Brandeis created a popular image of scientific management in the years before World War I that seemed public-spirited and humane but also modern, technical, and morally neutral.[18]

[17] Louis D. Brandeis, "What Is the Relation between Efficiency and Modern Trusts?" p. 6. Louis D. Brandeis to Robert M. La Follette, Sr., May 26, 1913, *Brandeis Guide*, p. 55. Mason, *Brandeis: A Free Man's Life*, chap. xxii. But what if the trusts somehow did turn out to be more efficient? When cornered with this question, Brandeis fell back upon the argument that the social and political ills resulting from trustification make medium-sized enterprise the more desirable form. "Testimony of Louis D. Brandeis," *Hearings before the Senate Committee on Interstate Commerce Pursuant to S. Res. 98*, 62d Cong., 1st Sess. (1911), I, 1168, 1174.

[18] Among those who testified against the Brandeis appointment were Clifford Thorne, midwestern reformer and Brandeis' associate in the Eastern Rate Case; Hollis R. Bailey, who aided Brandeis in inaugurating his savings-bank life insurance plan; William S. Youngman, an ally in the Boston Elevated Fight; and Edward P. Warren, a fellow reformer in the Public Franchise League. Rexford G. Tugwell, *The Art of Politics* (Garden City, N.Y.: Doubleday, 1958), p. 247. Samuel J. Konefsky, *The Legacy of Holmes and Brandeis: A Study in the Influence of Ideas* (New York: Macmillan, 1956), p. 163.

Though his immediate audience was more limited than Brandeis', Herbert D. Croly's influence on progressive thought was not less important. Croly came from a family dedicated to reform. His mother was a prominent feminist and his father a journalist with an itch for unusual causes.[19] Young Croly was closely tutored in Comte's ritualistic and hierarchical Religion of Humanity — once described by T. H. Huxley as Catholicism minus Christianity — but broke with those doc-trines in the search for more rigorous belief. During his much interrupted college education at the City College of New York and Harvard, which allowed for two years of study and travel in Europe, Croly drifted from an early interest in teaching philosophy to a career in serious journalism and art criticism. He established himself at the art colony in Cornish, New Hampshire (which had been founded by Augustus Saint-Gaudens and his admirers), and joined the staff of the *Architectural Record*, where he remained for thirteen years, serving as editor for six years.[20]

Croly came to the field of American architecture when there was an increasing concern for professionalism, similar to that which Taylor witnessed in engineering and Brandeis observed in law. American colleges of architecture were grow-ing in number and the many students trained at the Ecole des Beaux Arts in Paris were beginning to influence the American scene. The special training which infused American architecture drew its rules not so much from science as from the arts, and the importance of this training was often not recognized by the architect's client. The architect's posture,

[19] Oswald Garrison Villard, "Herbert David Croly," *Dictionary of American Biography*, ed. Harris E. Starr (New York: Charles Scribner's, Sons, 1944), XXI, 209. Croly's father campaigned against the use of black and white print, expressed sympathy for race improvement through stir-piculture, for polygamy, and for the idea of transforming prostitution into a proper vocation for women. David Goodman Croly, *Glimpses of the Future* (New York: G. P. Putnam's Sons, 1888), pp. 48–54, 55–61, 171–73; Carl Bode, "Columbia's Carnal Bed," *American Quarterly*, XV (Spring, 1963), 57–60. However, many of the father's less unusual ideas appear again in the works of the son. For example, the advocacy of an active, centralized state, strong trade unions, regulated trusts, and the rejection of equality in democracy, of deliberative legislatures, etc. D. G. Croly, pp. 10–17, 20–21, 25–26, 110–12, 138.

[20] Eric F. Goldman, *Rendezvous with Destiny* (New York: Alfred A. Knopf, 1953), p. 191; Villard, "Croly," DAB, XXI, 209; Jesse Lynch Williams, "Herbert Croly," *Metropolitan Magazine*, XXXIII (March, 1911), 742–44; Philip Littell, "A Look at Cornish," *Independent*, LXXIV (June 5, 1913), 1297–98.

therefore, was more self-conscious and self-justifying than the engineer's.[21]

In his work for the *Architectural Record,* Croly did much to supply justification for the professionalization of architecture. There was little instinctive love of art in America, Croly declared. The great mass of building in this country was directed by men who were simply trying to build for as little money as possible something which would sell or rent. Even those who seemed concerned with beauty had the most barbarous taste. Art, which in most countries grew almost unconsciously, in America had to be pursued consciously if at all. This required a trained elite. In architecture, progress depended absolutely upon increasing the authority of the architect with his client — upon the ability of the architect to get his own way.

Yet Croly did not adopt an unqualified aesthetic elitism. For he also believed that art was a social expression, and in its greatest periods a thoroughly popular growth. Somehow the American architect must be popular and influential without surrendering to the demands of business and popular taste, and without compromising the integrity of his work.[22]

How was this to be done? How could the artist be "good" and yet "formative in a large way" while America "resents exclusive technical standards and refuses to trust men who through their training have earned the right to represent such standards?" In his writings on architecture and his similar discussion of literature, Croly never resolved the dilemma. Yet when he generalized the problem and placed it in a broader social and historical setting, he did find what he thought to be the answer.[23]

[21] For example, compare Barr Ferree, "What Is Architecture?" *Architectural Record,* I (1891–92), 199, and A. D. F. Hamlin, "The Difficulties of Modern Architecture," *ibid.,* (1892–93), p. 137, with R. H. Thurston, "President's Inaugural Address," in *Trans. ASME,* I (1880), 13, or Oberlin Smith, "The Engineer as a Scholar and a Gentleman," *ibid.,* XII (1891), 42.

[22] Herbert D. Croly, "Criticism That Counts," *Architectural Record,* X (1901), 404, "American Artists and Their Public," *ibid.,* pp. 256, 258–61, "Rich Men and Their Houses," *ibid.,* XII (1902), 28, "What Is Indigenous Architecture?" *ibid.,* XXI (1907), 437–38, "Art and Life," *ibid.,* I (1891–92), 227, and "The New World and the New Art," *ibid.,* XII (1902), 151.

[23] Herbert D. Croly, "Henry James and His Countrymen," *The Lamp: A Review and Record of Current Literature,* XXVIII (February, 1904),

That answer was embodied in *The Promise of American Life*, Croly's most important work. This book, the author wrote, was "an attempt to justify the specialized contemporary intellectual discipline and purposes against the tyranny of certain aspects of our democratic tradition." The way to that justification lay in the formula, "a constructive relation between democracy and nationality." Democracy could not realize itself without a strong state, a strong executive, and an efficient administrative apparatus. The more democratic institutions were used to provide for the needs of the people, the more the people must resort to nationalized government organization. This organization would make use of men's varying individual abilities by giving each a sufficient sphere of exercise. Individualism and distinction were to be rescued not by smallness, as Brandeis thought, but by bigness and the specialized competence that bigness required. The commercialism which Croly condemned as destructive of individuality was precisely the small competitive model which Brandeis was trying to modify and preserve.[24]

Croly saw Theodore Roosevelt as America's exemplary political leader. He used strong government action for social purposes and "exhibited his genuinely national spirit in nothing so clearly as his endeavor to give men of special ability, training and eminence a better opportunity to serve the public." Croly's ideal was a democracy with an emphasis on distinction rather than equality, on "exceptional men" rather than "the popular average." It was a government which would use democratic organization "for the joint benefit of individual distinction and social improvement."[25]

Croly's vigorous state was also designed to prevent the social divisions within America from dissolving society. The magnitude and specialization which he urged upon government had already been realized in society at large. Since the Civil War, America had changed from a nation which was

47–53, and "The Architect in Recent Fiction," *Architectural Record*, XVII (Feb. 1905), 138. "The Case of the statesman, the man of letters, the philanthropist, or the reformer does not differ essentially from that of the architect." Herbert D. Croly, *The Promise of American Life* (New York: Macmillan, 1909), p. 446.

[24] Herbert D. Croly, "Why I Wrote My Latest Book: My Aim in 'The Promise of American Life,'" *World's Work*, XX (June, 1910), 13086, and *The Promise of American Life*, pp. 33–34, 185–214, 272–79, 408–15.

[25] Croly, *The Promise of American Life*, pp. 170, 207, 409–15.

agricultural and relatively homogeneous to one which was industrial and highly differentiated. The unconscious social bonds of a homogeneous society had been shattered, Croly observed, and must be replaced by a conscious national ideal which would harness the special interests and purposes of the country to the general welfare.[26] Croly's new nationalism would fulfill the people's needs, provide sanction for individual excellence, and maintain social order. These themes were carried through almost all of his subsequent writings.

His next book, *Progressive Democracy*, was clearly less impressive than the *Promise of American Life*. Already in the *Promise* Croly had suggested a belief that the center of experience was moral and even mystical, but he had carefully restrained this feeling. He wished to avoid the usual reformer's vice of recklessly cutting through complexities with simple moral verities. Croly's moralism was always more abstract and even abstracted. Yet in *Progressive Democracy*, these leanings brought him to a faith which was "emancipated . . . from bondage to a mechanical conception of social causation."[27] He came to neglect those circumstances and forces which condition and constrict the operation of the human will. The importance of social understanding, therefore, decreased and exhortation increased. *Progressive Democracy* is laced with calls to sacrifice, social righteousness, moral stamina, and risk, and with glorifications of the creative power of the will, the moral value of democracy, and the mystical unity of human nature. At some points it sounds like Friedrich Nietzsche presiding as a YMCA discussion leader.

Croly projected his mixture of moralism and mysticism into society as a "moving democratic faith." This faith, which was to provide a new social cement, temporarily diminished the role of the national ideal and even the state in his writings. *Progressive Democracy*, however, gave Croly's other guiding concepts — expertism and popular entry into and use of government — even more extreme application. The "moving democratic faith" downgraded law, constitutions, deliberating legislatures, and the party system, while it exalted direct democracy. The extension of direct government allowed for

[26] *Ibid.*, pp. 138–40.
[27] *Ibid.*, pp. 452–54, 145–46; Herbert D. Croly, *Progressive Democracy* (New York: Macmillan, 1914), p. 174.

fluid majorities which would quickly and easily register their desires. But this very fluidity made necessary an enlarged and powerful administrative division of experts to "discover and define better methods of social behavior and . . . secure cooperation in the use of such methods by individuals and classes." [28] Croly's proposal was for some sort of plebiscitarian administocracy.

The first issue of the *New Republic*, with Croly as its editor-in-chief, was on the newsstands about a month after the publication of *Progressive Democracy*. It was to be a political journal with high intellectual standards, addressed to that select audience interested in serious but unconventional social inquiry. "We shall be radical without being socialistic," wrote Croly. "We are seeking to build a body of public opinion believing in a more thoughtful and radical form of progressivism." The financial suport came from Willard and Dorothy Straight. They had become interested in Croly's ideas through the *Promise of American Life* and were willing to subsidize the new magazine with almost no strings attached. [29] The very existence of the *New Republic* could be seen as support for Croly's belief that America would find place for professional competence and integrity. It seemed to prove that he who paid the piper need not call the tune, providing the piper played exceedingly well.

The *New Republic* quickly won a reputation for fresh comment on current events in the light of much cleverness and information. The enthusiastic mysticism and exalted moralism of *Progressive Democracy* were not reflected in its pages, nor even in Croly's signed articles. At this point, Croly seems to have been less interested in their direct relevance to politics. The *New Republic* reached for intelligence rather than moralism and science rather than mysticism. As "the facts" were to provide Brandeis with the basis of a social program free from bias, so the scientific method was to do something similar for Croly and his staff. The *New Republic* championed expert administration and social control through active government. Within this context it also supported

[28] *Ibid.*, pp. 44–62, 236–37, 284–302, 330–31, 349–77, 368.
[29] Herbert Croly to Randolph Bourne, June 3, 1914, in the Randolph Bourne Collection, Butler Library, Columbia University. Herbert D. Croly, *Willard Straight* (New York: Macmillan, 1924), pp. 473–74.

"radical democracy" but often in such a manner as purportedly to save democracy from itself.[30]

An odd and interesting illustration of the *New Republic*'s line of thought was its support for the Cincinnati Unit Plan. This scheme, for which Croly won Dorothy Straight's financial backing, set up geographically based bicameral councils of consumers and professional groups which would "break down the barriers between the expert and the community," provide for various local needs, and even replace conventional political forms. The Social Unit Plan combined efficiency and democracy; it wed the experts to the masses. "Bosses" were to give way to "leaders," and the usual political party, in which the sincere efforts of the "college-bred" too often came to naught, was to be replaced by this new type of organization, in which such efforts would gain importance. After some tentative successes, the Social Unit Plan was overwhelmed and crushed in the Red Scare and the mass rush for normalcy.[31]

[30] For the *New Republic*'s views on expert administration see "The Expert and American Society," *New Republic*, XV (May 4, 1918), 5–7, IV (Sept. 25, 1915), 194–95, VI (March 18, 1916), 170, VII (July 8, 1916), 240–41, XV (June 8, 1918), 160; Herbert Croly, "Unregenerate Democracy," *ibid.*, VI (Feb. 5, 1915), 18. See also George Santayana, "Natural Leadership," *ibid.*, III (July 31, 1915), 333–34; "Philonous," "Intellectual Leadership in America," *ibid.*, I (Nov. 14, 1914), 17. On social control through active government see "Innocuous Frankenstein," *ibid.*, II (May 20, 1915), 169–70; "The Future of the Two Party System," *ibid.*, I (Nov. 14, 1914), 10–11; "Municipal Ownership versus Regulation," *ibid.*, (Nov. 28, 1914), pp. 12–14; *New Republic*, V (Nov. 6, 1915), 6. On democracy see "True Democracy," *ibid.*, III (June 26, 1915), 186; H. G. Wells, "What Democracy Means," *ibid.*, XIV (April 13, 1918), 316–18. After the smash-up of progressivism, when Croly began to lose interest in politics and became disillusioned with the social engineer, mysticism and moralism often reappeared in his writings. Herbert D. Croly, "Disordered Christianity," *ibid.*, XXI (Dec. 31, 1919), 136–39, "Regeneration," *ibid.*, XXIII (June 9, 1920), 40–47, and "Better Prospect," *ibid.*, XXVII (Aug. 24, 1921), 344–49. For Croly's disillusionment with the social engineer, see the introduction to Eduard C. Lindeman's *Social Discovery* (New York: Republic Publishing Co., 1924), pp. v–xx.

[31] A description of the Cincinnati Unit Plan is found in its inventor's autobiography. Wilbur C. Phillips, *Adventuring for Democracy* (New York: Social Unit Press, 1940), pp. 148–259, 370. For the enthusiastic support given to the Cincinnati Unit Plan by the New Republic see "The Expert and American Society," *New Republic*, XV (May 4, 1918), 7; "Who Makes Bolshevism in Cincinnati," *ibid.*, XVIII (April 19, 1919), 365–67. See also E. T. Devine, "Social Unit in Cincinnati: An Experiment in Organization," *Survey*, XLIII (Nov. 15, 1919), 115–26.

From its first issues, the *New Republic* seemed to be drawn to scientific management. "Mr. Taylor and his followers," a leading article asserted, "have made a major contribution to civilization." The *New Republic* not only condemned the AFL campaign against Taylorism but urged the application of scientific management to diverse social issues.[32] One editorial, presumably written by Croly, proposed setting up industrial colonies under the charge of a corps of expert scientific managers to which tramps and loafers would be committed. These camps would provide training in industrial habits and "disembarrass society of the workshy." Another editorial reported that many manufacturers were not efficient enough to pay their workers a decent salary and still stay in business. It recommended that the State Industrial Commission hire efficiency experts to inspect the factories' efficiency (just as it provided inspectors for safety and sanitation) and impose business efficiency upon all employers. In the pages of the *New Republic* the problem of industrial peace was often seen primarily as a question of business organization.[33]

The basis for the support of scientific management becomes apparent in Croly's own writings. Croly singled out the planning department for special attention. It was to replace the "adventurers" and "amateurs" with experts and substitute broad social purposes for selfish and hidebound goals. It was in the planning department that the college-bred man, in a position of influence, could impose technical standards for the general good. The discerning reader, Croly admitted, would note the parallel between the program of scientific management for the factory and his own suggestions for an enlarged administrative body for the state.

The parallelism is, as a matter of fact, extremely close. The successful conduct of both public and private business is becoming more and more a matter of expert administration, which demands similar methods and is confronted by the solution of similar problems.

[32] "Trade Unions and Productive Efficiency," *New Republic*, XV (May 11, 1918), 40–41; "Anti-Efficiency in War," *ibid.* (May 4, 1918), 8–9; *ibid.*, IX (Dec. 23, 1916), 204; *ibid.*, VII (May 27, 1916), 75; *ibid.*, VI (April 18, 1916), 252.
[33] "Salvaging the Unemployable," *New Republic*, IV (Oct. 2, 1915), 221–23; "Beyond Arbitration," *ibid.*, IX (Jan. 20, 1917), 315–17; *ibid.*, (Nov. 25, 1916), 84; *ibid.*, (Dec. 23, 1916), 204–05.

Moreover, Taylor's vision of the harmony of the classes through a common commitment to production afforded an economic analogy to the national ideals which would stand above class and avert social dissolution.[34]

The *New Republic*'s interest in scientific management did not hinge solely upon Croly's influence. Walter Lippmann, a brilliant young member of the editorial board, had come to these interests largely without Croly's help and followed them to somewhat different uses. Lippmann, like Brandeis, came from a well-to-do German-Jewish family and, like him, had made an outstanding record at Harvard. Yet while Brandeis embraced New England traditions and was, at least in the early years, accepted by its heirs, Lippmann kept and was kept at a distance. He was on good terms with the faculty but worked most closely with such outsiders as Graham Wallas and George Santayana.[35]

At Harvard, Lippmann became a socialist. Socialism in the America of the day was a various and loosely defined movement containing many contrasts in belief and temperament. Lippmann's youthful career in socialism consisted in a rapid sampling of its many varieties. He was influenced by the Fabianism of Graham Wallas, dipped into settlement work, served for four months as secretary to Rev. George R. Lunn, socialist mayor of Schenectady, and at one point led a left-wing local of the Socialist party.[36]

These rapidly succeeding socialisms had at least two connecting themes: a desire to bring a better life to the lower classes and a desire to bring order out of the disorder of capitalism. It was particularly among those socialists who laid special stress on setting things in order that a predisposition for elite leadership appeared. For a while, Lippmann

[34] Croly, *Progressive Democracy*, pp. 395–97, 398, 399, 400, 403–05.

[35] David Elliott Weingast, *Walter Lippmann* (New Brunswick, N.J.: Rutgers University Press, 1949), p. 6.

[36] *Ibid.*, pp. 7–11. For a while, Lippmann was an assistant muckraker to Lincoln Steffens. Though some of Steffens' "discoveries" were dazzling, he provided no consistent constructive program. Perhaps sensing his young assistant's dissatisfaction, Steffens wrote a friend, "We have been the blind leading the blind, but we have led. . . . I suppose that some young fellow like Lippmann will expose us some day, and I say let 'em expose." Lincoln Steffens to Francis J. Heney, December 23, 1910 in Francis J. Heney Papers, Bancroft Library, University of California, Berkeley.

took James MacKaye's *Economy of Happiness*, a learned socialist treatise on political engineering, as his bible.[37] With one hand Lippmann held to science and order, but he stretched to grasp indeterminacy, emotion, imagination, and even mysticism with the other. He praised the city planners and the efficiency experts, but he also praised the William James, who respected the findings of the spiritualists, and Henri Bergson, who taught the doctrine of Life Force. Lippmann became a regular visitor at Mabel Dodge's famous Fifth Avenue salon of artists, reformers, and radicals where a cheerful gospel of passionate living was preached.[38]

Lippmann respected both the non-rational and the rational, impulse and order, art and politics. He attempted to reconcile these apparently conflicting allegiances in his first two books, *Preface to Politics* and *Drift and Mastery*. In the *Preface* not only did the perspectives of the statesman and the artist sometimes merge, as in Croly's writings, but, more radically,

[37] Carl Binger, "A Child of the Enlightenment," *Walter Lippmann and His Times*, ed. Marquis Childs and James Reston (New York: Harcourt, Brace, 1959), p. 34. Walter Lippmann, "Basic Sanity," *New Republic*, II (April 3, 1915), 241. MacKaye had presented five lectures at Harvard on "An Outline of Political Engineering" while Lippmann was there as a student. "James MacKaye," *National Cyclopedia of American Biography*, XIV (New York: White, 1917), 159. Lippmann's clearest description of his brand of socialism was in his articles for the *New Review*. See Walter Lippmann, "The I.W.W. — Insurrection or Revolution," *New Review*, I (August, 1913), 701–6, and "Walling's 'Progressivism and After,'" *ibid.*, II (June, 1914), 340–44. The elitist currents in American socialism of the day and the stress on the rational restraints of socialism have not been discussed by the historians of the movement; however, these both become apparent in even a cursory glance at socialist literature. See for example Lena Morrow Lewis, "Jeffersonian vs. Social Democracy," *Masses*, III (April, 1912), 17; Rufus W. Weeks, "The Socialized Efficiency Expert To Be," *ibid.* (May, 1912), 16. Max Schrabisch, "Is American Democracy a Failure? Its Evils and the Way Out," *New York Call*, May 26, 1912, p. 13; "By the Editor," *Metropolitan Magazine*, XXXVII (April, 1913), 4. The *New Review*, which strained to avoid any taint of the Marxist "Classics" and Marxist orthodoxy, featured Engels' hard-boiled essay "The Principle of Authority" II [April, 1914], 222.

[38] Walter Lippmann, "Lewis Jerome Johnson," *Amer. Mag.*, LXXIII (Feb. 1912), 418, "More Brains — Less Sweat," *Everybody's Magazine*, XXV (Dec. 1911), 827–28, "An Open Mind: William James," *ibid.*, XXIII (Dec. 1910), 800–801, and "The Most Dangerous Man in the World," *ibid.*, XXVII (July, 1912), 100–101. For a discussion of the Mabel Dodge salon and its importance for the young intellectuals of the prewar years see May, *The End of American Innocence*, pp. 310–14.

the underlying force of art and politics were held to be one and the same. Man was a bundle of desires. In politics as well as art, emotion, will, and fantasy bubbled beneath. The statesman was to recognize these forces. Though they were initially destructive, the statesman should not suppress them, but rather direct them toward socially constructive paths. The state was not the effect of the agreement of rational men; it was the supreme instrument of civilization.[39]

But who would wield the instrument? Lippmann left this and other important issues unclear. He did emphasize the role of leaders and experts but placed them in a broad frame of a popular government. Lippmann's insistence upon the importance of the irrational also threatened the standing of objective knowledge itself. He liked the arguments of Nietzsche, Bergson, and Sorel that ideas were disguised impulses. Yet, if ideas were disguised impulses, did not that apply to this idea as well? Was anything safe from subjectivism? At some points the *Preface to Politics* threatened to turn into a postscript.[40]

Actually Lippmann only flirted with this radical form of irrationalism. It seemed to be out of character for him. Mabel Dodge described the Lippmann of those days as always rational, well-balanced, and in complete possession of himself. She recalled that he even felt the need for more organization to eliminate chaos and confusion at her soirées. And in fact, already within the *Preface to Politics* was a path from the quagmire of subjectivism, which he followed in his later *Drift and Mastery* and his articles in the *New Republic*. This path was the scientific method. Scientific method, to Lippmann, was a practical device which was free from bias and could provide a discipline for intellectual order and social co-operation.[41]

[39] Walter Lippmann, *A Preface to Politics* (New York: Mitchell Kennerley, 1913), pp. 47–52, 77–85, 112–21, 266–67.

[40] *Ibid.*, pp. 18, 155, 195–96, 212–13, 225–36, 302. H. Stuart Hughes, in *Consciousness and Society* (New York: Alfred A. Knopf, 1958), discusses the European origins of the irrationalist thought reflected in Lippmann's work.

[41] Mabel Dodge Luhan, *Intimate Memories: Movers and Shakers*, II (New York: Harcourt, Brace, 1936), pp. 92, 118; Lippmann, *Preface to Politics*, p. 301; *Drift and Mastery* (New York: Mitchell Kennerley, 1914), pp. 274–76, 281–85, 289–334; "Unrest," *New Republic*, XX (Nov. 12, 1919), 320–21.

Lippmann's social Freudianism was the model of his proposed integration of science and irrationality. For Lippmann, Freud was a scientist who provided an objective guide to the realm of the unconscious. He called upon Freud to prove the folly of suppression of basic instincts. Yet, unlike the other members of the Mabel Dodge circle, Lippmann emphasized the sublimation of desire rather than its gratification. One should not surrender to impulse nor suppress it, but direct it toward a higher aim. Lippmann believed that Freud had emphasized the repressed impulses rather than the repressive mechanism, simply because his interests were primarily therapeutic. Therefore, to make Freudianism available for social progress, Lippmann proposed a scientific understanding of the nature and possibilities of the "psychic censor." [42]

From this viewpoint, social reform appeared as a problem of social control. It involved a strong and active state, like Croly's, which would use its powers to minimize social conflict and promote the development of social harmony. This state would be dedicated to a social program "carried out against the active opposition of class interest and sectional prejudices." The trusts were to be regulated vigorously, and the labor movement was not to become "the plaything of its own vision." Both must be disciplined and joined to the other interests of civilization. [43]

Lippmann believed that as part of the increased scale and complexity of all social and economic life, reform had shifted from moral to technical issues. Political problems derived not from corruption and dishonesty but rather from lack of insight and intelligence. One must, therefore, appeal less to honesty and more to expertise. All efficient organizations produced natural pyramids of power, thought Lippmann; therefore, a strong and active state must have strong leader-

[42] Walter Lippmann, "An Epic of Desire," *New Republic*, VII (May 6, 1916), 21–22, *Preface to Politics*, pp. 51–52, *Drift and Mastery*, pp. 258, 271–72, and "Trotter and Freud," *New Republic*, IX (Nov. 18, 1916), Supp. 18.

[43] Lippmann, *Drift and Mastery*, pp. 72–76, 145–46, 169, 327, 328, and "Integrated America," *New Republic* VI (Feb. 19, 1916), 63–65. Lippmann was later to propose a plan to eliminate strikes, which he felt caused too much economic disruption. "Can the Strike Be Abandoned?" *New Republic*, XXI (Jan. 21, 1920), 224–27.

ship. This leadership, as Croly had advised, would be tempered by the forms of direct democracy. Yet the leaders would create issues with a view to the needs of the people and organize for popular support.[44]

Such issues were the nationalization of the railroads and comprehensive social insurance. These would give the country a basis for order, purpose, and discipline. They would serve as Hamiltonian devices in the twentieth century, just as funding the national debt had served in the eighteenth. However, it was the broad mass of the people rather than the rich and well-born who would be given a vested interest in their government. The nation's misfortune was that the rudderless rich, "untrained and uneducated," were born to power. Lippmann's nationalized America, given direction and discipline by expert administrators, would rectify this.[45]

Lippmann's attachment to scientific management was to be expected. While the Eastern Rate Case was still in progress, he wrote an article praising the scientific management experts who were "setting the world in order" and "humanizing" work. He saw them as the logical culmination of the muckraking movement, which had begun with questions of honesty and ended with questions of efficiency. The increased production which their discoveries yielded would provide the funds of progress. In addition, scientific management would help create a new type of business leader who could forsake the "cesspool of commercialism" for the independence and dignity of professionalism. Lippmann thought

[44] Lippmann, *Drift and Mastery*, pp. 10–26, 35–37, 261, *Preface to Politics*, pp. 16, 18, 59, 97–103, 115–16, 195–97, 250–51, 261, 263, 301–2, "Insiders and Outsiders," *New Republic* V (Nov. 13, 1915), 35; "The puzzle of Hughes," *ibid.*, VIII (Sept. 30, 1916), 213. Lippmann greatly admired H. G. Wells's novel, *The New Machiavelli*, which described a "student of social conditions and political theory" who entered Parliament and found little hope in radicalism, socialism, or the Liberal Party. He became a Tory in order to bring social regeneration from the top down.

[45] Lippmann, "Integrated America," pp. 62 ff., "Albert, The Male," *New Republic*, VII (July 23, 1916), 301, and "Mr. Rockefeller on the Stand," *ibid.*, I (Jan. 30, 1915), 13. Lippmann's foreign policy was a program of social control projected upon the world of nations. Absract justice was irrelevant. The fundamental problem was one of diplomatic anarchy, and "the ideal condition of the world would, of course, be the concentration of power in the hands of those whose purposes were civilized." Walter Lippmann, *The Stakes of Diplomacy* (New York: Henry Holt, 1915), pp. 220–21, 82 ff.

that the graduate schools of business, which Brandeis had praised, would play an important role in the new collective business organization in which the profiteer would give way to the "industrial statesman."[46]

Lippmann's concept of professionalism, like Croly's, was tied to bigness. The managers of the big corporations stood outside of "the higgling of the market" and could rise above the profit motive. The bigness of the corporations permitted the development of specialized competence which could be exercised independent of the shareholders, "the most incompetent constituency conceivable." In the great mass-production industries, "private property will melt away; its functions will be taken over by the salaried men who direct them, by government commissions, by developing labor unions." This socialized managerial revolution was to make big business cultured, magnanimous, and aware of "the larger demands of civilized life."[47]

Of course, there was the objection that bigness yielded inefficiency. Brandeis, using in part the facts of scientific management (the fact that the plants where it was used were of medium size), cast doubt upon the efficiency of bigness. Lippmann, using the logic of scientific management (the logic of the planning department and its generalized laws), came to the aid of bigness. Administration, Lippmann explained, was becoming a science capable of dealing with tremendous units.[48]

Lippmann, Croly, and Brandeis evolved social programs in which both scientific management and the trade union movement had important places. One of the difficulties in this position was that organized labor rejected scientific management, and most efficiency experts rejected trade unionism. This did not prove discouraging, however, for Lippmann,

[46] Lippmann, "More Brains — Less Sweat," pp. 827–28, *Drift and Mastery*, pp. 10–11, 23–26, 46–49, 115–17, 119–20, 328, and "Wilson and Little Business," *Metropolitan Magazine*, XL (August 1914), 23–25.

[47] Lippmann, *Drift and Mastery*, pp. 35–36, 38–39, 46, 48–49, 57–59, 60, 63. The romance of bigness occasionally pops up in progressive novels as part of the protest against acquisitiveness. Robert Herrick's *The Memoirs of An American Citizen* (1905) points out that little business is sordid and mean while big business may be poetic. Van Harrington, the hero, breaks with traditional commercial ethics, but his work is justified by its creativeness and its service to humanity.

[48] Lippmann, *Drift and Mastery*, pp. 39–42.

Croly, and Brandeis believed that science, expertism, and some form of democracy could be made to work together both in society and in the factory.

Their programs for the factory they usually called "industrial democracy." This term had been used earlier to describe the various shop-representation plans of the industrial betterment workers. These devices included "suggestion box" techniques and profit-sharing and even management-sharing plans based on stock purchases by workmen. Brandeis' "industrial democracy" derived directly from these schemes. Though stock-holding workers were not part of his program, shop representation in itself was a substitute for it. Property ownership, Brandeis believed, developed independence and responsibility. (This was one of the reasons for his support for smallness.) The worker, who could not own property, would gain his independence through his union and his sense of responsibility by having a say in shop affairs. Industrial democracy would eliminate the objections to scientific management on the part of the worker. The conflict between the unions and the efficiency engineers, Brandeis said, was based upon misunderstanding. Those aspects of management to which the laws of science did not as yet apply were to be subject to collective bargaining. Where science did apply, a union representative might serve as a watchdog to make sure that it was the laws of science and not class interest which was obeyed. That the laws of science might serve class interest did not seem to be a possibility.[49]

The whiff of guild socialism which was added to the already vaporous formula of "industrial democracy" in the years just before the war gave nothing to its precision but did make it more interesting to the younger reformers. Lippmann, who thought that guild socialism was a way to "ride the forces of syndicalism and use them for constructive purpose," incorporated some of its suggestions into his version of "industrial democracy."[50] The unions, as well as the man-

[49] "Testimony of Louis D. Brandeis," *U.S. Commission on Industrial Relations,* 64th Cong. 1st Sess. (Ser. Vol. 6936), pp. 7660 ff., and (Ser. Vol. 6929), pp. 991–92, 1004; Brandeis, *Curse of Bigness,* pp. 35 ff., and *Business – a Profession* (1933 ed.), pp. 53–56.

[50] Lippmann, *Preface to Politics,* pp. 287–89. Robert Grosvenor Valentine provided a link between Brandeis and the *New Republic* on the issues of scientific management and industrial democracy. Though af-

agers and the state, were to have a voice in the running of industry. The union with a say in management would protect the workers from exploitation and give them the discipline and interest in efficiency necessary for industrial advance. The real peril to the nation was not labor with power and responsibility but workers with "nothing to lose but their chains." For Croly, a form of co-management would not only protect the worker and bring him to accept efficiency methods, but would also preserve some dignity in the subordinate position he held in the factory. There was no loss of self-respect, Croly argued, when subordination was self-imposed. Industrial democracy became a staple program for the *New Republic*. A young Chicago lawyer, Donald Richberg, who later became better known as chief administrator of the NRA, suggested that industrial democracy might even lead the unions to lay aside the strike.[51]

Brandeis, Croly, and Lippmann shared a broad congruence of outlook. Stepping outside the dominant modes of progressivism, they tried to construct reform programs which could be fulfilled without a direct appeal to conscience. They attacked commercialism and acquisitiveness and wished to substitute the non-pecuniary posture of the professional. Acceptance of the age of mass participation in politics was balanced by an attachment to the expert and his guiding role in an active government. Scientific management, especially when placed within the conditions of industrial democracy,

fected by the guild socialist notions which had influenced the *New Republic* version of industrial democracy, he also worked with Brandeis to introduce scientific management techniques into the New York garment industry within the system of "industrial self-government" which Brandeis had set up. Louis Levine, *The Women's Garment Workers* (New York: B. W. Huebsch, 1924), pp. 306–9; "Robert Grosvenor Valentine," *New Republic*, IX (Nov. 25, 1916), 84 ff.

[51] Lippmann, *Drift and Mastery*, pp. 92–100; Croly, *Progressive Democracy*, p. 402, chap. xviii; "Tolerated Unions," *New Republic*, I (Nov. 7, 1914), 12; "Substitute for Violence," *ibid.* (Dec. 12, 1914), p. 9; "Another Cassandra," *New Republic*, III (July 17, 1915), 271; Donald R. Richberg, "Democratization of Industry," *ibid.*, XI (May 12, 1917), 50. Robert F. Hoxie's *Scientific Management and Labor* (New York: D. Appleton, 1915), which sympathized with the aspirations but was sharply critical of some of the practices of scientific management, led the *New Republic* to be more insistent on workers' consultation in scientific management. See Alvin S. Johnson, "Hoxie's *Scientific Management and Labor*," *New Republic*, V (Dec. 4, 1915), 127; "Democratic Control of Scientific Managment," *ibid.*, IX (Dec. 23, 1916), 264.

embodied in the factory the regime these progressive thinkers envisioned within society at large.

Their differences were often expressive of the changes taking place in American intellectual and social life. While Brandeis and Croly rejected the simple moralism prevalent in progressive reform, they clearly retained a belief that the ultimate direction of reform was toward moral improvement in a traditional sense. With Lippmann, this was much less clear. Brandeis' support for scientific management was accompanied by advocacy of resale price maintenance and open-price trade associations, devices for small business survival in an age of industrial giants. In contrast, Croly's and Lippmann's support of scientific management was accompanied by advocacy of bigness, and specialization and by a moderate anti-property bias.[52] Brandeis' reform program spoke to an old middle class. Croly's and Lippmann's spoke to the new.

[52] Croly, *Progressive Democracy*, p. 385; Lippmann, *Drift and Mastery*, pp. 50–65.

• CHAPTER VI

The Politics of Efficiency

"Two enemies," wrote Francis Parkman in 1878, "unknown before, have risen like spirits of darkness on our social and political horizon—an ignorant proletariat and a half-taught plutocracy." The greater danger, he felt, lay with the restless workmen, foreigners for the most part, "to whom liberty means license and politics means plunder, to whom the public good is nothing and their own most trivial interests everything, who love their country for what they can get out of it." "King Demos" raised barbers and butchers and dishwashers to positions of power and pushed aside the better class of citizens, who were forced to abandon politics in disgust. The source of the evil, Parkman said, lay in universal suffrage. The essential remedy was a "new reform" to counteract and neutralize this suffrage so that it would cease to be a danger.[1]

Parkman's views were expressed during the public discussion arising out of the Tilden Commission report. The Commission, formed in answer to the Tweed Ring exposures in New York, had recommended the restriction of suffrage on matters of taxation to property holders.[2] This was imme-

[1] Francis Parkman, "The Failure of Universal Suffrage," *North American Review*, CXXVII (July–August 1878), 3, 4, 7, 13, 20.

[2] For discussion of the work of the Tilden Commission, see James Bryce, *The American Commonwealth* (London and New York: Macmillan, 1888), II, 282–91; M. Ostrogorski, *Democracy and the Organization of Political Parties* (New York: Macmillan, 1902), II, 520–22; Chester L. Barrows, *William M. Evarts: Lawyer, Diplomat, Statesman* (Chapel Hill: University of North Carolina Press, 1941), pp. 194–96; John Bigelow, *The Life of Samuel J. Tilden* (New York: Harper, 1895),

diately attacked by Wendell Phillips in the same issue of the *North American Review* that carried Parkman's article. The times, Phillips admitted, were not without peril, but reformers must "save this sheet-anchor of the race — universal suffrage . . . , God's method of gently binding men into Commonwealths in order that they may at last melt into brothers." [3]

However, both Parkman's violent assault on "King Demos" and Phillips' unqualified sympathy for the underdog were extreme. More typical were the views of Edwin L. Godkin, editor of the *Nation*, who had actually served on the Tilden Commission. Godkin soon set aside the appeal for the direct restriction of suffrage as impractical, but persisted in his advocacy of the less contentious aspects of the Commission report. His program turned on three themes, characteristic of the reform of the day: non-partisanship, the strong executive, and the separation of politics from administration.

These themes pointed in the same direction as the Commission's proposal of restricted suffrage — giving political preponderance to the "better elements." This direction became clear when Godkin brought these principles to bear upon questions of New York municipal reform. The political shenanigans of the Tweeds and the Crockers, he believed, were based upon the electoral power of the Irish vote. Godkin thought that there was indeed a relation between the corrupt politicians and what Lincoln Steffens was later to call "the interests." But he saw this relation as a form of blackmail, backed by a threat of political harassment, levied by the bosses upon businessmen whose strongest wish was simply to go about their business. Godkin proposed the strengthening of the executive, in the belief that even a "debased electorate" did not easily break the salutary habit of putting notables in conspicuous executive offices. But his most emphatic pro-

I, 264–66. A condensed version of the Tilden Report was republished in *Municipal Affairs*, III (September, 1899), 434–54. Bryce considered the report of the Commission "classical" and, in general agreement with its point of view, held that the evils of American politics resulted from the low level of the electorate and the complexity of the governmental system.

[3] Wendell Phillips, "The Outlook," *North American Review*, CXXVII (July–August, 1878), 115–16. Phillips also opposed the Civil Service reform program as too aristocratic. Carlos Martyn, *Wendell Phillips, the Agitator* (New York: Funk & Wagnalls, 1890), pp. 465–66.

posal was the driving of partisanship from the city. The "respectable classes," he complained, split into two parties on national issues and remained divided in municipal affairs. "The dangerous classes," "the enemies of social order," did not split. The power of corruption could be destroyed by uniting "the intelligent and educated classes" under the banner of non-partisanship. While non-partisanship would challenge the bosses in the polling booths, Civil Service reform, the separation of politics from administration, could deprive them of the chief means of rewarding their agents.[4]

This was the program of much of reform in the last half of the nineteenth century. Urban political reformers in the period from the Civil War to World War I saw themselves as standing in the middle of the social order. Roughly, in the years before 1900, the greater dangers seemed to rise up from below, while in the years following they seemed to come from above. The mugwumps characteristically thought of themselves as a brake upon the lower classes, while the progressive reformers claimed to march with the people. Though marching with the people, the progressive reformers clearly marched at their head. Progressive political reform often seemed to involve a singular attempt to bring government close to the people and at the same time keep it somewhat distant.[5]

The three elements — non-partisanship, the strong executive, and the separation of politics from administration — which appeared in mugwump reform became even more prominent in the progressive era. The shift in social perspective, however, gave them new connotations. The strong executive was now seen as the public protector against "organized

[4] Edwin L. Godkin, "The Problems of Municipal Government," *Annals of the American Academy of Political and Social Science* (hereafter cited as *Ann. AAPSS*), IV (May, 1894), 866, 870–71, 879–88; *Unforeseen Tendencies of Democracy* (Boston: Houghton Mifflin, 1898), pp. 160–68.

[5] See, for example, Richard T. Ely, "Progressivism, True and False — an Outline," *American Review of Reviews*, LI (February, 1915), 209–11; Charles S. Slichter, "Industrialism," *Popular Science*, LXXXI (October, 1912), 360–61; F. W. Blackmar, "Leadership in Reform," *American Journal of Sociology*, XVI (March, 1911), 626–33; C. H. Grabo, "Education for Democratic Leadership," *ibid.*, XXIII (May, 1918), 763–78; Edward A. Ross, "The Outlook for the Plain-Folk," *Everybody's Magazine*, XIX (December, 1908), 755; Frank Henry Giddings, *The Responsible State* (Boston: Houghton Mifflin, 1918), pp. 107–8.

privilege." The executive was not only a man of high character, a barrier to social turbulence and corruption; he was also a leader who instigated and directed government action. He was given a representative as well as an executive function. For the executive had the "strongest claim to the right to voice the general will of the people of the whole state." [6]

Non-partisanship, in the progressive era, was more an expression of belief in the underlying harmony of society than a call for unity among the "better elements." Characteristically, as in the commission form of government and the nonpartisan ballot, it was a harmony put into force by legislation.[7] On the national level, non-partisanship found its most earnest advocates in the National Voters' League and among the Bull Moosers. With the latter, it was probably both a cause and a consequence of their break with traditional party allegiances. Senator Beveridge's declaration in the keynote

[6] Arthur N. Holcombe, "Organizing Democracy," *New Republic*, XI (July 7, 1917), 270. See also "The Executive's Duty," *Outlook*, XCV (June 4, 1910), 246–47; "The President and the People," *World's Work*, XIX (March, 1910), 12648–51; "Masterfulness of Presidents," *American Review of Reviews*, XLIV (July, 1911), 4–9; "Executive Leadership," *New Republic*, IV (Aug. 14, 1915), 31–32.

[7] A general discussion of the notion of non-partisanship in the progressive era would carry this study too far afield. It would have to deal with such remote questions as the influence of voteless but politically active upper-class women, and such interesting but distracting examples as the Boston 1915 movement. The spirit behind commission government is best seen in John J. Hamilton, *The Dethronement of the City Boss* (New York: Funk & Wagnalls, 1910), which was the most popular contemporary account. By February, 1913, approximately 225 cities had adopted the commission plan, and its proposals found an unusually diverse support. For a brief sampling see: W. B. Slosson, "New Galveston," *Independent*, LVI (June 16, 1904), 806–7; Don E. Mowry, "Governing Cities by Commission," *La Follette's Weekly Magazine*, I (March 27, 1909), 7; W. T. Arndt, "Municipal Government by Commission," *Nation*, LXXXIII (Oct. 18, 1906), 322; Charles W. Eliot, "Municipal Government," *New England Magazine*, N.S. LXX (June, 1909), 393–97. On the non-partisan ballot see Samuel M. Jones, "The New Patriotism, A Golden Rule Government for Cities," *Municipal Affairs*, III (September, 1899), 455–61; Robert Treat Paine, "The Elimination of National Party Designations From Municipal Ballots," *Proceedings of the National Municipal League*, 1909, pp. 291–308; M. D. Hull, "The Non-Partisan Ballot in Municipal Elections," *National Municipal Review*, VI (1917), 219–23; Frank G. Bates, "Nonpartisan Government," *American Political Science Review*, IX (May, 1915), 313–15; Robert E. Cushman, "Nonpartisan Nominations and Elections," *Ann. AAPSS*, CVI (March, 1923), 83–96.

address of the Progressive convention of 1912, "We stand for an undivided Nation," epitomized the sentiment.[8] The idea of the separation of politics from administration had been implicit in much of mugwump reform. It was not until the end of the nineteenth century, however, that this idea received systematic formulation. This was the work of Professor Frank J. Goodnow. Goodnow, in a series of influential studies, proposed the radical separation of governmental ends and means. Questions of ends, he said, were within the realm of politics and legislation. Governmental means were in the realm of administration and could be treated impartially and — as those who later developed this line of reasoning claimed — scientifically.[9] This was more than a matter of classification. Behind these definitions lay the attempt to create a realm of government free from both class prejudice and the ballot box. For Goodnow, to define was to plead a cause.

Many of the progressive reformers who seized upon Goodnow's formula did so with the intent of creating an honored and important profession of administrators having special skills and a special ethic.[10] The image of the government

[8] S. J. Duncan-Clark, *The Progressive Movement* (Boston: Small, Maynard, 1913), p. 37, chap. ii; Amos R. E. Pinchot, *History of the Progressive Party, 1912–16*, ed. Helene Maxwell Hooker (New York: New York University Press, 1958), p. 34; *A Nonpartisan Party: Address before National Conference on Popular Government, December 6, 1913*, by George W. Norris, 63d Cong., 2d Sess., Sen. Doc. 372 (Ser. Vol. 6593); Lynn Haines, *Your Congress* (Washington, D.C.: National Voters' League, 1915), chap. iii, iv, v.

[9] Frank J. Goodnow, "The Place of the Council and of the Mayor in the Organization of Municipal Government," *A Municipal Program: Report of a Committee of the National Municipal League, Adopted by the League, November 17, 1899* (New York: Macmillan, 1900), pp. 74–87, and *Politics and Administration: A Study in Government* (New York: Macmillan, 1900). Goodnow's work had been preceded by some isolated and relatively uninfluential attempts, most notable of which was Woodrow Wilson, "The Study of Administration," *College and State: Educational, Literary and Political Papers, 1875–1913*, ed. Ray Stannard Baker and William E. Dodd (New York: Harper, 1925), pp. 1, 130–58.

[10] "There can be no higher ambition than that of serving the state, nothing more creditable than to serve it well" — read the motto of the *Public Servant*, a journal devoted to the promotion of training for public service and issued from Madison, Wisconsin. It proposed a West Point for the Civil Service which would turn out a cadre of trained intelligence for public service. *The Public Servant*, I (February, 1916), I, 91.

official, which had been hazy in the writings of the Civil Service reformers, became somewhat clearer to the progressive reformers. Top officials, at least, would be college-bred administrators with broad powers.[11]

Goodnow's separation of politics from administration was to reconcile expertism with democracy. This reconciliation, however, rested upon the optimistic belief that the demos would accept such a separation, and upon restrictive definitions that would deprive experts of almost all direct social influence. Yet, progressive reformers had optimism in good store, and the subtle restrictions might be overlooked. In fact, once a seemingly impartial role had been fashioned for the administrators, many of Goodnow's adherents showed an amazing doctrinal absent-mindedness with regard to the restrictions that Goodnow's formula placed upon that role. Politics was not only separated from administration but often subordinated to it.[12]

The scientific expert became the prototype of all administrators. He brought scientific wisdom down from the ivory

[11] It is instructive to compare Dorman B. Eaton's classic work on the Civil Service in Great Britain (Eaton was the author of the Pendleton Act) with Robert Moses' study, published a generation later. For Eaton, an important result of Civil Service reform was the creation of an environment which would naturally lead "the purest and wisest minds into positions of honor and control." Robert Moses thought this left too much to chance and even to false notions of democracy. He proposed putting all higher administrative positions into a special classification and reserving them for men of the highest college and university training. Dorman B. Eaton, *Civil Service in Great Britain: A History of Abuses and Reforms and Their Bearing Upon American Politics* (New York: Harper, 1880), pp. 357, 419, 427–28; Robert Moses, *The Civil Service of Great Britain* (New York: Columbia University Press, 1914), pp. 5–9, 244–45, 257–70.

[12] This is clearly seen in the development of the City Manager movement. On paper, the City Manager plan was a strict construction of Goodnow's maxims. However, in the most celebrated city management municipalities, the manager soon eclipsed the elective council. The city managers were applauded for "taking the public gently by the hand and helping it to really understand what it wants." William H. Allen, "What City Managers Can Do To Further Advance Good Government," *Third Annual Report of the City Managers' Association, 1916*, p. 45; Ossian E. Carr, "Progress, Prospects, and Pitfalls of the New Profession," *Fifth Year Book of the City Managers' Association, 1919*, pp. 103, 107–8; "Waite, Master of Efficiency," *Independent*, LXXXVIII (Nov. 20, 1916), 300; W. W. Renwick, "Democracy Chooses an Autocrat," *Technical World Magazine*, XXI (March, 1914), 13–19; Chester E. Rightor, *City Manager in Dayton* (New York: Macmillan, 1919), chap. iv. Russell M. Story, *The American Municipal Executive* (Urbana: University of Illinois Press, 1918), pp. 218–20.

tower and set it to work for the man in the street. "The practical man," declared Comptroller Metz, New York City's administrative reformer, "knows *how*. The scientific man knows *why*. The expert knows *how* and *why*."[13] The expert's authority derived from his science, and the range of that authority often remained somewhat indefinite. For most progressives the expert was to be neither on top nor on tap. He would do less than command but more than advise. He would surely count for something.

From this standpoint even the most circumspect notions of Goodnow drew interest and vitality.[14] It is not surprising to find Professor W. F. Willoughby, who borrowed and elab-

[13] Quoted in F. W. Taylor to Carl G. Barth, Nov. 18, 1910, in Frederick W. Taylor Collection, Stevens Institute of Technology, Hoboken, N.J.

[14] Some of the connotations that collected around the word "administration" may be seen in an extraordinary book, *Philip Dru, Administrator*, published in 1912. The author was anonymous but rumors quickly pointed to a man prominent in politics, most commonly thought to be Colonel Roosevelt. It was not until years later that another colonel, Edward Mandell House, Wilson's "silent partner," stepped forward as the author. The book combines the literary styles of the American political party platform and the juvenile adventure story. Its simple-minded depiction of human beings and human motives is not unrelated to the political and social programs for which they are the fictional underpinning. Philip Dru, a West Point graduate, is caught up in a new American Civil War stemming from a plot to corrupt the Presidency, the Senate, and the Supreme Court for "organized capital." Dru preaches moderation, and, immediately, leadership of the popular forces is thrust upon him. He sets up headquarters at Madison, Wisconsin, for the inevitable military conflict. The issue is decided in one grand battle which kills 63,000 men and wounds fifty times that number. Dru then declares himself "Administrator of the Republic" and dispenses with constitutional government for seven years. With the aid of a "Council of Twelve" expert advisers, he proceeds to set things in order. "Our civilization," Dru believed, "was fundamentally wrong, in as much as among other things it restricted efficiency." If society were properly organized, none would be without food, clothing, and shelter. The administration of public affairs would become at once simple, direct, and businesslike. Dru could "permit no misplaced sentiment to deter him." Obsolete and useless laws were cut out; a graduated income tax, revenue tariff, women's suffrage, the short ballot, flexible currency, effective trust regulations, and even a touch of single-tax reform were brought in. Labor and government were given representation on the boards of corporations; profit-sharing programs were set up and strikes outlawed. Canada and Mexico were brought under the American flag, the second as a result of a minor war and with some bloodshed. With everything straightened out, Dru gave over his power to the simplified and improved representative institutions which he had created and took off for Russia, apparently to lend a hand there also. [Edward Mandell House], New York: Huebsch, [1913].

orated upon Goodnow's definitions, agreeing with Pope that "The government best administered is best."[15]

Administration seemed to open a road to social influence for those not adept at hand-shaking, back-slapping, and back-stairs negotiations. From Wisconsin, Professor John Rogers Commons, who held various important administrative posts, advertised the advantages of administration over legislation and predicted that administration would become a fourth branch of government.[16] The "Wisconsin idea" (symbolized by State Street in Madison, which ran from Capitol Hill to University Hill) described a new role for trained intelligence in government. "In Wisconsin, wealth is sanctified by commonwealth and the people of the State willingly let University professors write their laws and administer their departments," wrote an enthusiast. This was an inaccurate description of Wisconsin politics but an accurate expression of the hopes of many progressive reformers.[17]

To the mugwump and the progressive, these three principles of reform — the strong executive, non-partisanship, and the separation of politics from administration — suggested the need for leadership of the educated and the competent

[15] William F. Willoughby, "Agencies for Studying Public Administration Generally: Unofficial," in Gustavus A. Weber, *Organized Efforts for the Improvement of Methods of Administration in the United States* (New York: D. Appleton, 1919), p. 43. Willoughby doctored the quotation slightly. Pope's couplet reads: "For forms of government let fools contest, / What e'er is best administered is best."

[16] John Rogers Commons, *Myself* (New York: Macmillan, 1934), p. 107, *Labor and Administration* (New York: Macmillan, 1913), p. 396, and "A Fourth Branch of Government," *La Follette's Magazine*, V (July 26, 1913), 8.

[17] Frank P. Stockbridge, "University That Runs a State," *World's Work*, XXV (April, 1913), 699, 708; Charles MacCarthy, *The Wisconsin Idea* (New York: Macmillan, 1912), pp. 32, 46, 136–39, Appendix, pp. 313–17, and Theodore Roosevelt's introduction, pp. vii–xi; "Testimony of Charles MacCarthy," *U.S. Commission on Industrial Relations*, 64th Cong., 1st Sess., Sen. Doc. 415 (Ser. Vol. 6929), pp. 379–80; Edward A. Fitzpatrick, *McCarthy of Wisconsin* (New York: Columbia University Press, 1944), chaps. v, vi, viii, ix, xviii; William Hard, "A University in Public Life," *Outlook*, LXXXVI (July 27, 1907), 659–67; "University and the Public Service — The Wisconsin Idea," *Review of Reviews*, XLIV (December, 1911), 746–47; Frederick Jackson Turner, "Pioneer Ideals and the State University, Commencement Address at the University of Indiana, 1910," *The Frontier in American History* (New York: Henry Holt, 1920), pp. 285–89; Felix Frankfurter, *Felix Frankfurter Reminisces* (New York: Reynal, 1960), p. 166.

and for the creation of a realm in government where conflicting purposes would disappear. And it was especially where conflicting purposes disappeared and the "competent" had their way that questions of efficiency became important. Starting, at the latest, with the Tilden Commission report, and running through the progressive era, the comparison of government to a business corporation appeared repeatedly in the writings of the political reformers. It was not only the corporation's commercial efficiency, with its suggestions for tax cutting, that the reformers had in mind, but also the corporation's singleness of purpose and the discipline and effectiveness this singleness permitted. The reformer's commitment to governmental efficiency fitted closely with these themes of reform and shared their implications. Often the call for governmental efficiency turned out to be a plea for such things as public unity and leadership of the competent.[18]

At the time of the efficiency craze, the growing interest in government efficiency became more explicit and far-reaching. Frederick W. Taylor, in the introduction to the *Principles of Scientific Management*, had mentioned government as a field for the application of his ideas. He proposed to start, simultaneously, at the very top with the source of authority and at the very bottom with the simplest tasks. In an article entitled "Government Efficiency," Taylor suggested that someone who had made efficiency a life study be placed in the President's cabinet to unify and direct the introduction of efficiency into all government departments, and that "the scientific study of what should constitute a proper day's work for each government employee" begin immediately. Of course, the Taylor System had actually been introduced into the Navy yards and the Army arsenals, even before the efficiency craze. It was scuttled by the Navy, however, when it became an issue of factional rivalry, and was pushed out of the arsenals by trade union opposition. In his last years, Tay-

[18] This switch often appears in the writings of Croly, Lippmann, and Brandeis, and almost invariably in all the broader discussions of governmental efficiency. See, for example, Woodrow Wilson, "Democracy and Efficiency," *Atlantic Monthly*, LXXXVII (March, 1901), 289–99; Albert H. Wright, "Scientific Criteria for Efficient Democratic Institutions," *Scientific Monthly*, VI (March, 1918), 237–41; Vernice Earle Danner, "Making Government Efficient," *Forum*, LI (March, 1914), 354–64.

lor devoted much effort to trying to keep a foothold for his system in government.[19]

Despite all the ballyhoo about scientific management, reformers interested in the direct application of its techniques to government complained that there was a scarcity of relevant literature and few efficiency experts ready to offer assistance.[20] Most Taylorites seemed to feel more at home in the factory than in the government office building. Nevertheless, Hollis Godfrey and Morris Llewellyn Cooke, two orthodox Taylorites, as well as Harrington Emerson, the nonjuring practitioner, had their fling at government work.[21] It was Cooke who made the biggest splash. The two famous municipal non-partisan "efficiency administrations" of the day were those of John Purroy Mitchel in New York and Rudolph Blankenburg in Philadelphia.[22] While Mayor Mitchel relied

[19] Frederick W. Taylor, "Government Efficiency," *Bull. Taylor Soc.*, II (December, 1916), 9–10; Frank Barkley Copley, *Frederick Winslow Taylor: Father of Scientific Management* (New York: Harper, 1923), II, chaps. xi and xii.

[20] Henry Bruere, *The New City Government* (New York: D. Appleton, 1916), p. 375; Governor Robert P. Bass to Frederick W. Taylor, Jan. 24, 1911; Helen V. Bory to Frederick W. Taylor, May 19, 1914; Frederick A. Cleveland to Frederick W. Taylor, July 13, 1912, Taylor Collection.

[21] Godfrey served as expert consultant to the Iowa Survey of 1914 and as chief of the Bureau of Gas in Philadelphia under Morris L. Cooke. Harrington Emerson was an efficiency consultant to the Socialist administration in Milwaukee, and his brother Samuel worked for the cities of Seattle and Pittsburgh.

[22] No general study of Mitchel and his administration has been published. Some of the more helpful sources are: J. P. Mitchel, "Efficiency and the Government," *Independent*, LXXX (Nov. 30, 1914), 327, and "What We Have Done for New York," *ibid.*, LXXXII (May 10, 1915), 237–39; Albert Shaw, "New York's Government by Experts," *American Review of Reviews*, XLIX (February, 1914), 171–73; H. S. Gilbertson, "The Municipal Revolution under Mitchel," *ibid.*, LVI (September, 1917), 300–303; William Hard, "Political Leader and Efficient Administrator," *Everybody's Magazine*, XXXVII (October, 1917), 465–78; Charles A. Beard, "Appreciation," *Survey*, XL (July 13, 1918), 422; "John Purroy Mitchel," *New Republic*, XV (July 20, 1918), 332–33. For the work of Rudolph Blankenburg, see "Testimony of Rudolph Blankenburg," *U.S. Commission on Industrial Relations*, 64th Cong., 1st Sess., Sen. Doc. 415 (Ser. Vol. 6931), pp. 2699 ff.; Rudolph Blankenburg, "The Municipal Need of Technically Trained Men," *Scientific American*, CVIII (April 12, 1913), 342; J. D. Burks, "The Outlook for Municipal Efficiency in Philadelphia," *Ann. AAPSS*, XLI (May, 1912), 245–61; "The Blankenburg Reform Administration," *Outlook*, CV (Sept. 13, 1913), 58–59; Donald W. Disbrow, "Reform in Philadelphia under Mayor Blankenburg, 1912–1916," *Pennsylvania History*, XXVII (October, 1960), 379–96.

upon the Bureau of Municipal Research, then under the sway of Taylor's ideas, Mayor Blankenburg went directly to Taylor for help and came away with Morris L. Cooke as his Director of Public Works.[23]

Cooke did not hope to turn Philadelphia into a scientifically managed metropolis. Even in a much smaller city, he believed, that could be done only if the electorate would permit itself to be guided by scientific managers for five or ten years. Cooke was not given that kind of tenure or range of authority. Furthermore, stop-watch time study and intricate bonus systems, which many thought fundamental to Taylor's science, had become troublesome issues owing to trade union opposition. Cooke placed less emphasis on exact measurement of the tasks of those on the lower levels and more on redefining the authority and responsibility of those higher up. He set up a planning board in the Public Works Department, modeled on Taylor's factory planning department, and a program of "functionalized management." He reached beyond his own department and began a lecture series on scientific management for all public employees of Philadelphia. Frederick W. Taylor, Edwin F. Gay of the Harvard Graduate School of Business, and Cooke himself were among the speakers.[24]

The news of Cooke's work in Philadelphia spread quickly and he became an authority on scientific management in government and a sought-after lecturer on the subject of municipal efficiency. He translated the principles of scientific management into political terms which fitted nicely with the prevailing tendencies of progressive thought. "Expertism" and "democracy" were his watchwords. The expert must be given more scope and power. The "total of voting decisions" should be reduced and voting saved for "broader issues"

[23] Kenneth E. Trombley, *The Life and Times of a Happy Liberal: A Biography of Morris Llewellyn Cooke* (New York: Harper, 1954), p. 14.

[24] Morris Llewellyn Cooke, *Our Cities Awake: Notes on Municipal Activities and Administration* (New York: Doubleday, Page, 1918), pp. 63–65, 86, and "Scientific Management of the Public Business," *American Political Science Review*, IX (August, 1915), 488–95; William H. Connell, "Public Works and Engineering Services on a Public Service Basis," *Ann. AAPSS*, LXIV, (March, 1916), 106–15; John A. Dunaway, "Some Efficiency Methods in City Administration," *ibid.*, 101–2; "The Efficiency of the Cities," *Efficiency Magazine*, I (October, 1913), 68.

(left unspecified). Questions of government were becoming more and more questions of fact. Cooke pointed out that the movements for the short ballot, smaller legislative bodies, fewer juries, the city manager, longer terms for administrative offices, all stood for the same tendencies in politics that scientific management stood for in industry. These developments did not clash with democratic principles. For Cooke, "democracy" meant government for the people, not for selfish interests, and a more intense popular involvement within a narrowed sphere of political activity. The growing complexities of modern life, Cooke believed, made it difficult for the average man to act intelligently in public affairs. Here publicity was crucial. It was "the backbone of progress." Publicity presented the expert's understanding in words of one syllable and permitted that partnership of the expert and the citizen which was essential to good government.[25]

Where scientific management was applied without the supervision of efficiency engineers, in both industry and government, its effect is more difficult to appraise. There was much scientific-management patter bandied about. Remarks like that of Charles Steinmetz, the "wizard" of the General Electric Company, that "all that is necessary is to extend methods of economic efficiency from the individual industrial corporation to the national organism as a whole,"[26] were common. The most literal application of Taylor's techniques by laymen appeared in the cities. Secret time study of municipal workers (though Taylor frowned on concealment) was tried in New York and Chicago. Here, the trade unions, with their important voice in municipal politics, stood in the way of using these data to set up bonus systems. However the attempt at some measurement of tasks and accomplishments continued.[27]

Perhaps the most influential proponents of the transfer of

[25] Morris Llewellyn Cooke, *How About It?* (Lancaster, Pa.: New Era Printing, 1917), p. 17, *Our Cities Awake*, pp. 66–67, 97–104, chap. vii, and "Who Is the Boss in Your Shop?" *Bull. Taylor Soc.* (August, 1917), 4, 7; Charles A. Beard, "Training for Efficient Public Service, *Ann. AAPSS*, LXIV (March, 1916), 218.

[26] Charles Steinmetz "Industrial Efficiency and Political Waste," *Harper's Magazine*, November, 1916, p. 926.

[27] Robert Thurston Kent to Frederick W. Taylor, Nov. 24, 1911, Taylor Collection; Benjamin F. Welton, "The Problem of Securing Efficiency in Municipal Labor," *Ann. AAPSS*, XLI (May, 1912), 103–4; Guy C. Emerson, "Scientific Management in the Public Works of Cities," *National Mu-*

Taylor's methods to government were found in the Bureau of Municipal Research in New York. Reflecting the newer tendencies in reform, the Bureau invited reformers to deliver themselves from vague sentimentalities, to substitute knowledge for indignation, and to work for practical, constructive, and lasting results. It argued for efficiency within the context of those abiding themes of urban reform — the strong executive, non-partisanship, and the separation of administration and politics. The Bureau saw the government, which it would make efficient, as a welfare agency. Laissez faire was dead and the protection of property incidental. The efficiency of government was to be measured not only with reference to its established framework and goals, but also by taking into account those community needs that were not yet satisfied.[28] All three directors of the Bureau had served as functionaries in philanthropic organizations, and their understanding of community needs was based on the social workers' concept of "normal" — which in turn usually meant lower middle class.[29] Yet, characteristically, there was little talk of where efficient government was going and much rolling-up of sleeves and getting on with the business at hand.

In its early days, the Bureau proposed to create both effi-

nicipal Review, II (October, 1913), 571; "Government Efficiency and Labor," *100%*, IV (February, 1915), 80; Jesse D. Burks, "Efficiency Standards in Municipal Management," *National Municipal Rev.*, I (July, 1912), 364–71; Clarence E. Ridley, *Measuring Municipal Government* (New York: Municipal Administration Service, 1927), p. 47.

[28] Bureau of Municipal Research, New York, *Purposes and Methods of the Bureau of Municipal Research* (New York, 1907), pp. i, 19–28; Frederick A. Cleveland, *Chapters on Municipal Administration and Accounting*, pp. 102–4, 202–5, and "The Need for Coordinating State and National Activities," *Ann. AAPSS*, XLI (May, 1912), 24, 27; William H. Allen, *Efficient Democracy*, chap. v, pp. 286, 293; Henry Bruere, "Efficiency in City Government," *Ann. AAPSS*, XLI (May, 1912), 3, 6; Norman N. Gill, *Municipal Research Bureaus* (Washington, D.C.: American Council on Public Affairs, 1944), chap. i.

[29] A prime example is Edward T. Devine, *The Normal Life* (New York: Survey Associate, 1915). Bruere, "Efficiency in City Government," p. 6. The precocious image of the welfare state which the Bureau directors espoused takes on special interest when seen against the source of their revenues. The most ardent support came from Robert Fulton Cutting, a financier of a distinguished New York family active in church and philanthropic enterprises. Other financial "angels" were John D. Rockefeller, Andrew Carnegie, Mrs. E. H. Harriman, Kuhn, Loeb and Co., J. P. Morgan and Co., Henry Morgenthau, George W. Perkins, and Felix Warburg. "Testimony of F. A. Cleveland," *U.S. Commission on Industrial Relations*, 64th Cong., 1st Sess., Sen. Doc. 415 (Ser. Vol. 6937), p. 8325.

cient citizens and efficient officials; citizens armed with "the facts" and officials trained in new techniques. Yet even these efficient citizens were to remain somewhat detached from the actual workings of government:

Citizens of larger cities must frankly recognize the need for professional service in behalf of citizen interests. . . . Even efficient private citizens cannot deal helpfully with expert governmental questions. Efficient citizens will evidence their efficiency by supporting constructive efforts for governmental betterment.[30]

A member of the general public could rise only to a taxpayer's and not to an administrator's awareness of organizational effectiveness.[31] The Bureau proposed to aid the public servant and eventually replace him with a new and better type. A Training School for Public Service was established for training administrative executives and "to help make the public service a profession of equal standing with law and medicine."[32]

When the Eastern Rate Case brought news of scientific management before a broad public, the Bureau responded with excitement. "We are looking for the light," wrote Frederick A. Cleveland, technical director of the Bureau, to Taylor, "and I know that you and the men working with you can be of great service to us. . . ."[33] Cleveland joined the Taylor Society (he was one of the first members who was neither a businessman nor an engineer) and spoke before the important Dartmouth College Conference on "The Application of Scientific Management to The Activities of State and Municipal Government."[34] Bureau officials were quick to urge

[30] Bruere, "Efficiency in City Government," p. 21; Frederick P. Gruenberg, "The Engineer's Responsibility for Efficient Government," *Journal of the Engineers' Club of Philadelphia*, XXXVI (November, 1919), 426.

[31] Harold Braddock, "Efficiency Value of the Budget Exhibit," *Ann. AAPSS*, XLI (May, 1912), 157; Bruere, "Efficiency in City Government," pp. 21–22.

[32] Quoted in Weber, *Organized Efforts*, p. 176; William H. Allen, "Training Men and Women for Public Service," *Ann. AAPSS*, XLI (May, 1912), 307–12; Charles A. Beard, "Training for Efficient Public Service," *ibid.*, LXIV (March, 1916), 215–26; Luther Gulick, *The National Institute of Public Administration* (New York: National Institute of Public Administration, 1928), chap. iii.

[33] Frederick A. Cleveland to Frederick W. Taylor, Oct. 22, 1916, Taylor Collection.

[34] Dartmouth College, *Addresses and Discussion at the Conference on Scientific Management Held October 12, 13, 14, 1911* (Hanover, N.H.: Dartmouth College, 1912), pp. 313–35.

the use of principles of scientific management in municipal activities and to paraphrase Taylor on the need to "functionalize work" and "to specify tasks to be performed by each employee with reference to kind, quantity and time of performance." Like Taylor, the Bureau directors argued that correct methods rather than extraordinary persons opened the way to lasting reform. In the Bureau's Training School, the "literature of efficiency" became required reading, and Saturday luncheon meetings were set up for discussion of it.[35]

In the Bureau's work, as in that of Morris Llewellyn Cooke, stop-watch time study was usually unfeasible. However, Taylor's insistence upon the exact measurement of tasks did find a parallel in the Bureau's campaign for job standardization in public employment. This involved the orderly arrangement of titles and salaries tied to accurate "work values," so as to enable the public executives to supervise employees closely. Again, as in Cooke's work, the more significant contribution of scientific management seems to have been in the higher ranges of authority and responsibility. Taylor created a neat, understandable world in the factory, an organization of men whose acts were planned, co-ordinated, and controlled under continuous expert direction. "The full meaning of Scientific Management," explained Frederick A. Cleveland, "is comprehended in the word 'planning' and in the phrase 'the execution of plans.'"[36]

An attempt to transfer some forms of "planning" into the realm of public administration is clearly seen in the proposed reforms of President Taft's Commission on Economy and Efficiency. Since the Civil War, there had been occasional inquiries into the efficiency of government departments, but

[35] Bruere, "Efficiency in City Governement," p. 5; Braddock, loc. cit., p. 151; George A. Graham, Education for Public Administration (Chicago: Public Administration Service, 1941), pp. 137, 135; Annual Report of the Training School for Public Service, 1913, p. 49; William H. Allen, "Municipal Research," The [Cincinnati] Citizen's Bulletin, VI (April 18, 1908), 5.

[36] Cleveland, Dartmouth address, p. 314. The new interest in "planning" appeared as one of the important factors in the Bureau's support of the city manager idea. See Henry Bruere, A Plan of Organization for New York City (New York: M. B. Brown, 1917), pp. 12, 20; "Standardization of Public Employments," Municipal Research (November, 1915), pp. 10, 16–19, 31; "Standardization of Public Employment," ibid. (August, 1916), pp. 6–9, 98.

these had scarcely risen above the problems of office procedure and accounting.[37] President Taft's selection of Frederick A. Cleveland as chairman of his Commission gave promise of important innovations. The two fundamental proposals of the Commission were the executive budget and a bureau of central administrative control. The executive budget had had a quiet and respectable career of its own, prior to contact with scientific management. But now it was loaded with new meaning and expectations. It was no longer simply a financial device; it was now a "plan" through which the needs of the country were to be taken into account and direction given to the activities of the government in meeting them.[38] The proposed bureau of central administrative control would help draw up this budget and exercise "control over the subject of the efficiency of personnel and over the character of the results obtained in the several departments."[39] These recommendations did not find favor in Congress. Congressmen especially resented any attempt to weaken their power over the purse. When the Wilson administration took office the Commission was dissolved and replaced with a Bureau of Efficiency, tied more closely to Congress and content to work, for the most part, within the existing administrative structure.[40]

[37] For a discussion of the results and lack of results of these investigations see Weber, *Organized Efforts*, pp. 49–83; Leonard B. White, *The Republican Era, 1869–1901: A Study in Administrative History* (New York: Macmillan, 1958), pp. 84–92.

[38] Frederick A. Cleveland, *Organized Democracy* (New York: Longmans, Green, 1913), p. 458; *The Need for a National Budget*, 62d Cong., 2d Sess., House Doc. 854 (Ser. Vol. 6306), 10, 132–142; Frederick A. Cleveland, "The Evolution of the Budget Idea in the United States," *Ann. AAPSS*, LXII, 17.

[39] *The Need for the Organization of a Bureau of Central Administrative Control*, 62d Cong., 3d Sess., Sen. Doc. 1113 (Ser. Vol. 6353), p. 194. In a more limited realm, the possible influence of Taylor's work might be seen in the Commission's proposal that "efficiency records," used in the executive departments since the days of Carl Schurz, be changed from subjective evaluations of employees by their superiors to a quantitative measurement based on work actually performed. *Report to the President on Methods of Keeping Efficiency Records*, 62d Cong., 3d Sess., House Doc. 1252 (Ser. Vol. 6470), pp. 763, 774.

[40] Brandeis, Mayor Mitchel, John R. Commons, Charles McCarthy, and Morris L. Cooke used their influence in Congress and with the President to save the Commission. Wilson favored the Commission but was willing to give it up in exchange for congressional support for tariff and currency measures. Frederick A. Cleveland to C. A. Royse, May 31, 1913, Box

The states were quick to follow the lead of the federal government, and they soon set up their own efficiency commissions. Beginning with Wisconsin in 1911, at least sixteen states formed such commissions in the next half-dozen years. The specific influence of scientific management was less noticeable in the state capitals than in Washington. New Jersey and Iowa did call upon "efficiency experts," but their influence was limited by the narrow scope given them in New Jersey and by the impolitic thoroughness of their recommendations in Iowa. Generally, the achievements of the state commissions of efficiency and economy came down to the consolidation of state agencies, improvement of cost accounting techniques, and, most important, the grant of more power to the governor.[41]

Efficiency was also the hallmark of the New York State constitutional convention of 1915, one of the most widely discussed efforts at rewriting a state constitution in the progressive era. Significantly, the convention devoted itself chiefly to administrative reforms and called upon the Bureau of Municipal Research for surveys and recommendations. Here the proposals of the Taft Commission for an executive budget and for administrative planning departments reappeared,[42] accompanied by suggestions for consolidation of bureaus, the short ballot,[43] and a more powerful governor. But here, as in the case of the Taft Commission and the state

080.2, *Records of the President's Commission on Economy and Efficiency*, National Archives; Joseph P. Tumulty to Louis D. Brandeis, telegram, April 1, 1913, Box NMF 54, Louis D. Brandeis Collection, University of Louisville Law School, Louisville, Ky.; Weber, *Organized Efforts*, pp. 89–91, 104–12; *Congressional Record*, 64th Cong., 1st Sess., LIII (March 2, 1916), 3446–7; Carroll H. Wooddy, *The Growth of the Federal Government, 1915–32* (New York: McGraw-Hill, 1934), pp. 58–60.

[41] Raymond Moley, "The State Movement for Efficiency and Economy," *Municipal Research* (October, 1917), pp. 2, 8, 39–45, 56–59, 70, 86, 138; Frank E. Horack, "Reorganization of State Government in Iowa," *Iowa Applied History* (Iowa City: State Historical Society, 1914), pp. 53–57.

[42] Charles A. Beard, "Reconstructing State Government," *New Republic*, IV (Aug. 21, 1915), supp. 1–16; George W. Wickersham, "The New Constitution and the Work of the Bureau of Municipal Research," *Real Estate Magazine*, X (October, 1915), 1–6; Frederick A. Cleveland, "A State Budget," *Municipal Research*, February, 1915, pp. 147–68; Bureau of Municipal Research, New York, *The Constitution and Government of the State of New York: An Appraisal* (Albany: Bureau of Municipal Research, 1915), pp. 94, 135.

[43] The short ballot was, in effect, a device for enlarging the powers of the executive. It was generally accorded the honor of being a "Reform"

commissions on efficiency and economy, few of the proposals survived the buffetings of what the reformers called "petty politics." [44] Beyond the realm of municipal reform, the efficiency movement in government during the progressive era left a record of high-spirited attempts rather than durable accomplishments.

Yet these attempts call our attention to an aspect of the progressive movement which is often ignored. Alongside the well-known campaign for direct democracy was a less familiar but equally important campaign to carve out an inviolable realm of altruistic expertism in American government. At times, both of these aims could attract the same men — in the name of a revitalized government of, by, and for the people. More often, however, those who were most eager to hasten the coming of the expert, though they sincerely welcomed government for the people, were troubled by the middle term of the classic Lincolnian triad, government by the people. This group of reformers usually led the campaign for governmental efficiency and found scientific management a corroborative and invigorating idea. Efficiency provided a standpoint from which progressives who had declared their allegiance to democracy could resist the leveling tendencies of the principle of equality. They could advance reform and at the same time provide a safeguard to the "college-bred."

---

in its own right because it found a sizable following willing to consider it a panacea. The short ballot would convert many elective officers into appointive officers. Supposedly this made the administrative system beholden to the elected executive rather than to the political boss and allowed the executive to organize his administration with an eye to discipline and efficiency. Politics was to be made simple enough for the average citizen to understand. Actually, only the ballot was made simple. Politics remained as complex as before, but these complexities were now entrusted to the executive. The short ballot drew a diverse group of supporters united in the belief of the inadequacy of the citizen when confronted by the intricate workings of government and his need for leadership. Richard S. Childs, *Short-Ballot Principles* (Boston: Houghton Mifflin, 1911), chap. i, ii, iii; "The Short Ballot Movement and Simplified Politics," *Ann. AAPSS*, LXIV (March, 1916), 168–71; Albert M. Kales, *Unpopular Government in the United States* (Chicago: University of Chicago Press, 1914), chap. i, ii, iii; Arthur George Sedgwick, *The Democratic Mistake: Godkin Lectures of 1909 Delivered at Harvard University* (New York: Charles Scribner's Sons, 1912), chap. iii, iv; H. S. Gilbertson, "Extremes Meet," *Equity*, XVII (January, 1915), 78–79.

[44] The work of the Convention was rejected by the voters in a tangled and confusing contest. Alexander C. Flick (ed.), *History of the State of New York* (New York: Columbia University Press, 1935), VII, 229–37.

• CHAPTER VII

The War Machine

It is sometimes said that World War I killed progressivism, that reformers put aside reform to fight the War to End Wars and then found that they had lost their winning combination, and for some time to come could score only sporadically. There is much to be said for this view, especially if one concentrates on the legislative achievements of the years during and after the war. But a look beyond the *Congressional Record* to the sequence of popular attitudes suggests some changes in this picture. The war appears as an occasion when important progressive principles were put into service rather than pushed aside. In fact, the absence of legislative milestones of reform can be seen, in part, as a characteristic of a period when administration superseded legislation—in itself a dream of many reformers in the prewar years. In the Overman and Lever Acts, Congress placed the most important problems of the country in the hands of administrative agencies set up by the President. Senator Brandegee offered an ironical amendment to the Overman Act, providing that "if any power, constitutional or not, has been inadvertently omitted from this bill, it is hereby granted in full."[1]

The administrative arm of the government was suddenly, almost recklessly, enlarged. Washington was glutted with dollar-a-year-men, and these were outnumbered by the professors, the engineers, the "college-bred." The term "white collar" came into use.[2] Wesley Clair Mitchell, who had just

[1] Quoted in Frederick L. Paxson, *America at War* (Boston: Houghton Mifflin, 1939), p. 226.

[2] Charles Earle Funk, *Heavens to Betsy! And Other Curious Sayings* (New York: Harper, 1955), p. 29.

moved from Columbia University to the Division of Planning and Statistics of the War Industries Board, conveyed the exuberance of these new administrators in a letter to his wife: "Indeed I am in a mood to demand excitement and to make it up when it doesn't offer of itself. I am ready to concoct a new plan for running the universe at any minute. . . ."[3] Petty politics had been thrust aside, and it seemed that a new industrial regime had taken its place.

The War Industries Board marshaled the resources of the country through a system of priorities and price-fixing. The War Labor Board, backed by threats of government seizure and warnings of "work or fight," moved to put an end to class conflict. When the Smith and Wesson plant at Springfield rejected a Labor Board ruling, it was commandeered. When the machinists at Bridgeport refused to obey, they were confronted with the draft. This was the type of "positive government" which the *New Republic* had been talking about for so long.[4] A surprising number of reformers and radicals called it socialism or the first steps toward socialism.[5]

The United States found a singleness of purpose similar to the Union Sacrée of France and the Burgfriede of Germany during the early years of the war. "The supreme test of the nation has come," Wilson announced. "We must speak, act, and serve together."[6] This was much like the spirit of civic unity which had carried Galveston to commission government after its great tidal wave and Dayton to the city manager

[3] Quoted in Lucy Sprague Mitchell, *Two Lives: The Story of Wesley Clair Mitchell and Myself* (New York: Simon & Schuster, 1953), p. 299.

[4] "Springfield and Bridgeport," *New Republic*, XVI (Sept. 14–21, 1918), 185–86, 216–17.

[5] William Dean Howells, "Editor's Easy Chair," *Harpers' Monthly*, CXXXVI (April, 1918), 756; Charles Nagel, "The Growth of Socialistic Influence," *Speeches and Writings of Charles Nagel, 1900–28*, ed. Otto Heller (New York: Putnam, 1931), I, 64–67; *American Labor Year Book, 1917–1918*, ed. Alexander Tractenberg (New York: Rand School of Social Science, 1918), pp. 40–42. For H. L. Gantt's appraisal, see "Tool Power, Not Wealth Supplies Sinews of War," [*Philadelphia*] *Public Ledger*, April 10, 1917, p. 14. For similar observations on European experience see Albert Bushnell Hart, "The War and Democracy," in *Problems of Readjustment after the War* (New York: D. Appleton, 1915), pp. 19–20; "Practical Socialism in War Time," *American Review of Reviews*, LIII (June, 1916), 730–31; Alvin Johnson, "Socialism of Modern War," *Unpopular Review*, IX (January, 1918), 139–53.

[6] *Americanism: Woodrow Wilson's Speeches on the War*, ed. Oliver Marble Gale (Chicago: Baldwin Syndicate, 1918), p. 50.

system after its disastrous floods. Where singleness of purpose was accepted, questions of efficiency usually became important, and the analogy between society and the machine became more agreeable.

Even John Dewey, who had spent a good part of his early career explaining the shortcomings of the mechanical analogy, inadvertently fell under its spell. The image of the machine lay beneath the peculiar distinction between "force" and "violence" upon which Dewey built his argument against pacifism and his eventual justification of American entry into the war. Force, he said, was the energy necessary for the accomplishment of social ends. Violence was simply force used wastefully. Law, then, became "a method for employing force economically, efficiently, so as to get results with the least waste." Following this logic, it was sensible to oppose all use of violence but silly to oppose all use of force. Of course, it is a machine, in particular, which works only through the application of force. The hidden mechanical analogy helped make the argument powerful. Other forms and characteristics of human organization — voluntary agreement and co-operation, and the fundamental contrast between compulsion and choice — were neglected. Having once taken this ground, Dewey, when he condemned persecution of the opponents of the war, could only argue that the government's strong-arm tactics were, in this case, inefficient.[7]

Efficiency became a patriotic duty. Conservatives often presented their criticism of the Wilson war effort in terms of efficiency; and liberals, for their part, insisted that efficiency was a liberal thing.[8] This was complicated by the fact that Germany had popularly been considered the paragon of effi-

[7] Dewey's argument is found in his *Character and Events* (New York: Holt, 1929), II, 567, 636–41, 782–89. Morton White presents a sharp critique from a different angle in his very helpful book, *Social Thought in America: The Revolt against Formalism* (Boston: Beacon Press, 1957), pp. 161–68, chap. xiii.

[8] George Harvey, "Wanted a Leader: Can Pacifists Win the War?" *North American Review*, CCVII (March, 1911), 321–29, and "Constructive Criticism," *ibid.*, CCVIII (August, 1918), 161–68; Warren G. Harding, "Causes of Our War Delay," *Forum*, LIX (Jan. 26, 1918), 661–66; "Is the Administration Staggering under the Burdens Assumed?" *Current Opinion*, LXIV (February, 1918), 80–82. For liberal views see William Hard, "Victory for Efficiency," *New Republic* XII (Aug. 11, 1917), 40–42, "Efficiency and the 'He-Man,'" *ibid.*, XIV (March 9, 1918), 165, and "Efficiency and Slackers," *ibid.* (March 16, 1918), pp. 201–3.

ciency. Before America entered the war, propagandists for the Allies had advanced an image of German inhumanity derived from her supposed machine-like efficiency. However, once America was in the war, efficiency became a necessary virtue and, like many virtues, it was decontaminated of "Prussianism." [9]

Industrial efficiency, especially in the armament industries, was an urgent matter. Taylor's advocacy of unrestrained production became common sense. In wartime England, interest in scientific management boomed, and by 1916 even the Fabian Society offered its conditional endorsement. In France, Clemenceau ordered that Taylor's principles be applied in military plants. One patriotic Taylorite began to worry that the spread of Taylorism abroad might mean that the United States would be outstripped in the industrial world. [10]

In America, a Conservation Division in the War Industries Board was charged with cutting out unnecessary uses of labor, materials, and capital. Standardization agreements eliminated styles and sizes, thus placing strict limits on consumers' choices and giving production problems precedence over sales problems. [11]

Yet even in these seemingly favorable circumstances there

[9] Compare, for example, the reports of Edison's trip to Germany with later accounts of that country. Allen Louis Benson, "Edison Says Germany Excels Us," *World To-Day*, XXI (November, 1911), 1356–60; "What Edison Learned in Germany," *Literary Digest*, XLIV (June 1, 1912), 1156–57; "Made in Germany," *Scientific American*, CV (Dec. 16, 1911), 550; Robert H. Davis and Perley Poore Sheehan, *Efficiency: A Play in One Act* (New York: Doran, 1917); Fletcher Durell, "Germany from the Efficiency Standpoint," *National Efficiency Quarterly*, I (May, 1918), 18 ff.; Herbert F. Small, "The Legend of German Efficiency," *Unpopular Review*, VII (April, 1917), 230.

[10] Horace Bookwalter Drury, *Scientific Management: A History and Criticism* (3d ed., New York: Columbia University Press, 1922), pp. 189–90; George H. Seldes, "American Efficiency in England," *Bellman*, XXII (Feb. 3, 1917), 122–23; Sidney Webb and Arnold Freeman, *Great Britain after the War* (London: Allen & Unwin, 1916), chap. viii; H. S. Person, "Opportunities and Obligations of the Taylor Society," *Bull. Taylor Soc.*, IV (February, 1919), 5; Frank Barkley Copley, *Frederick W. Taylor: Father of Scientific Management* (New York: Harper, 1923), I, xxi; H. K. Hathaway, "Discussion," *Bull. Taylor Soc.*, III (March, 1917), 6. As of 1917, the foreign countries with the most numerous applications of scientific management were Russia, Japan, France, England, and Canada, in that order. C. Bertrand Thompson, *The Theory and Practice of Scientific Management* (Boston: Houghton Mifflin, 1917), p. 39.

[11] Bernard M. Baruch, *American Industry in the War* (New York: Prentice-Hall, 1941), chap. v.

was no great run on scientific management. "We could not sell scientific management thirty years ago," complained a prominent member of the Taylor Society; "we can hardly sell it today." [12] There were new installations — most notably that at the Winchester Repeating Arms Company. However, some previously Taylorized plants weakened their system to take advantage of the new business opportunities. On a cost-plus contract, all costs, including the costs of waste, were less pressing than the demand for whopping production. [13]

Another reason for the lack of impressive advances of scientific management in private industry lay in the exodus of Taylorites from commercial work to government service. All of the officers and a large part of the membership of the Taylor Society went to work for Uncle Sam. [14] Many found their place in the Ordnance Department, where scientific management had already gained a foothold, as a result of the running battle to Taylorize the arsenals. Others were drawn to the Shipping Board and the Emergency Fleet Corporation. (Shipping was the first industry which the government was empowered to take over and run as a unit.)

The Taylorites gathered to discuss the problems of war production amid widespread criticism of what were alleged to be the lax war policies of the administration. The call for centralized power and control, [15] a frequent refrain among the critics of Wilson's wartime policies, was now heard at the Taylor Society meetings. "There is nothing to do," remarked Ernest Hopkins, president of Dartmouth College and a good friend of scientific management, "except to make a complete democratic move, to commandeer everything and everybody and every resource of this country for the common purpose." [16] Henry P. Kendall, manager of a model Taylor fac-

[12] Morris L. Cooke, "Discussion," *Bull. Taylor Soc.*, IV (April, 1919), 7.

[13] R. G. Scott, "Discussion," *ibid.*, VI (December, 1921), 232.

[14] *Ibid.*, IV (February, 1919), 1.

[15] "Call for a War Lord," *Literary Digest*, LVI (Jan. 26, 1918), 10–11; "Cerebral Congestion at Washington," *Nation*, CV (Dec. 27, 1917), 708; "The Conduct of the War," *Independent*, Dec. 29, 1917, pp. 577–78; "The Conduct of the War," *New Republic*, XIII (Dec. 8, 1917), 136–38; Joseph Henry Odell, "Passing of the Buck in Washington," *Outlook*, CXVIII (Feb. 13, 1918), 241–43.

[16] Ernest Martin Hopkins, "Discussion," *Bull. Taylor Soc.*, IV (April, 1919), 17. The minutes of this discussion were not published until 1919. Hopkins had been interested in scientific management since the Dartmouth

tory, deplored the fact that Wilson did not understand the principles of organization. The time had come for an "organization of experts with complete responsibility." America should break with tradition and set up "a single machine," "the most efficient, democratic autocracy." [17]

But the very bluntness of these demands for control from the top produced, as a reflex action, a "democratic" counterargument which stressed the importance of "response from below." Morris L. Cooke, who had often talked about the need for decisive leadership, now led those Taylorites who thought that things might be going too far toward high-handed assertions of authority. What is most significant, however, is that even the Taylorites who stressed the importance of "response from below" accepted a hierarchy of authority and initiative, as well as a unity of interest, in their "democratic" concept of organization. The disagreement could therefore be construed somewhat innocuously as a matter of emphasis. "My own feeling," said Cooke, "is that we should have the maximum of decentralization that is consistent with a strong and able and far-sighted central control." [18]

Even before the Armistice, public interest turned from the problems of the "war machine" to those of "reconstruction." To most progressives, it seemed that there had never been a time more favorable for serious reform. The war, Wilson told the nation, was "a peoples' war" which would bring "a full and unequivocal acceptance of the principle that the interest of the weakest is as sacred as the interest of the strongest"; it would bring "the final triumph of justice and fair dealing." [19]

College Conference in 1911. He became a pioneer in "employment management," and during the war held a position on the War Labor Policies Board.

[17] Henry P. Kendall, "Discussion," *ibid.*, pp. 18, 19.

[18] Morris L. Cooke, "Discussion," *ibid.*, pp. 5, 7.

[19] "Address delivered in New York at the opening of the Fourth Liberty Loan Drive," Sept. 27, 1918, in *Americanism:Woodrow Wilson's Speeches on the War*, pp. 130–36. In private, Wilson expressed views which might be considered socialistic. He thought the world was going to change radically after the war. Governments would have to do many things which had hitherto been left to individuals and corporations. The government would have to take over such things as water power, the coal mines, and the oilfields. Ray Stannard Baker, *Woodrow Wilson* (New York: Doubleday, Doran, 1939), VIII, 241–42. Theodore Roosevelt advocated compulsory peacetime industrial service for young men and women. John M. Blum, *The Republican Roosevelt* (Cambridge, Mass.: Harvard University Press, 1954), p. 158.

William Allen White announced that the back of the profit system was broken,[20] and Charles M. Schwab of U.S. Steel described the coming new order as "a world for the workers, a world in which mere possession will no longer rule, a world which will yield honor not to those who have but to those who serve." [21] The journals of reform declared that progressivism would go forward.[22] This was seconded by the pro-war socialists, who saw the wartime "collectivism" as a step leading to the further "conscious organization of society." [23]

There were many plans of "reconstruction." [24] Almost all of them, with the important exception of that of the American Federation of Labor, made much of the idea of worker partic-

[20] Quoted in William J. Ghent, *The Reds Bring Reaction* (Princeton, N.J.: Princeton University Press, 1923), p. 3.

[21] Quoted in Charles W. Wood, *The Great Change: New America as Seen by Leaders in American Government, Industry, and Education Who Are Remaking Our Civilization* (New York: Boni & Liveright, 1919), p. 125.

[22] "The Aim of Reconstruction," *Nation*, CVII (Nov. 9, 1918), 545; "The Meaning of Reconstruction," *New Republic*, XVII (Dec. 14, 1918), 182–83; Edward T. Devine, "Nation Wide Drive for Social Reconstruction," *Survey*, XLI (March 1, 1919), 784–85; Thorstein B. Veblen, "The Modern Point of View and the New Order," *Dial*, LXV–LXVI (Oct. 19, 1918–Jan. 25, 1919), 19–24, 75–82, 289–93, 349–54, 409–14, 482–88, 543–49, 605–11; Frederick M. Davenport, "The Spirit of Political Reconstruction in America," *Outlook*, CXXI (Jan. 8, 1919), 61–62; D. Joy Humes, *Oswald Garrison Villard* (Syracuse, N.Y.: Syracuse University Press, 1960), pp. 129–30.

[23] Algie M. Simons, *The Vision for Which We Fought* (New York: Macmillan, 1919). See views of Walter Lippmann, Algie M. Simons, John Spargo, J. G. Phelps Stokes, and William English Walling in "Socialists and the Problem of War: A Symposium," *The Intercollegiate Socialist*, V (April–May, 1917), 7–27. In addition, there is an interesting series of articles by Harry W. Laidler: "War Collectivism and Wealth Conscription," *ibid.*, VI (April–May, 1917), 4–7, " 'State Socialism' in War Time," *ibid.* (February–March, 1918), pp. 11–18, "War Time Control of Industry," *ibid.*, VII (October–November, 1918), 11–14, and "Washington and the Coming Reconstruction," *ibid.* (December-January, 1918–19), 8–11.

[24] Among them was that of the National Catholic War Council (with the official sanction of the Catholic hierarchy) which pleased and displeased many by its "socialistic" proposals, and that of the AFL, which pleased and displeased many by its non-socialistic proposals. The Catholic program recommended a legal minimum wage, compulsory sickness insurance, labor participation in management, profit-sharing, and "considerable modifications" in income distribution and in "the present system." Raymond E. Swing, "The Catholic View of Reconstruction," *Nation*, CVIII (March 29, 1919), 467–68; "Catholic Reconstruction," *Survey*, XLI (Feb. 22, 1919), 727; Ralph M. Easley, "Radicals Mislead Churches about Labor," *National Civic Federation Review*, IV (March 25, 1919), 3–4; "Practical vs. Visionary Program," *ibid.* (Jan. 25, 1919), p. 10.

ipation in management. Before the war, industrial democracy (as worker participation in management was often called) had been linked with the audacious proposals of Brandeis, Croly, and Lippmann but also with the prudent system of industrial representation set up by John D. Rockefeller, Jr., at the Colorado Fuel and Iron Company.[25] During the war, the growth of workers' representation programs as a means of extra-union collective bargaining had been encouraged by the War Labor Board's policy of maintaining the status quo in industry while insisting on collective bargaining.[26] However, it was not until the months following the Armistice that the notion of industrial democracy took hold of a large and zealous following. On May 20, 1919, President Wilson sent a message to Congress which proposed "the genuine democratization of industry, based upon a full recognition of the right of those who work, in whatever rank, to participate in some organic way in every decision which directly affects their welfare or the part they are to play in industry."[27]

The great variety of programs of industrial democracy were animated by a great variety of motives. Some advocates wanted a Christian capitalism, some wanted to fight off the trade unions, and others wanted a new social order. Fundamentally, these programs were of two kinds: those which seemed to challenge the traditional source of authority in the factory and those which left it intact, and perhaps even strengthened it.

The most popular primer of the second group was John Leitch's *Man to Man*.[28] Reading the book today, without the assumptions of 1919, one finds it difficult to understand how so many thoughtful men could have taken Leitch so seriously. How, for example, Justice Oliver Wendell Holmes could have dropped his much-vaunted skepticism and written to Harold

[25] "John D. Rockefeller, Jr., Puts over His Industrial Peace Plan with the Colorado Miners," *Current Opinion*, LIX (December, 1915), 415–16; John D. Rockefeller, Jr., "There's a Solution for Labor Troubles," *System*, XXX (August, 1916), 115–21.

[26] William L. Stoddard, *The Shop Committee* (New York: Macmillan, 1919), chap. ii.

[27] Woodrow Wilson, *War and Peace: Presidential Messages, Addresses, and Public Papers (1917–1924)*, ed. Ray Stannard Baker and William E. Dodd (New York: Harper, 1927), I, 488.

[28] *Man to Man: The Story of Industrial Democracy* (New York: B. C. Forbes, 1919).

Laski: " I read John Leitch's *Man to Man.* . . . It gave me more hopefulness than anything I have read. He talks as one who had applied his ideas and succeeded in making employers and employees work together heartily." [29] Leitch simply presented a literal-minded application of Brandeis' rhetorical pronouncement that the nineteenth century had been the century of political democracy and the twentieth would be the century of industrial democracy. He transferred the apparatus of a modified American constitution to the factory. There was a "House of Representatives," usually elected by a meeting of all employees below the rank of foreman; a "Senate," consisting of superintendents and foremen; and a "Cabinet," composed of executive officers and presided over by the president. There were speakers of the House, presidents of the Senate, legislative committees, bills passed, Roberts' Rules of Order followed, etc. Of course, this was closer to Alexander Hamilton's ideal government than to Brandeis'. Leitch wished to have the worker see his employer, and the employer see himself, as the executive of the workers' best interest. Yet one wonders whether this insistence that the government of the shop under his system was just like the government of the country, fostered loyal workers or disloyal citizens. In any event, Leitch assured his readers that the adoption of his plan would increase efficiency, end strikes, and further the Americanization of the immigrant worker. His program seemed to appeal especially to those who were just coming to accept the existence of the large, permanent working class of large-scale industry but who longed for the old, supposedly harmonious, employer-worker relationship of small-scale enterprise; a relationship which, as Leitch's title indicates, was man-to-man.[30]

Of quite a different order was that variety of industrial democracy which challenged the rights of ownership and sometimes placed limits on the powers of management. This was the industrial democracy that shaped the Plumb plan [31]

[29] *The Holmes-Laski Letters: The Correspondence of Mr. Justice Holmes and Harold J. Laski, 1916–1935,* ed. Mark DeWolfe Howe (Cambridge, Mass.: Harvard University Press, 1953), I, 212.

[30] Leitch, pp. 70, 228, chaps. vii and viii.

[31] Glenn E. Plumb, "Let the Workmen Run the Railroads," *Independent,* XCIX (Aug. 30, 1919), 288–89, and "Should Labor Participate in Management?" *Ann. AAPSS,* LXXXVI (November, 1919), 222–26.

for the railroads and looked to Mary Parker Follett's *The New State*[32] rather than Leitch's *Man to Man* for guidance. Characteristically, Miss Follett placed industrial democracy in a broad frame. It was but one of the applications of the "Group Principle," which was to serve as the basis for the reorganization of all society. Only in later years did she turn her attention fully to the factory and become one of the leaders in the field of industrial administration.

Mary Parker Follett was a Boston settlement worker and friend of the Brandeis family; a gifted, well-to-do, well-educated woman who found in the settlement house a door to a wider world. Her book, *The New State*, was first published in December, 1918, and soon ran through four printings. It contained most of the fashionable notions to be expected of an up-and-coming serious thinker of that day. Here was the "New Psychology" (which Miss Follett credited to McDougall's social psychology, Freud, and behaviorism), as well as Roscoe Pound's sociological jurisprudence. Allusions to the Bergsonian *élan vital* were included, along with Hegelian patter from the works of T. H. Green, Bosanquet, and the British idealist school. (There is something intriguing about a high-minded, deeply religious New England spinster repeatedly propounding the fundamental importance of "the law of interpenetration.") Finally, the book finished off with generous helpings from the functionalist and anti-state doctrines of the political pluralists, Leon Duguit, J. N. Figgis, and Harold Laski.

Miss Follett pointed this odd mixture of doctrines toward a new concept of democracy, political and industrial. She attacked representative government, the "fictitious democracy" which spoke in terms of equal rights, consent of the governed, and majority rule, and proposed the "true democracy," which was to be based on the "group process."[33] This process was characterized by "integration" rather than domination or the compromise of differences.[34] It was not opposed to aristocracy;

[32] Mary Parker Follett, *The New State*, introduction by Lord Haldane (4th imp., New York: Longmans Green, 1923). For information on her life and writings see *Dynamic Administration: The Collected Papers of Mary Parker Follett*, ed. Henry C. Metcalf and L. Urwick (New York: Harper, 1940), esp. pp. 9–29.

[33] Follett, *New State*, pp. 5, 173, chaps. xvi–xxi.

[34] She lists "good words": integrate, interpenetrate, compenetrate,

it included aristocracy. This was an aristocracy of function, rather than of birth or property, which found its justification in expert service to the group. The war, Miss Follett declared, had taught the startling spiritual truth of unity. Now the task at hand was to convert this sentiment into a system of organization, into a "cooperative collectivism." This was the New State, to be compounded of small neighborhood groups (the Social Unit of Wilbur Phillips), occupational groups (of the guild socialists), and factory groups (the "industrial democracy" idea).[35]

Miss Follett was trying to reassert the primacy of community, to establish more open yet more intense relationships between men than modern social institutions seemed to afford. The group meant fellowship, co-operation, altruism, and increased creative force, but also increased discipline. It stood opposed to the uncontrolled individual and the unprincipled class; against egoism, conflict, the scramble for power and wealth. The "group process" somehow made the traditional distinctions between ruler and ruled, powerful and powerless, public and private, consent and compulsion, irrelevant.[36]

When Miss Follett wrote that "every department of our life must be controlled by those who know most about that department, by those who have most to do with that department," she attacked the rights of property. At one point, she proposed state ownership and "producers' control" of industry. This, apparently, did not mean workers' control but the application of the group process to the factory. This "group process" which was to create harmony — by integration, interpenetration, compenetration, etc. — meant guidance by the expert and did not mean "the rule of numbers." The functional principle attacked the rights of property but left other rights vulnerable as well. It beckoned toward popular participation through "groups" but clearly not toward popular rule within "groups" or by "groups."[37]

Under orthodox Taylorism the worker's participation in <u>management</u>, if it could be called that, had been restricted

compound, harmonize, correlate, co-ordinate, interweave, reciprocally relate or adapt or adjust, etc. *Ibid.*, p. 39.

[35] *Ibid.*, pp. 117–21, 139, 158, 175, 239, 324–30, chap. v.
[36] *Ibid.*, pp. 42, 47, 141, 189, 276.
[37] *Ibid.*, pp. 7, 142, 145, 328.

to his understanding orders and the bonus system. In cases of insubordination or repeated failure, the "shop disciplinarian" in the planning department would take the matter in hand. When Brandeis and others suggested that the workers might accept scientific management more readily if some form of worker consultation were to be used, the reply was that no one could install scientific management "and simultaneously participate in a debating society or risk the results of unfavorable decisions by a well-meaning but uninformed board of arbitration." [38]

There had been, however, even in the prewar period, a few Taylorites who had departed from this view.[39] These unorthodox Taylorites were responding to the opposition of organized labor, trying to overcome the objections of otherwise sympathetic reformers, or simply yielding to the ambiguous democratic enthusiasms of the era. An important influence upon these Taylorites was Professor Robert F. Hoxie's investigation of scientific management, conducted on behalf of the Commission on Industrial Relations. Hoxie had concluded that scientific management was a major step forward in industrial progress but that it held immediate dangers for the worker and in the long run spelled the doom of craft unionism. Many of the friends of scientific management, therefore, decided that the workers needed the protection of some sort of democratic control. Even some of the model Taylor shops cautiously introduced elected shop committees with limited authority.[40]

[38] Frank Bunker Gilbreth, *The Primer of Scientific Management* (New York: D. Van Nostrand, 1912), pp. 48, 86; Frederick W. Taylor, "Shop Management," *Trans. ASME*, XXIV (1902–3), 1393–94; Louis D. Brandeis, "Organized Labor and Efficiency," *Survey*, XXVI (April 22, 1911), 148–51; Meyer Bloomfield, "Scientific Management: Cooperative or One-Sided," *ibid.*, XXVIII (May 18, 1912), 312–13; Frank T. Carlton, "Scientific Management and the Wage Earner," *Journal of Political Economy*, XX (October, 1912), 834–45.

[39] The most radical departure was that of Robert G. Valentine, "Scientific Management and Organized Labor," *Bulletin of the Society for the Promotion of the Science of Management*, I (January, 1915), 3–9. Also see chapter III in this book, above. In addition, see Morris L. Cooke, "Who Is Boss in Your Shop," pp. 167–85; Horace B. Drury, "Scientific Management and Progress," *Bull. Taylor Soc.*, II (November, 1916), 7; H. S. Person, "The Manager, the Workman, and the Social Scientist," *ibid.*, III (February, 1917), 4–5.

[40] Robert Franklin Hoxie, *Scientific Management and Labor* (New York: D. Appleton, 1915), pp. 123–39, and "Scientific Management and

During the war, the many Taylorites in the Ordnance Department and Emergency Fleet Corporation were confronted by all manner of industrial democracy programs.[41] Industrial democracy proved to be harmless, if not helpful. When the Taylorites returned from war, what had previously been the dissenting view became the view of the majority. The Society became a rostrum for the ideas of industrial democracy.[42] A speech in vigorous defense of the powers of the executive and the need for maintaining the discipline of management found but few supporters, and met chiefly hostile reactions from the audience, at a Taylor Society meeting.[43] Morris L. Cooke proposed "industrial institutes," joint councils of workers and managers, to discuss production problems. And when Lenin called for the adoption of the techniques of Taylorism as part of a policy of centralization of authority in Russian factories, Taylorites were gratified by the references to scientific management but objected to "the spirit of the super-boss and the industrial autocrat" in his program.[44]

Changes within the body of ideas which went to make up the Taylor system also left it susceptible to the notions of in-

Labor Welfare," *Journal of Political Economy*, XXIV (November, 1916), 833–54; Alvin Johnson, "Hoxie's Scientific Management and Labor," *New Republic*, (Dec. 4, 1915), 127. Alvin Johnson, *Pioneer's Progress* (New York: Viking Press, 1952), presents important background information on the Hoxie report. Milton J. Nadworny, *Scientific Management and the Unions: 1900–1932* (Cambridge, Mass.: Harvard University Press, 1955), pp. 94–95, chap. vi; Mary Barnett Gilson, *What's Past Is Prologue: Reflections on My Industrial Experience* (New York: Harper, 1940), chap. x.

[41] "Vigilans," "Industrial Democracy at Rock Island," *Nation*, CIX (Sept. 13, 1919), 366–67; Dean Acheson, "Rock Island," *New Republic*, XXIII (Aug. 25, 1920), 358–61; John A. Fitch, "Manufacturing for Their Government," *Survey*, XLII (Sept. 13, 1917), 846–47; Horace B. Drury, "Labor Policy of the Shipping Board," *Journal of Political Economy*, XXIX (January, 1921), 1–28. Paul H. Douglas and French E. Wolfe, "Labor Administration in the Shipbuilding Industry during War Time," *Trade Unionism and Labor Prolems: Second Series*, ed. John R. Commons, (New York: Ginn, 1921), pp. 318–20, 347–48.

[42] Keppelle Hall, "The New Day," *Bull. Taylor Soc.*, IV (June, 1919), 5–7; George D. Babcock, "Discussion," *ibid.* (December, 1919), p. 25; Felix Frankfurter, "Discussion," *ibid.*, pp. 13, 14, 16; Henry W. Shelton, "Discussion," *ibid.*, pp. 45–46.

[43] John E. Otterson, "Industrial Relations," *ibid.*, pp. 34–43, and the "Discussion," following.

[44] Morris L. Cooke, *An All American Basis for Industry* (Philadelphia: Morris L. Cooke, 1919), pp. 13–15; [H. S. Person], "Comment," *Bull. Taylor Soc.*, IV (June, 1919), 2.

dustrial democracy. Some influential writers on management had begun to examine Taylor's psychological assumptions and find them unfashionable. By 1919, the differential piece rate, through which Taylor had first presented his new vision for the factory, had "ceased to be a major principle." The differential piece rate, it must be remembered, was Taylor's method for securing the co-operation of the worker and giving him an incentive for hard work. With its decline, other possible sources of incentive and discipline became of interest. Even before the war, one prominent defender of the Taylorite orthodoxy began to speak of "the type of discipline which wells up from beneath and is at least partially self-enforcing." The claims that worker participation in management led to increased output gave it new drawing power.[45]

For the public at large, the drawing power of industrial democracy lay partly in its vagueness. The boom in the shop committee programs owed much to those who thought of them as substitutes for the trade unions, those who thought of them as supplements to the trade unions, and those who thought of them as the basis for a new social order. During the war, the AFL had recommended that its unions take part in the shop committees which were being set up in war industries. The locals, however, were often openly hostile to these programs. They feared that the shop committees would usurp their functions as agents of collective bargaining and would be used to break the unions. The craft unions, moreover, for which only a fraction of the workers were eligible, were put in a difficult position with respect to the companies' programs of "factory solidarity." At the 1919 Convention, the AFL condemned the shop committee system and began its fight to unionize the steel industry where Rockefeller-type plans were in force.[46]

The opponents in the steel strike of 1919 laid waste to the middle ground of which many reformers were so fond. The

[45] Ordway Tead, *Instincts in Industry: A Study of Working Class Psychology* (Boston: Houghton Mifflin, 1918), pp. 50–51, 54–55, and "Problems of Incentives and Output," *Ann. AAPSS*, LXXXIX (May, 1920), 170–79; H. S. Person, "The Opportunities and Obligations of the Taylor Society," *Bull. Taylor Soc.*, IV (February, 1919), 3; "Comment," *ibid.*, V (April, 1920), 49; Bertrand Thompson, *The Theory and Practice of Scientific Management* (Boston: Houghton Mifflin, 1917), p. 168.

[46] *Trade Unionism and Labor Problems: Second Series*, ed. John R. Commons, pp. 319–20, 345, 346–48.

steel companies made it clear that their shop committees eliminated the need for unionism, and the AFL insisted that unions would replace the shop committees. For many advocates of industrial democracy, this turn of events was the signal for retreat. At the Taylor Society, however, there was little sign of distress. The optimistic belief that there was no necessary conflict between industrial democracy and trade unionism was reaffirmed. Morris L. Cooke went so far as to suggest that the Taylor Society should actively support both industrial democracy and the trade unions, not in order to strengthen the bargaining power of the worker, but rather to lay the basis for the national planning of the future. This would require national unions; shop committees unaffiliated on a national basis would not do.[47]

The postwar discussions of industrial democracy at the Taylor Society were much like the wartime debates on centralization and decentralization. Even the most ardent partisans of the shop councils had no intention of destroying hierarchy in the factory. Ordway Tead, who brought the teachings of Miss Follett and the guild socialists to the Taylorites, pointed out that there "must be executive direction which employs a high order of intelligence. There must be unified control and there must be the machinery which secures prompt decisions and assures prompt carrying out of decisions."[48] The over-all significance of industrial democracy for the Taylor Society was twofold: first, it provided a way station for many Taylorites en route to an acceptance of the trade union, and second, it provided a pattern for the absorption of democratic criticism within Taylor doctrine.

[47] William F. Willoughby, "American History," *American Year Book, 1919*, ed. Francis G. Wickware (New York: D. Appleton, 1920), pp. 24–26; John B. Andrews, "Labor and Labor Legislation," *ibid.*, pp. 458–59; Samuel Crowther, "The Fetish of Industrial Democracy," *World's Work*, XXXIX (November, 1919), 23–27; compare this with his earlier "What I Found British Labor Planning," *System*, XXXVI (July, 1919), 35–38. See also Elmer H. Fish, "Some Dangers in the Shop Committee," *Industrial Management*, LVIII (September, 1919), 205; Albert W. Atwood, "Industrial Democracy and Human Nature," *Saturday Evening Post*, CXCIV (Aug. 20, 1921), 21; Henry S. Dennison, "The President's Industrial Conference," *Bull. Taylor Soc.*, V (April, 1920), 82, 90; Morris L. Cooke, "Discussion," *ibid.*, p. 91.

[48] Ordway Tead, "The Technician's Point of View," in *New Tactics in Social Conflict*, ed. Harry W. Laidler (New York: Vanguard Press, 1926), p. 123.

The discussions of industrial democracy were encouraged by the enthusiasm for new ideas and new measures so common in the first months after the Armistice. "Certain it is that the old order has passed never to return and that a new day is here," declared a speech to a meeting of Taylorites.[49] This was the kind of fervor which inspired the reorganization of the Taylor Society after the war. In place of the somewhat informal arrangements of the prewar days, a substantial organization was set up to support more ambitious activities and to carry the message of Taylorism to the country. An important change was the creation of the post of managing director, to conduct the Society's affairs. This, now the most influential office, was given to Harlow S. Person, who had served as president before the war. Person was neither an engineer nor a businessman but a college professor with a strong interest in the social consequences of Taylorism. The office of president became something of an honorary position. And E. W. Clark and Company, a Philadelphia banking house with close ties to the Taylor family, supplied the treasurer and probably underwrote any deficits.[50]

Moreover, when the work of the Taylor Society was redefined in the light of war experience, new undertones of radicalism were heard. "The businessmen as a class," Person reported, "failed to measure up to the reputations which they brought with them from private industry." The businessman's talents could not be transferred from the very specific conditions in which he had achieved his success. Therefore, there was a great need for "trained managers with universal and adaptable managerial principles, free and able to organize and direct enterprises — national, state, municipal or private — wherever at any moment or in any emergency their services may be in demand." Taylorism would serve as the foundation of the new profession of "transferable administrators" or "engineer-administrators." For it was the only unified system of management which applied the methods of the exact sciences and incorporated the findings of the other sciences as well.[51]

Many members of the Taylor Society saw themselves as

[49] Keppelle Hall, loc. cit., p. 5.
[50] Bull. Taylor Soc., IV (April, 1919), supp. 1–6.
[51] Person, "Opportunities and Obligations," pp. 3, 4, 6–7.

peculiarly fitted to act as disinterested spokesmen for the community at large. They were dedicated to greater production — the sustenance of an advancing America. In the factory, these "engineer-administrators" stood between the owners and the workers. Beyond the factory, they might muster their forces to hold the balance of power in the conflict of industrial classes and bring a return to productive efficiency. By 1919, many prominent Taylorites had moved closer to labor and were apt to present efficiency as a criticism of existing institutions. The *Bulletin of the Taylor Society* sided with the workers in the bituminous coal strike of 1919 and later supported the eight-hour shift in the steel industry. When the *Dial* published the series of Veblen essays which were later to form the book, *The Engineers and the Price System*, the *Bulletin* reprinted an excerpt with favorable comment. It gave prominence to an open letter from one of its members that condemned the waste of private control of the power industry and recommended a plan of government ownership.[52]

The Taylorites had absorbed some of the social concerns of the progressive era and included them in their program. "Our profession," declared Cooke, "that of industrial engineering, has come of age at a time when the interests of society and not the interests of individuals is the master test. This is one advantage which our profession has over all others, and it carries with it a very deep significance."[53]

[52] Keppelle Hall, *loc. cit.*, p. 5; Henry H. Farquhar, "Positive Contributions of Scientific Management," *Bull. Taylor Soc.*, IV (October, 1919), 24; Person, "Opportunities and Obligations," p. 5; [H. S. Person], "Comment," *Bull. Taylor Soc.*, IV (August, 1919), 2, 27; Cooke, *An All American Basis for Industry*, p. 2, and, "Discussion," *Bull. Taylor Soc.*, IV (October, 1919), 47, 49, 50; *ibid.*, V (April, 1920), 49; Walter N. Polakov, "Open Letter," *ibid.*, IV (October, 1919), 49–50.

[53] Morris L. Cooke, "Discussion," *Bull. Taylor Soc.*, V (June, 1920), 128.

• CHAPTER VIII

Boston Is a State of Mind

One of the distinctive elements of the progressive era was the widespread feeling among many urban, middle-class reformers that there was little to fear from below. Social gospel ministers and similarly minded sociologists, social workers, and publicists, working initially from a broadened concept of Christian charity, created a sympathetic image of the lower classes. The motto of the progressive era was "uplift." In part, this meant lifting up the lower classes into the middle class. Generally this elevation was to be moral, but often it acquired economic connotations. The goal of making the worker a home owner, for example, runs through much of progressive literature on industrial welfare.

When 1919 ended, however, many of the bonds of sympathy with the lower classes seemed to be breaking. Incitements to domestic reform were still evident through most of the year, but gradually these became alloyed with a feeling of danger from below which lessened their force. Inflation, which had vexed the middle classes in the prewar years, and which lay behind the excitement of the Eastern Rate Case, became an even more pressing problem in 1919.[1] The result was a campaign again the "profiteers" (the Big Five Meat Packers bearing the brunt of the attack) and the granting of new regulatory powers to the federal government. This had many of the characteristics of the prewar battles against "the

[1] Paul A. Samuelson and Everett E. Hagen, *After the War, 1918–20* National Resources Planning Board Pamphlet [Washington, D.C.: Government Printing Office, 1943]), pp. 13–15.

interests." But the leaders of the campaign against the high cost of living were now also leaders of the campaign against radicalism.[2]

In January, 1919, the *Commercial and Financial Chronicle* announced that Bolshevism in America was inconceivable. This confidence was shaken some weeks later by the Seattle general strike but restored through its failure. The *Seattle Times* thought the strike had been a good thing, since it had cleared the air and proved the strength of law and order. Beyond the West Coast, the memory of the strike and its factitious hero, Mayor Ole Hanson, faded quickly, not to be resurrected until the end of the year.[3] The Senate committee to investigate Bolshevism, which met in February and March, spent most of its time discussing conditions in Russia, not America, and gave John Reed and Albert Rhys Williams the opportunity to present the Bolshevik side of the story. The star witness was Catherine Breshkovskaya, a member of the Russian Social Revolutionary party, who condemned the Bolsheviks for their dictatorship and not for their socialism. In fact, American socialists provided much of the early postwar criticism of Russian Bolshevism.[4]

As for the domestic radicals, there was a movement in the first months of 1919 for a general amnesty for those convicted under the Espionage Act. Reacting to these pressures, A. Mitchell Palmer asked the president for clemency for fifty-two persons on April 11, and Attorney General Gregory, before

[2] William F. Willoughby, "Cost of Living," *American Year Book, 1919*, ed. Francis G. Wickware (New York: D. Appleton, 1920), pp. 18–21. A. Mitchell Palmer and Clayton R. Lusk were prominent in both campaigns. A. Mitchell Palmer, "How Can We Bring Down the High Cost of Living," *World Outlook*, V (December, 1919), 5–6, and "How To Bring Down Prices," *Independent*, Dec. 13, 1919, p. 167; *New York Times*, May 26, 1920.

[3] *Commercial and Financial Chronicle*, CVIII (Jan. 18, 1919), 204; "The Meaning of the Western Strikes," *Literary Digest*, LX (March 1, 1919), 15; Frederick L. Paxson, *American Democracy and the World War* (Boston: Houghton Mifflin, 1948), III, 31.

[4] "Bolshevism Probed by Senate," *National Civic Federation Review*, IV (March 5, 1919), 1–3; Gustavus Myers, "Bolshevik 'Industrial Government,'" *ibid.* (Dec. 20, 1918), pp. 8–9; William English Walling, "Bolshevism Convicted out of Its Own Mouth," *ibid.* (Jan. 10, 1919), pp. 7–9; Algie M. Simons, "Bolshevism and Shop Stewardism," *ibid.* (March 5, 1919), p. 17; J. G. Phelps Stokes, "The New Tragedy of the War," *ibid.* (April 10, 1919), p. 9.

him, had appealed on behalf of others. There was a noticeable change in attitude after the postal bomb explosions in June, yet a sampling of the American press to see whether Bolshevism was considered a real peril still brought equivocal answers.[5]

With the Boston police strike in September, however, what had been a sporadic campaign against radicalism moved rapidly toward the "Red Scare." The police strike was one of the cardinal events in American domestic affairs in 1919, for it not only heightened the fear of radicalism but linked this radicalism to the labor movement. It sounded the alarm. There was real danger below.

Woodrow Wilson reacted strongly to the events in Boston, taking time from a speech in Helena, Montana, in support of the League of Nations, to denounce the strike as "a crime against civilization." [6] The general reaction was even more vehement. Boston was compared to Belgium, with some periodicals carrying descriptions of women being dragged off streetcars and carried into alleyways.[7] Even the *New Republic*, which had been moving toward the left and had proposed a labor party for the United States, now came out against the strike. It denied the right of policemen to strike or even to

[5] William F. Willoughby, "National Campaign against Radicalism," *American Year Book, 1919*, p. 59; "Is Bolshevism Becoming a Real Peril? The Extent of Our Social Unrest and Suggested Remedies," *Curren Opinion*, LXVII (July, 1919), 4–6. Up to this point, even the NAM did not seem to think Bolshevism was an immediate danger in America. "Bolshevism — What Is It?" *American Industries*, XIX (February, 1919), 2; Michael J. Hickey, "Bolshevism — Old Wine in New Bottles," *ibid.*, p. 13; William A. Pinkerton, "How To Deal with the Bolsheviki," *ibid.* (July, 1919), p. 30.

[6] *New York Times*, Sept. 12, 1919. When Coolidge defeated the Democratic candidate for governor in the Massachusetts fall elections, Wilson, the official leader of the Democratic party, took the extraordinary step of sending a telegram to Coolidge congratulating him on his election as "a victory for law and order. . . . when that is the issue, all Americans stand together." Quoted by James Albert Woodbury, "Politics and Parties," *American Year Book, 1919*, p. 65.

[7] F. Roswell Burgess, "Governor Calvin Coolidge, All American," *National Magazine*, LXVIII (October, 1919), 394; "The Guardians of Order Abdicate," *Independent*, XCIX (Sept. 20, 1919), 392; Gregory Mason, "No Bolshevism for Boston," *Outlook*, CXXIII (Sept. 24, 1919), 124–25; "When the Police Strike," *Literary Digest*, (Sept. 20, 1919), 2–3; "Can Public Servants Strike?" *Public*, XXII (Sept. 20, 1919), 1006–7; "Boston's Police Strike," *American Review of Reviews*, LX (October, 1919), 341–3; D. C. Brewer, "Executive Action," *American Industries*, XX (December, 1919), 26.

join the AFL. The AFL itself, owing in part to internal conflicts, had been among the first to battle against radicalism and to champion Americanism.[8] This was to no avail, for soon the AFL was classed with the Bolsheviks. Labor had committed the major sin against progressivism; it had put class interest above public interest.

The changing image of the lower class and its dangers is perhaps most clearly seen in the magazines of entertainment; magazines with few beliefs of their own to uphold and a desire to violate none of those of their readers'. The *National Magazine*, for example, which thrived chiefly upon mawkish fiction and lavish illustrations, in May had announced, without any qualms, that power was passing into the hands of the proletariat, but in October published a call for "a strike against strikes."[9] Now Albert J. Beveridge spoke out against the predatory labor organizations, which were trying to dictate to the government.[10] And a relatively unknown Chicago lawyer rose to a brief popularity as a lecturer and author by his single-minded attack on the word democracy, a key word for the whole progressive era.[11] When the Red Scare subsided, fear of those below on the part of the urban middle class

[8] "Why a Labor Party?" *New Republic*, XVIII (April 26, 1919), 397–400; "Police Strike," *ibid.*, XX (Sept. 24, 1919), 217–18; "Policeman and the Police Power," *ibid.* (Oct. 1, 1919), 247–48; "Samuel Gompers' Great Message," *National Civic Federation Review*, IV (Dec. 5, 1918), 1–2; *New York Times*, April 13, 1919; Ralph M. Easley complained that prominent businessmen were coddling the socialists while Samuel Gompers was fighting them. "It is the American labor movement that is entitled to all the credit today for our freedom from Bolshevism, anarchy, and revolution in this country," "Forces of Disorder," *National Civic Federation Review*, IV (Dec. 5, 1918), 19.

[9] "America after the War," *National Magazine*, XLVIII (May, 1919), 164; F. Roswell Burgess, *loc. cit.*, p. 393. The journals of public affairs also reflected this shift. See "Public Opinion Defeating the Strikes," *Lit. Digest*, LXIII (Nov. 22, 1919), 11–14; "Red Threats of Revolution Here," *ibid.* (Nov. 8, 1919), pp. 15–16; "The Radicalism of American Labor," *ibid.*, LXVI (July, 1920) pp. 24–26; "Labor Omnia Vincit," *Independent*, CI (Feb. 21, 1920), 282.

[10] The speech was printed and widely distributed, prefaced with the statement that "a most hopeful omen of the present day is the turn of the public sentiment against labor unions." He followed this first success with a speech on "Organized Labor's Assault on American Institutions." Claude G. Bowers, *Beveridge and the Progressive Era* (Boston: Houghton Mifflin, 1932), pp. 509–11.

[11] He proposed to return to the word "republic" which had no connotations of majority or mass rule. Harry F. Atwood, *Back to the Republic* (Chicago: Laird & Lee, [1919]).

went with it, but the estrangement remained. A middle-class self-consciousness had appeared.[12] Gone was the simple optimism and confidence which had led to a program of up-lifting the lower classes into the middle. The year 1919 had opened with a good many progressive reformers, especally those of the urban middle class, looking forward to new triumphs. The year 1919 closed with many of these same re-formers beset with gloom and bewilderment.[13]

The Taylor Society, which had accepted some of the atti-tudes of progressivism into its orthodoxy, did not shift so rapidly. This apparent constancy made the Taylor Society ap-pear somewhat radical, in a period when many Americans were turning their backs on reform. In these circumstances scientific management attracted unexpected sympathizers. Or-ganized labor, the socialsts, and even the Wobblies (IWW) were now drawn to it. Such men as Thorstein Veblen and John Rogers Commons, who had remained somewhat distant during the efficiency craze, now moved closer to the Taylorites.

While before the war an alliance of Thorstein Veblen and his followers with a group of Taylorite engineers would have seemed unlikely, in the new circumstances of postwar Amer-ica such a tie-up appeared to be almost inevitable. Thorstein Veblen was an outlander. Yet the appeal of his critique of America owed much to the fact that it was based on moral

[12] Homer Hoyt, "If the Middle Class Should Strike," *Outlook*, CXXIII (Nov. 26, 1919), 337; Theodore L. Stoddard, "Common People's Union," *World's Work*, XXXIX (November, 1919), 102–4; Glenn Frank, "Butt, Buffer, and Burden-Bearer," *Century Magazine*, XCIX (April, 1920), 798–99; John Corbin, "Forgotten Folk," "The New Poor and the Old," "Liberty Above Equality," *North American Review*, CCXII (September, November, December, 1920), 308–18, 618–30, 741–53. Even the *New Re-public*, which was dedicated to middle-class selflessness, showed signs of middle-class "class consciousness." See H. L. Mencken, "Meditation in E Minor," *New Republic*, XXIV (Sept. 8, 1920), 38–40.

[13] Contributing to this loss of vigor and idealism in the progressive movement were the divisions created within progressivism by the war, the confused and contradictory reactions of progressives to the Versailles Treaty, and the very accomplishments of a decade of reform which in-creased the numbers of those not too unhappy with the existing state of things. A study addressed more directly to the history of progressivism would, of necessity, deal with these important factors and their bearing upon the shift in social perspective discussed here. Such a study would also discuss the profound cultural revolution within which this shift took place. See Henry F. May, *The End of American Innocence* (New York: Alfred A. Knopf, 1959), especially Part IV.

standards that were familiar and widely held. For many, this morality was made even more forceful because it denied morality. He scorned preaching and hid his own preachments behind an ironic manner and beneath the guise of seemingly objective instincts — workmanship, parental bent, and idle curiosity. From this vantage point he claimed to "describe" America, while covertly he condemned luxury and waste and approved simplicity and work. Veblen resembled Frederick W. Taylor in this respect. Not only was their list of virtues similar, but both frequently slipped their preachments behind the protection of "science." Furthermore, both Veblen and Taylor pictured the industrial system as a machine process whose major goal was production and whose underlying code was efficiency.[14]

At this point their differences became more important. Taylor, coming from an eminent Philadelphia family, looked down the social scale and found the initial obstacle to efficiency in the "soldiering" of the worker. Veblen, the son of a Norwegian immigrant farmer, looked up the social scale and found the obstruction in "interstitial disturbances," the sabotage of production by the profit takers. While Taylor was later to complain that most of his trouble came from those on top in the factory, and Veblen was to admit the complicity of the workmen in the "conscientious withdrawal of efficiency," it was their initial emphasis which gave direction to most of their work.

Another difference lay in Taylor's insistence upon harmonies where Veblen underscored conflicts. Taylor saw no necessary opposition between the classes, nor a necessary clash between commercial and mechanical efficiency for the capitalist or the worker. For Veblen, under the system of private property and pecuniary logic, an indispensable method of making money was not making goods. This position derived from Veblen's dichotomy between business and industry. Here again, incidentally, Veblen was touching on notions which were familiar and widely held. Veblen's contrast between technology and credit (one aspect of his all-encompass-

[14] Veblen's view of the industrial system was already suggested in *The Theory of the Leisure Class* (New York: Macmillan, 1899), and presented in full in *The Theory of Business Enterprise* (New York: Mentor Books, 1958), chap. ii.

ing dichotomy) was a sophisticated rendering of a sentiment which reached back at least to the Jacksonian hard-money debates and was later to erupt in the economic wisdom of Henry Ford and Ezra Pound.[15] However, when Veblen clearly turned his dichotomy into a distinction between productive and non-productive classes, with the lower classes the productive ones, he probably found approval only among the Populists and socialists. Furthermore, he thought he cut himself off even from these. Veblen nowhere said that the lower classes would be the saviors of society. He saw himself as an observer, a scientist, and declared that "teleology" was a grave intellectual sin.[16]

Veblen had been unmoved by the popular enthusiasm for efficiency engineers in the years before the war. At that time, he had thought that the engineer's addiction to commercial notions of efficiency differed from that of the capitalist and the laborer only in degree. The efficiency engineers, he had argued, were trying to combine the functions of the accountant and the technologist; they accepted the dispensation which made questions of efficiency incidental to questions of profit.[17]

[15] In a contemporary novel, written by a businessman, this contrast was personified by the contrast between the hero, a rough but honest manufacturer, and the villain, a stock market speculator, slick, effete, well-groomed, popular with the ladies, who spent most of his time at the country club playing golf. Arthur Jerome Eddy, *Ganton and Co.: A Story of Chicago Commercial and Social Life* (Chicago: A. C. McClurg, 1908). See also Cedric B. Gowing, "Market Speculation in the Muckraker Era: The Popular Reaction," *Business History Review*, XXXI (Winter, 1957).

[16] See especially Veblen's criticism of Marx, "The Socialist Economics of Karl Marx and His Followers," *The Place of Science in Modern Civilization and Other Essays* (New York: B. W. Huebsch, 1919), p. 416, 430. Teleology, wrote Alvin Johnson, "is Veblen's specialty. Let another scientist produce a generalization, however abstract, Veblen will extract a teleological element, an ulterior motive from it. He is like a skilled pathologist, competent to prove that all the world is suffering from his pet disease." Then with much justice, Johnson adds, "Such a pathologist usually ends by taking the disease himself, if it ıs communicable; and even if it is not, he is likely to reproduce the symptoms." Alvin Johnson, "Review of 'The Instinct of Workmanship,'" *Political Science Quarterly*, XXXI (December, 1916), 631. See also Lewis S. Feuer, "Thorstein Veblen: The Metaphysics of the Interned Immigrant," *American Quarterly*, V (Summer, 1953), 99–112, for the suggestion that Veblen's early stance of the observer was due in part to the restrictive conditions of academic life in this era.

[17] Thorstein Veblen, *The Instinct of Workmanship and the State of the Industrial Arts* (New York: Viking Press, 1943), pp. 342, 345–46. This was due to the contamination of the sense of workmanship by pecuniary institutions. While fundamental instincts, as well as the intellectual habits with which machine technology imbued the engineer (and to a

During the war, Veblen gave up the attitude of the disinterested observer, to which he had been long accustomed, for that of the reformer. He saw the possibility of a sweeping social change arising from the exigencies of modern war, and he joined the vast white-collar army which the war called into being. He served on Colonel House's inquiry on peace terms and then in Herbert Hoover's Food Administration, urging radical measures on both.[18] With many others, Veblen saw "reconstruction" as "a revision of vested rights for the common good." He recommended that the vested rights of organized labor and employers be set aside and control be exercised by some third group which had no pecuniary interest in industry and was therefore free to manage it in the interests of the entire community, that is, for productive efficiency. Now, he assigned this role specifically to the engineers. (Veblen was even ready to place the making of peace in their hands.)[19] and it appeared that the engineers might be receptive. For "right lately these technologists have begun to become uneasily 'class-conscious' and to reflect that they together constitute the indispensable General Staff of the industrial system," Veblen reported.[20]

---

lesser extent the worker and society in general), were in conflict with these pecuniary institutions, for Veblen the ultimate outcome of this conflict was as yet uncertain. *Theory of Business Enterprise*, pp. 149, 189, chap. ix; *Instinct of Workmanship*, p. 303, chap. vii; "Christian Morals and the Competitive System," *Essays in Our Changing Order*, ed. Leon Ardzrooni (New York: Viking Press, 1934), pp. 200–218.

[18] The shift is clearly seen in his book, *The Nature of Peace*. This work begins with the announcement that it is not concerned with the merits of peace or war but rather with the systematic knowledge of things as they are. However, when Veblen came to write the preface he was ready to affirm that the quest for peace was "a paramount and intrinsic human duty." Lasting peace was to be achieved through the unconditional surrender of Germany, and, somewhat inconveniently, Japan, and by the establishment of a league of neutrals in which the United States would play a leading role. Thorstein Veblen, *An Inquiry into the Nature of Peace and the Terms of Its Perpetuation* (New York: B. W. Huebsch, 1919), pp. viii, 2–3, 194–203, 233–44, 250–52; *Essays in Our Changing Order*, pp. 267–336, 361–82.

[19] Thorstein Veblen, "A Policy of Reconstruction," *Essays in Our Changing Order*, pp. 391, 392, 395. This essay was first printed in the *New Republic*, XIV (April 13, 1918), 318–20; Veblen, *The Vested Interests and the Common Man* (New York: B. W. Huebsch, 1920), p. 89, and "Peace," *Essays in Our Changing Order*, p. 419, reprinted from *Dial*, May 17, 1919.

[20] Thorstein Veblen, *The Engineers and the Price System* (New York: Viking Press, 1944), p. 71. This chapter was first printed as "The Cap-

Undoubtedly, the engineers were but a small minority of the population. This, however, was an advantage and not an obstacle. It favored the formation of a compact, homogeneous, effective organization of those key men who were essential for the working of the industrial system.[21] The overthrow of the old order was to be primarily a technical affair. One could not rely upon the AFL, which had a vested interest in the system, nor the Wobblies, "the flotsam of industry, . . . whose contribution to the sum total is loose talk in some foreign tongue." A Bolshevik revolution, which Veblen saw as a mass uprising, was possible only in a backward country and out of the question in the United States. Here, the initiative and direction was to come from the country's technicians. A self-selected group of engineers could bring the old order tumbling down through the simple expedient of a general strike "for such time as may be required to enforce their argument." This move meant the concerted action of no more than a fraction of 1 per cent of the population.[22]

The new government was to consist primarily of a small "self-selected" central directorate of engineers and "production economists," whose concerns were to be chiefly technological. Absentee ownership was to be discarded and a regime of workmanship set up to liberate the productive powers of the economy (increasing the output of industry by 300 to 1,200 per cent!). To sustain this new regime, the "Soviet of Technicians" would need the support of the industrial rank and file. However, since the material needs of this rank and file would be taken care of, they were expected to co-operate. Their co-operation would be clearly in a subordinate capacity.[23] Veblen's was a syndicalism for an industrial elite.[24]

tains of Finance and the Engineers," in *Dial*, LXVI (June 14, 1919), and reprinted in the *Bulletin of the Taylor Society*, IV (August, 1919). Actually Veblen thought he found this new awareness more typically among the younger engineers, (pp. 73–74).

[21] Veblen, *The Engineers and the Price System*, pp. 79–80.

[22] *Ibid.*, pp. 79–80, 90, 98–99, 138, 167.

[23] *Ibid.*, pp. 71, 142–46, 166.

[24] This was not the stable, self-confident elitism more often found in traditionally stratified societies. There was always an unresolved wavering between elite and mass, engineer and Wobbly, in Veblen's thought; yet the elitist tendencies predominated. Veblen's outlook, like that of other syndicalists and elitists, contained elements of disgust with, and a sense of helplessness with regard to, democratic mass politics. It re-

The feeling for elite leadership was not unusual among American reformers. Lester Frank Ward, whom Veblen admired, had urged a similar view in his famous "sociocracy." Even John Dewey, at one time, had been eager to establish an "Intelligence Trust" at the head of society to work in the interest of all classes.[25] Veblen's choice of the engineer followed from his over-all technological bias; one is tempted to say, technological hallucination. In the machine age, Veblen thought, the machine was the undeniable fact. From it came a work discipline, and from the work discipline came the intellectual habits of the bulk of the community. The engineer, above all others, was compelled to come to terms with the discipline of the machine. Therefore, he would think in terms of cause and effect: he would tend to be skeptical, matter of fact, materialistic, unmoral, unpatriotic, and undevout.[26]

Modern civilization as a whole, Veblen thought, rested upon a technological system which he described as an increasingly comprehensive interlocking mechanical process. At times the distinction between the society and the mechanical process on which it rested was blurred in his writings. And Veblen, who found the engineer in a strategic position in the factory, granted him a strategic position within the social order. Furthermore, the engineers were becoming radical. Their workmanlike instincts and machine-disciplined habits of mind, which, in the past, had been "contaminated" by pecuniary institutions, were now becoming decontaminated.

In the months which followed the Armistice, the Taylor Society entered what appeared to be a period of growing radicalism. Gantt's New Machine began to reassemble. Fred J. Miller, one of Taylor's active supporters and a close friend of Gantt, was elected president of the American Society of Mechanical Engineers — signifying the ascendency of the "progressives." Through his worshiping disciple Leon Ardzrooni, Veblen now came into contact with an assortment of restive engineers and architects. This included the new lead-

sembled Charles Ferguson's utopian habit of mind and the mood of those political reformers who found refuge in "administration." It is difficult to read *Engineers and the Price System* today without thinking of Ayn Rand's *Atlas Shrugged*.

[25] Lewis Feuer, "Dewey and the Back to the People Movement," *Journal of the History of Ideas*, XX (October–December, 1959), 550–52.

[26] Veblen, *Theory of Business Enterprise*, p. 149, chap. ix.

ership in the American Society of Mechanical Engineers, Gantt and his followers, and other prominent members of the Taylor Society. Veblen planned to form the nucleus of the "Soviet of Technicians" from this group and to use the New School for Social Research, where he was teaching, as its headquarters. At one meeting of this nucleus "there was substantial agreement as to the part the technician plays in the scheme of things and his responsibility to society to lead in the direction of order." [27]

However, the prospects for the venture were not promising. There were important differences between Veblen and even the most radical of the engineers. Veblen spoke in terms of inevitable and comprehensive contradictions. Maximum production and efficiency could be achieved only by bringing down the old order. Gantt, on the other hand, the foremost of the radical engineers, thought in piecemeal terms. He agreed that considerations of profit sometimes hampered efficiency, but he proposed to place restrictions on profits rather than abolish them. The engineers talked of holding a balance of power, the terms of which they would have liked to change, but they did not talk about destroying the balance itself. [28]

Veblen's Soviet never amounted to much. Gantt, who might perhaps have played an important role, died before things got started. The more prominent engineers drifted away quickly and left a scattering of younger men who maintained their ties with Veblen for a while. Among these men was Otto Beyer, who worked in the Taylor tradition and later gained renown for introducing efficiency techniques into the Baltimore and Ohio Railroad shops with the co-operation of the unions. Another was Howard Scott, who later became famous as the leader of technocracy. (Though Scott attended meetings of the Taylor Society, he was not a follower of Taylor.) Scott soon set up an organization of his own, the Technical Alliance, with more limited objectives than Veblen's projected Soviet. [29]

On June 14, 1919, Veblen spoke of the growing "class

[27] Leon Ardzrooni, "Veblen and Technocracy," *Living Age*, CCCXLIV (March, 1933), 40; Joseph Dorfman, *Thorstein Veblen and His America* (New York: Viking Press, 1941), p. 454.
[28] See chap. iii, above. See also Charles W. Wood, *The Great Change* (New York: Boni & Liveright, 1919), chap. iv.
[29] Dorfman, *Veblen*, pp. 459–60.

consciousness" of the engineers, and on October 4 he gave credence to the suggestion that the overturn of the system would probably take place within two years.[30] But two weeks later he asserted that this view was too sanguine. The general strike of technicians was a remote contingency, since the engineer had turned out to be harmless and docile. This was true not only of the older generation but even the younger generation of engineers in which he had placed his hopes. They deferred to the older men "with such a degree of filial piety as should go far to reassure all good citizens." Veblen returned to his earlier view that the engineers had a "hired-man's loyalty" to the established order.[31]

Much closer to the outlook of the radical engineers were the views of John Rogers Commons, Wisconsin's noted administrator, reformer, and scholar. Commons believed that conflicts of interests made for progress, but he also stressed the mutual dependence of the contending forces and the need to impose some order upon them.[32] Veblen was sour, unfair, and addicted to fixed ideas, yet sometimes brilliant and exciting. Commons was easygoing, sober, and tolerant, but a lesser mind. Commons self-consciously followed a course which Veblen accused others of doing unawares. He cast the lessons of personal experience into a loose, all-inclusive mathematics of abstractions. While Veblen had stood aloof from the uproar of American pre-war reform, Commons had been in the thick of it.[33]

Many of the ideas scattered through progressivism are brought together in Commons' works. To free politics from

[30] Veblen, *Engineers and the Price System*, p. 101.

[31] *Ibid.*, pp. 116, 134, 135, 137, 141, 151. Veblen later became even more pessimistic about the engineers and their devotion to the established order. Thorstein Veblen, *Absentee Ownership and Business Enterprise in Recent Times: The Case of America* (New York: B. W. Huebsch, 1923), pp. 281–83, 442–45.

[32] John R. Commons, *Labor and Administration* (New York: Macmillan, 1913), pp. 71–84, and *Institutional Economics: Its Place in Political Economy* (Madison: University of Wisconsin, 1934), p. 4.

[33] See Commons, *Institutional Economics*, pp. 1–9; Commons entered politics as a Christian Socialist and was converted to the single tax. He served as an investigator for the U.S. Industrial Commission and moved on to the National Civic Federation and finally to the University of Wisconsin, where he drafted important legislation for the La Follette regime and sat on various administrative boards. While serving Wisconsin, he took time out to work for the Pittsburgh Survey and to accept an appointment to President Wilson's Commission on Industrial Relations.

political parties and class conflicts, he advocated proportional representation. The first edition of his book on the subject included a rejection of initiative and referendum, but the revised edition ten years later held out only on the question of the initiative, which seemed to demand too much of the average voter. Commons was one of the foremost proponents of the advantages of administration as against legislation. Administration, he suggested, should become the fourth branch of government.[34]

Of course, Commons was most famous as the pioneer historian of American labor. He wrote of the "lower idealism" of working-class demands and the safe and sane disposition of the modern trade unions. He found little to fear from the rank and file of labor, but not much to admire in it either. It was the labor leaders and leading capitalists whom he respected. He based his theory of institutional economics "not on the assumptions of natural equality of the Declaration of Independence . . . but on leaders, bosses, and conquerors of the Malthusian more or less stupid and passionate masses."[35]

Commons proposed the control of "collective action" through guidance by experts to those in positions of power. "One can sense almost on every issue," wrote one of the most sympathetic and perspicacious students of his work, "that Commons is attempting a formulation that will be relevant to the decision which some strategically placed person must make — such as a judge, legislator, governor, or especially the head of an administrative commission."[36] His formulations were usually ethical notions given "scientific" teeth — ill-fitting as they generally turned out to be. From this perspective, Commons' interest in scientific management is understandable.

[34] Compare the first edition of Commons' *Proportional Representation* (New York: T. Y. Crowell, 1896) with the second (New York: Macmillan, 1907); John R. Commons, *Myself* (New York: Macmillan, 1934), p. 107, *Labor and Administration*, p. 396, and "A Fourth Branch of Government," *La Follette's Magazine*, V (July 26, 1913), 8.

[35] *Labor and Administration*, pp. 33, 259–64; *Myself*, pp. 88, 89, 139–40.

[36] Kenneth H. Parsons, "John R. Commons' Point of View," in John R. Commons, *The Economics of Collective Action* (New York: Macmillan, 1950), p. 374.

Commons busied himself with questions of efficiency early in his career. He was the chief author of a government report on restriction of industrial production which aimed at the practices of businessmen as well as workers. He believed that in the interest of industrial progress, restrictive practices should be lifted but without leaving the workers open to abuse. When the socialist mayor of Milwaukee decided to set up a Bureau of Efficiency and Economy (this one government-owned, as distinguished from the bureaus of municipal research which lived off subscriptions of private benefactors), Commons was called in. He, in turn, consulted Harrington Emerson and descended upon Milwaukee with a flock of graduate students to boost efficient government.[37] Commons liked scientific management, as did President Charles R. Van Hise, Charles McCarthy, and other notables at the University of Wisconsin. Commons visited model installations of scientific management and recommended scientific management for other factories.[38]

He demurred, however, on one of its features. He had little doubt of Taylor's devotion to truth or of the truth of many of his discoveries or the importance of these discoveries to the solution of labor problems. Yet he felt that Taylor's fondness for bonus plans, designed to separate laborers into individual bargaining units, was unfortunate. Scientific management had to accept collective bargaining, he argued, for it was the inescapable response of workers to modern industrial conditions. The real task lay beyond the comparatively simple problems of production. It was necessary to bring the

[37] *Eleventh Special Report of the Commissioner of Labor: Regulation and Restriction of Output*, by John R. Commons, in collaboration with others, 58th Cong., 2d Sess., House Doc. 734 (Ser. Vol. 4732); Commons, *Labor and Administration*, chap. ix, viii, *Myself*, p. 151, and "Municipal Reform in Milwaukee, *Outlook*, XCVIII (June 10, 1911), 275–76.

[38] F. W. Taylor to William Crozier, Dec. 6, 1913, Carl G. Barth file in Taylor Collection; Commons, *The Economics of Collective Action*, p. 99; Charles McCarthy, *The Wisconsin Idea* (New York: Macmillan, 1912), pp. 12, 16; Edward A. Fitzpatrick, *McCarthy of Wisconsin* (New York: Columbia University Press, 1944), p. 220. When the university itself was subjected to a crude efficiency survey, many on the faculty (but not Commons, McCarthy, or Van Hise) assailed efficiency experts indiscriminately. Merle E. Curti and Vernon Carstensen, *The University of Wisconsin: A History, 1848–1925* (Madison: University of Wisconsin Press, 1949), II, 272–73.

two conflicting requirements — efficiency and the workers' need for self-protection — into harmony through "a higher principle of organization." Commons was one of the first to argue that scientific management and collective bargaining could and should flourish together.[39]

After the war, when many prominent Taylorites gave their support to programs of industrial democracy, Commons moved yet closer to scientific management. Efficiency was elevated to the rank of one of his five fundamental principles of economic action. In the realm of economic theory, Commons believed that scientific management restored the labor theory of value of Ricardo and Marx. Taylor, he asserted, reduced the abstractions of these profound thinkers to measurement.[40] In the realm of economic practice, he saw scientific management as "the most productive invention in the history of modern industry." He admonished the unions that pushed anti-stop-watch laws and that made the removal of those devices an unnegotiable demand. Of course, Commons still argued that the findings of the Taylorites should be imposed through collective bargaining.[41] Yet this now seemed to be a less difficult requirement. For Commons became a supporter of the Leitch plan of industrial democracy, which offered a form of collective bargaining that did not oblige the efficiency expert to work with the regular trade unions.[42] Direct dealing between workers and employers on a shop level appealed to Commons. He wanted the shop committees to discuss time and speed standards, wage and piece rates, the accuracy of stop-watch statistics, and also those important factors not measurable by a watch. These recommendations were not intended to undermine the authority of the employer in his factory. Commons warned the enthusiasts of industrial democracy that labor could not and did not want the responsibilities of managing industry. It was "immoral," he thought, to hold this up

[39] Commons, *Labor and Administration*, chap. x.
[40] Commons, *Institutional Economics*, pp. 65, 85, chap. viii; *The Economics of Collective Action*, chap. vii, p. 98.
[41] John Rogers Commons, *Industrial Goodwill* (New York: McGraw-Hill, 1919), pp. 12–16, 123–25, 161.
[42] Commons and others, "Why the Leitch Plan Makes Good," *Independent*, CIII (July 3, 1920), 7; Commons and others, *Industrial Government* (New York: Macmillan, 1921), chaps. vii–x.

to labor as a hope. The members of a family, Commons insisted, could not do without a head of the family.[43]

For Commons, the advances in management had meaning which reached beyond the factory. They were indications that capitalism was "not the blind force that socialists supposed; and not the helpless plaything of demand and supply. . . ." They were demonstrations of intelligence and self-consciousness, proof that capitalism was not inevitably doomed but, on the contrary, that it could save itself.[44]

Not only the friends of labor but even the leaders of labor could be found mingling with the efficiency engineers in the postwar years. The first gestures toward co-operation came from Taylor's followers. Morris L. Cooke, who in the past had carried the message of scientific management into unfamiliar realms,[45] now became the outstanding advocate of co-operation between the Taylorites and the unions. Cooke came to this view gradually. Enthusiasm for a nebulous brand of industrial democracy served as an intermediate step before he came to accept the idea of full co-operation with organized labor.[46] The unusual reversal on the part of union leadership with regard to scientific management (at least in the realm of convention speeches if not in day-to-day tactics) [47] came about during the early twenties in a public atmosphere unfriendly to the unions.[48]

[43] *Industrial Goodwill*, pp. 113–17, 121, 124, 195, 226–27.

[44] *Ibid.*, pp. 272, 269.

[45] He had applied the principles of scientific management to the universities and municipal governments. Morris L. Cooke, *Academic and Industrial Efficiency: Bulletin #5 of the Carnegie Foundation* (New York, 1910).

[46] Cooke's changing outlook is seen in "Who Is Boss in Your Shop," *Annals of the American Academy of Political and Social Science*, LXXI (May, 1917), 167–85, *An all American Basis for Industry* (Philadelphia: Morris L. Cooke, 1919), pp. 13–15, and "Discussion," *Bull. Taylor Soc.*, V (April, 1920), 91.

[47] The restrictions on the use of the stop watch and bonus in arsenals and Navy yards were renewed yearly until 1949, when through the efforts of Senators Taft of Ohio and Flanders of Vermont they were removed. Milton J. Nadworny, *Scientific Management and the Unions, 1900–1932* (Cambridge, Mass.: Harvard University Press, 1955), pp. 103, 104–9.

[48] For a thoroughgoing study of the change of mind on the part of the Taylorites and the union leaders, see Nadworny, *Scientific Management and the Unions*, especially chapters vii and viii. See also Jean T.

The attempt to placate an increasingly hostile public was probably an important element in the AFL's new devotion to increased production and efficiency. Yet, as often happens in such cases, labor did not completely escape its own public relations program. In addition, some union leaders saw the use of scientific management methods, under the supervision of employers and the union, as a means of strengthening those shops which employed the more costly union labor. This was especially true in the clothing industry, where competition was bitter. Sidney Hillman, the most persistent supporter of this approach, overrode violent opposition from the rank and file to bring his union to accept "production standards." In the late twenties, union and management co-operation for increased production through scientific management techniques was an important component of the "New Unionism." [49]

At the time of the efficiency craze, the Taylorites had gained the respect of some important socialists. American socialists denounced capitalism not only because it lacked heart but also because it lacked head. The longing for order, discipline, and capable leadership was apparent in a line of socialism stretching from Bellamy and Gronlund to the young Walter Lippmann. This was compounded with a Marxist theory that stressed technological growth, and a reforming practice that preferred class co-operation to class struggle (leading to an attack on waste rather than on exploitation). These three elements in prewar American socialism had made it susceptible to the ideas of scientific management.

Pro-war socialists, who had left the Socialist party in the war period, often did not find a political group in which they could place their trust. Some fell back on what seemed to be economic fundamentals. "The man who can organize a work-

McKelvey, *A.F.L. Attitudes toward Production, 1900–1932* (Ithaca, N.Y.: Cornell University Press, 1952), chap. v; Horace Bookwalter Drury, *Scientific Management: A History and Criticism* (3d ed., rev. and enl.; New York: Longmans, Green, 1922), pp. 21–28.

[49] Matthew Josephson, *Sidney Hillman* (Garden City, N.Y.: Doubleday, 1952), chaps. iii, viii; Nadworny, *op. cit.*, chap. viii; Sumner H. Slichter, *Union Policies and Industrial Management* (Washington, D.C.: Brookings Institution, 1941); Arthur W. Calhoun, "Labor's New Economic Policy," in J. B. S. Hardman (ed.), *American Labor Dynamics* (New York: Harcourt, Brace, 1928), p. 320.

shop for the most efficient production," wrot[
Ghent, "is more truly the herald of the future
the man who can merely frame a revolut:
phrase." [50] Those socialists who looked to Sovi(
hope and guidance found Lenin resorting to sc
agement techniques. Lenin's pamphlet, which ar
new regime for the factory, was published in N
the Rand School of Social Science in at least two
and five editions. [51] Another printing appeared in
a foreword by Anna Louise Strong. She praised 1
flinching, almost cynical realism" and pointed o[
cialism itself can only succeed if it produces w
efficiently than capitalism." [52] The most popular (
on socialism for college classes and study group
pertinent excerpts from the Lenin pamphlet. And
presented even more extensive portions to a yet br
lic under the heading "Scientific Management an(
ship of the Proletariat." Scientific management v
on the agenda of the Intercollegiate Socialist Soci

[50] See, for example, William J. Ghent, "Capitalism and tl
Alternative," *The Review*, I (Aug. 9, 1919), 272–73, and *The*
Reaction (Princeton, N.J.: Princeton University Press, 1923)
[51] See Foreword to Nikolai Lenin, *The Soviets at Work*
New York: Rand School of Social Sciences, 1919), p. 2.
[52] Nikolai Lenin, *The Soviets at Work: A Discussion of th*
Faced by the Soviet Government of Russia After the Revolu
word by Anna Louise Strong (Seattle, Wash.: Seattle Uni(
[1918]), pp. 2, 3. Miss Strong claims that 20,000 copies we[
Anna Louise Strong, *I Change Worlds: The Remaking of an*
(New York: Henry Holt, 1935), p. 68. Interestingly, Miss S
described her conversion to socialism as resting on a youthful :
Bellamy's *Looking Backward*, the lessons of which later became
in the years before World War I. "The only remedy would b
quite differently organized, where work and jobs and wages w(
matters, and everything that conditioned them was publicly own
society organized assignment of work and cut everybody's ho
work and looked after all workers, and all children learning
and all old people after their work was done. That was comm(
it was efficiency; it was abolition of chaos and waste. I knew e
know that such a society was called socialism, and that I m
socialist.
"Thus I came to condemn capitalism, not through any op
endured by me personally, but through that very deification of e
which capitalism had taught me. . . . the standards of efficienc
capitalism sets up in the minds of technical men and administrat(
many of them to condemn capitalism in the end" (pp. 40–41).

ner conference on "Problems of the Revolutionized Order."[53] And Lenin's adoption of scientific management was one of the few steps of which John Spargo, veteran American socialist, seemed to approve in his general denunciation of the Bolshevik regime.[54] No opposition to the introduction of scientific management would be encountered under socialism, one socialist explained, since the interest of all persons in the factory would be the same.[55]

One result of this concern with scientific management was the attraction to the Taylor Society of many who at one time called themselves socialists. Robert W. Bruere, Edward Eyre Hunt, N. I. Stone, William M. Leiserson, William H. Leffingwell, Ordway Tead, and Algie Simons were among them. Algie Simons' career is one of the more interesting. He entered the Socialist party via the route of charity and social settlement work and became an editor of various socialist journals. At one time he was a leader of the party's left wing.

[53] Harry W. Laidler, *Socialism in Thought and Action* (New York: Macmillan, 1920), pp. 347–48; John R. Commons (ed.), *Trade Unionism and Labor Problems*, 2d ser. (Boston: Ginn, 1921), pp. 179–98; "The June Conference 'Problems of the Revolutionized Order,'" *Intercollegiate Socialist*, VII (April–May, 1919), 6.

[54] John Spargo, *The Greatest Failure in All History: A Critical Examination of the Actual Workings of Bolshevism in Russia* (New York: Harper, 1920), p. 234. In an earlier work he had remarked that the supreme task of the socialist state would be the greatest possible increase in industrial efficiency. "We shall destroy nothing of social value, abandon no height of culture or productive efficiency — not even for the sake of equality!" John Spargo, *Applied Socialism* (New York: B. W. Huebsch, 1912), pp. 284, 280–81. The pairing of culture and efficiency is interesting. Both presumably were products of highly trained elites.

[55] James MacKaye, *Americanized Socialism: A Yankee View of Capitalism* (New York: Boni & Liveright, 1918), p. 167. The non-socialist response to Lenin's adoption of Taylorism provides interesting sidelights. The *Independent* commented favorably: "Lenine's advice to the Bolsheviki in the pamphlet 'Soviets at Work,' might be published in any of our efficiency magazines with some changes of phraseology, for it is devoted to urging increase of production, speeding up processes, iron discipline during work, careful accounting, business devices, the Taylor system of scientific management, and the like. . . .

"Mazzini, the Italian patriot, defined democracy as 'progress of all thru all under the leadership of the best and the wisest.' Plato in describing his socialist republic said it must be ruled by philosophers. He did not mean professors of metaphysics, but rather what we should call efficiency experts or men of science. If such definitions of democracy are adhered to we may view the advent of industrial democracy with great hopefulness." "Industrial Democracy," *Independent*, XCVII (March 8, 1919), 320.

His early writing already contained hints of an interest in waste and the role of the "brainworker." Compared with socialism, Simons observed, "no other philosophy has ever so clearly pointed out the value and historical function of the labor of organization and direction." In 1914, he published a pamphlet called *Wasting Human Life*, which indicted the capitalists "not so much for their greed, their luxurious idleness and their brutal indifference to human suffering, as for their colossal stupidity as managers of industry." If the increased product were given to those who produced it, scientific management would be welcomed in every shop. Yet in a society which inevitably bred class struggles, the greatest of all wastes, this was impossible. Simons conducted a rough survey of the inefficiency of American industry and arrived at the conclusion that 105 billion dollars a year was wasted. He asked that the capitalist "give us only the waste." But this meant taking industry out of the hands of the capitalist class and placing it with those who could make it happy, healthful, and plentiful in its production.[56]

Simons was one of those who broke with the Socialist party on the issue of supporting American entry into the war. He gave his energies and talents as a writer to Creel's Committee on Public Information and he was among the many who saw in the war the possibility of a social revolution which would bring "the conscious organization of society." He joined the short-lived National party, an interesting attempt to unite prowar socialists and "hard-core" Progressives, but, in the vast disillusionment of the early twenties, he gave up any belief in a "sudden millennial conquest." He turned his attention toward the factory and became a writer and lecturer on industrial management. He carried the bluntness of his socialist writings, which dispensed with shadings in favor of stark black and white, to his works on industrial management,

[56] A. M. Simons, *The Philosophy of Socialism* (Chicago: C. H. Kerr, [189–]), pp. 19–20, *The Man under the Machine* (Chicago: C. H. Kerr, [189–]), pp. 4, 28, "Wasting Human Life," *Intercollegiate Socialist*, II (February–March, 1914), 14 (this article is a summary and discussion of the pamphlet), and *Wasting Human Life* (Chicago: Socialist Party of the United States, [1914]), pp. 89, 93–96. The argument that the benefits of increased efficiency made possible by scientific management would not be justly distributed was the subject of an exchange between Upton Sinclair and Frederick W. Taylor in the *American Magazine*, LXXII (June, 1911), 243–45.

making them somewhat unusual in the field. "The fundamental function of industry is to produce the goods needed by society," Simons wrote, "and to this everything else must be secondary. Whatever interferes with production threatens industry and society built upon it. Whatever increases production strengthens, improves, and develops industry and makes possible a higher social evolution."[57]

From this viewpoint, Taylor was seen as the genius who had applied a broad scientific vision to industry. Scientific management helped introduce the idea of law into industrial relations. The efficiency experts discovered the facts of production and reduced these facts to scientific laws. Disputes about fact could not be compromised, Simons argued, and until they were settled scientifically there would be violent struggles and autocratic assertions of power rather than common action. Within the structure of scientific law, industrial democracy could find room in which to thrive. Into industrial democracy Simons introduced the distinctions which some administrative reformers had brought to political democracy. "The actual executive function — that is, the function of getting things done — must always be autocratic."[58]

The influence of scientific management upon the IWW was indirect. Their contact with Howard Scott was probably as close as they came to orthodox Taylorism. (This was not very close at all.) There were, however, some interesting points of similarity between the Taylorites and the Wobblies. Before the war, C. Bertrand Thompson, an orthodox Taylorite, had spoken of separating "the real principles of syndicalism from its crudities." The IWW, he thought, represented modern tendencies, in part because of "its greater consonance with the principles of scientific management."[59] This consonance lay in the rejection of the existing craft loyalties, and perhaps in the concentration upon the factory rather than broad political action as the hinge of social advance. "Forget Marx," said

[57] "The National Party," *Independent*, XCII (Dec. 29, 1917), 578; A. M. Simons, *Personal Relations in Industry* (New York: Ronald Press, 1921), pp. iii, 3.

[58] Simons, *Personnel Relations in Industry*, pp. 13, 22, 264–65, chaps. xvii–xix, and *Production Management: Control of Men, Material, and Machines* (Chicago: American School, 1922), I, 27–29, 134.

[59] C. Bertrand Thompson, *The Theory and Practice of Scientific Management* (Boston: Houghton Mifflin, 1917), p. 151.

Ben Williams, a Wobbly notable, in 1907, "and study the industries." [60]

In the early months of 1919, when it seemed that the old order might topple, members of the IWW began talking of training workers to take over and run the industrial machine. The Wobblies thought that the industrial chaos in Russia which followed the revolution could be avoided here if workers had more knowledge of industrial technique. Lenin's pamphlet dealing with scientific management was distributed in large quantities. A Bureau of Industrial Research was established to make extensive industrial surveys and to investigate the problems of increased production and industrial management. The unions were renumbered on the basis of an organization chart of the prospective industrial order. *One Big Union Monthly*, one of the major IWW magazines, changed its name to the *Industrial Pioneer*. And a reporter for the *New York World* was surprised to find the Wobblies talking of "uninterrupted production," the "coordination of industrial processes," and "the necessity for accurate research and an exact determination of the facts" instead of class consciousness, exploitation, and revolution.[61]

The IWW launched a "drive on the technician." Their only important catch was Howard Scott, who had just left Veblen's Soviet to set up his Technical Alliance. Scott preached "the engineering approach to social change" through a series of industrial surveys which were published in the *Industrial Pioneer*.[62] While the IWW soon lost interest in industrial research and the problems of production, from time to time a discussion of the harmony of its program with the movement to apply science to industry could be found in its journals.[63]

Although the Taylorites found themselves in unfamiliar

[60] Quoted by Art Shields, "The New Turn of the I.W.W.," *Socialist Review*, X (April–May, 1921), 69.

[61] *Christian Science Monitor*, May 20, 1919, p. 1; Shields, "The New Turn of the I.W.W.," p. 71; John S. Gambs, *The Decline of the I.W.W.* (New York: Columbia University Press, 1932), p. 174, appendix iii; Charles W. Wood, "The Unemployment Conference in New York City," *New York World*, Feb. 27, 1921.

[62] For Scott's version of this liaison see Gambs, *Decline of the I.W.W.*, pp. 157–62. Ralph Chaplin, *Wobbly* (Chicago: University of Chicago Press, 1948), pp. 295–96, presents another view.

[63] See, for example, "Science and Labor Organization," *Industrial Pioneer*, II (July, 1924), 45–46.

radical company after the war, they did not significantly alter their newly found, yet moderate, social program. A clear presentation of the Taylor program could be seen in *Waste in Industry*, a survey published in June, 1921. Ostensibly, this report was the work of a committee of the Federated American Engineering Societies, headed by Herbert Hoover. Actually, it was more like a Taylor Society report. A large majority of the committee making the survey were recognized advocates of scientific management, and there was some complaint that the Taylor Society was behind it all.[64]

Hoover and the Wobblies were on opposite fringes of the scientific management movement. Yet the fact that Hoover's right-hand man, at the time, was Edward Eyre Hunt (who had been a young literary and political radical before the war, a founder of the Harvard Socialist Club and a director of the famous Madison Square Garden pageant on the IWW strike in Paterson) suggests an image of Hoover unlike that which was to become familiar a decade later. It should be noted that the Hoover presidential boom of 1920 began in the offices of the *New Republic*.[65] Though the Hoover of 1919 and 1920 spoke of personal initiative, he was also interested in those areas where he believed personal initiative by itself was not enough. He called for national guidance, national planning, and national efficiency.[66] Where Hoover was silent, many of his admirers inferred progressive policies. Insofar as he was practical, thought the *New Republic*, he was bound to be progressive. This had been a mode of thought common in the prewar years. It rested on a usually unexamined assumption that Christian morals or progress, or even progressive principles, were written into the laws of the universe.[67]

[64] Morris L. Cooke, "The Influence of Scientific Management upon Government — Federal, State and Municipal," *Bull. Taylor Soc.*, IX (February, 1924), 35; *ibid.*, VII (October, 1922), 198.

[65] Walter Lippmann, "Notes for a Biography of Herbert Croly," *New Republic*, LXIII (July 10, 1930), 250–52; E. E. Hunt, "Herbert Clark Hoover," *ibid.*, VII (Sept. 30, 1916), 213–15.

[66] Herbert Hoover, "Nationalized Power," *Nation*, CVI (Sept. 18, 1920), 318–19; "The Only Way Out," *Mining and Metallurgy*, I (March, 1920), 7; "Division of Profits," *Journal of the Engineers' Club of Philadelphia*, XXXVI (October, 1919), 365–69.

[67] "Hoover and the Issues," *New Republic*, XXI (Feb. 4, 1920), 281–83. See Henry F. May's illuminating discussion of "practical idealism" and "practicalism" in *The End of American Innocence*, pp. 14–20, 128–

It was the conservatives who were impractical, who were bucking against reality and bringing unnecessary suffering when power was in their hands. The good, the true, and the practical were fused and confused. All three were associated with Herbert Hoover, engineer and humanitarian.[68]

The Taylorites were delighted with Hoover. At the Institute of Mining Engineers, discussions of public issues were considered taboo, and here was their foremost representative preaching the social responsibility of engineers. Perhaps the Taylorites were also pleased that the public sometimes mistook him for an efficiency engineer.[69]

The idea of a survey of the waste in industry was not a new one, but previously it had usually accompanied radical social programs. Sidney Reeve and Algie Simons, both socialists, had conducted rough surveys of waste on their own. And Veblen thought that such a survey, revealing the efficiencies to follow from the elimination of the business system, would be a step toward his Soviet of Technicians. The advocacy of a survey of waste was almost the only guiding principle of Howard Scott's chimerical organization, the Technical Alliance. In fact, the IWW was publishing the results of the Scott surveys while the committee of the Federated Engineering Societies was deep in its work.[70]

---

38. "Practical idealist" was the most common description of Hoover in these days.

[68] See Robert Herrick, "For Hoover," *Nation*, CX (June 5, 1920), 750–51; French Strother, "Herbert Hoover, Representative American and Practical Idealist," *World's Work*, XXXIX (April, 1920), 518–85; Edwin E. Slosson, "Hoover to the Rescue," *Independent*, XCVIII (Sept. 6, 1919), 318; "Independent Progressive," *Nation*, CX (March 20, 1920), 355.

[69] *Bull. Taylor Soc.*, V (April, 1920), 78; Edward G. Lowry, *Washington Closeups* (Boston: Houghton Mifflin, 1921), pp. 211, 212; "Efficient American," *Bellman*, XXV (Nov. 23, 1918), 566; "Herbert Hoover, Master of Efficiency," *Independent*, LXXXIX (March 19, 1917), 477.

[70] For the radical surveys see Sidney A. Reeve, *The Cost of Competition* (New York: McClure, Phillips, 1906), chap. x; Simons, *Wasting Human Life*, p. 89; Veblen, *Engineers and the Price System*, p. 152; Dorfman, *Veblen*, pp. 459–60; "Report on Waste: Part I, Oil Division," *Industrial Pioneer*, I (February, 1921), 33–37; "Wasteful Methods of Distributing City Milk," *ibid.* (May, 1921), pp. 53–58; "Wastes in the Coal Industry," *ibid.* (July, 1921), pp. 53–58. The National Conservation Commission's inventory of natural resources provided a more respectable precedent. Charles Richard Van Hise, *The Conservation of Natural Resources* (New York: Macmillan, 1911), pp. 8–9, 11–12.

"This survey," Hoover announced, "will attempt to visualize the nation as a single industrial organism and to examine its efficiency towards its only real objective — maximum production." [71] Roughly, the report dealt with three areas of national waste — factory management, industrial conflict, and the business cycle. The engineers' real interest was the factory. They seemed concerned with the other problems only insofar as these interfered with stable production schedules and the efficiencies such schedules made possible. For the factory, the report recommended improvements in organization and production control. (Of course no specific system was endorsed; that would have been indiscreet.) The report suggested that labor give up its restrictive practices and understand that "science is an ally and not an enemy." The unions ought to join forces with "the technicians who serve with them to increase production which will inure to the ultimate benefit of all." The acceptance of "performance standards" was essential. As for industrial conflicts, here the government was to play an important part. While it was the duty of management to adopt the best personnel methods, the government still should create and operate "agencies endowed with sufficient power and vision to adjust or stop the destructive and needless controversies over labor questions." The Kansas compulsory arbitration law was mentioned, but it was too new for comment. [72]

The further the report moved from the factory, the less distinct its vision became. The reliance on trade associations and labor exchanges to promote business stability was probably Hoover's suggestion. (Gantt, a short while before he died, had proposed the creation of cartels, regulated by the government as public service corporations, to control all questions of selling.) [73]

So far, there was little in the report to clash with the growing conservative mood of the country. The increased role for government in industrial disputes and possibly in support of

[71] Herbert Hoover, "Industrial Waste," *Bull. Taylor Soc.*, VI (April, 1921), 77.
[72] Committee on Elimination of Waste in Industry of the Federated American Engineering Societies, *Waste in Industry* (New York: McGraw-Hill, 1921), pp. 24–29, 31, chap. xiii.
[73] Wood, *The Great Change*, p. 53.

trade associations was surely not radical. But when the report specified that "over 50% of the responsibility for these wastes can be placed at the door of management and less than 25% at the door of labor," it was sure to excite resentment. At the Taylor Society, of course, the response to the report was overwhelmingly favorable. H. S. Person emphasized the fact that technical organization and methods rather than profits were used as the index of efficiency.[74] The specific assigning of responsibility for waste was but a quantitative rendering of Taylor's dictum that most of the trouble came from those on top. This, of course, fitted well with the social perspective of the progressives, who saw the greater danger coming from above rather than below.[75] But now these sentiments were out of favor, and the Federated American Engineering Societies rejected the report of its committee. The isolation in which the Taylorites found themselves was underscored when *Industrial Management,* a magazine usually sympathetic to scientific management, accused the authors of the report of adding to the "spirit of class antagonism."[76] The leading Taylorites had arduously adjusted to the modes of progressivism, and now most Americans were in process of rejecting them.

[74] *Waste in Industry,* p. 9; Person, "Discussion," *Bull. Taylor Soc.,* VII (April, 1922), 77.

[75] Howard Scott and Walter N. Polakov were dissatisfied with the report. They thought it did not go far enough. "Discussion," *Bull. Taylor Soc.,* VII (April, 1922), 80.

[76] *New York Times,* June 4, 1921, p. 7; "Disappointing Report," *Industrial Management,* LXII (July 1, 1921), 53.

• CHAPTER IX

Postscript:
Taylorism in the Twenties

By the time of the publication of *Waste in Industry*, there were signs that the Taylor Society might relinquish its place in the rear guard of retreating progressivism and fix upon a more acceptable role in the *avant garde* of onrushing business. This did not require a sudden or radical change but rather a shift in emphasis. The shift appeared, at first, as a call to make scientific management yet more scientific. Such an appeal had often been heard at Taylor Society meetings. In the new social climate of the 1920's, however, this appeal took on new meaning. Scientific management was to be made more scientific not only by more exacting methods of time and motion study (Gilbreth was now invited back to the society to argue for his micro-motion study), new statistical techniques, and refined and precise measures of production control, but now, more significantly, by restricting it to the realms which seemed most appropriate for scientific treatment.

H. S. Person, the director of the Taylor Society, proposed a distinction between the terms "administration" and "management." The moral, social, and political aspects of an enterprise were to be classed under the first and the technical aspects under the second. While management was to be dealt with scientifically, the use of scientific methods in administration remained open to question. In some ways this new separation between management and administration, which became popular among the Taylorites in the 1920's, resembled the distinction between mechanical and commercial efficiency and the distinction between administration and politics. All three set off areas of expert knowledge—but each with differing connotations. Person's distinction, more clearly than the others, pointed to a separation of fact and value. This was more than a philosophical subtlety. In the general usage at the Taylor Society, administration soon came to be linked with the work of the chief executive of the firm and management with the work of the plant manager. Not only were fact and value separated, but they were ascribed to different ranks in the hierarchy of the enterprise.[1]

Harrington Emerson, a dependable weathercock for the changing winds of doctrine, quickly shed the effusive idealism which had been his specialty just before the war. "When I was much younger," he announced,

I thought that the function of the industrial engineer was to spread himself all over the map. He was concerned with the health of the operators, with their education, their morals and their happiness—all that was part of the function of the industrial engineer. As I went along I discovered it was none of his business whatever; that he was there to secure industrial competence. . . . Happiness, of course is a great thing for the human race, but it is not the business, as I see it, of the industrial engineer to take up the subject of happiness.[2]

Elton Mayo, a rising luminary in the management movement, suggested that management was the same irrespective of social system; that it did not matter whether one con-

[1] Person's first mention of this distinction was in "Scientific Management," *Bulletin of the Taylor Society*, IV (October, 1919), 10 ff. The implications of this distinction were not discussed until J. William Schulze's paper, "Planning Applied to Administration," *ibid.*, V (June, 1920), 120 ff. See also H. S. Person, "Scientific Management and the Reduction of Unemployment," *ibid.*, VI (February, 1921), 50. In the late 1920's, the separation of fact from value sometimes suggested the rejection of morality. F. A. Silcox, friend of Rexford Tugwell and future New Deal official, asserted that "The acquisition of power is the primary thing that counts . . . that an inherent quality of power is that it knows no limits . . . that the only limit in the use of power is an opposing force . . . that with a favorable balance of power there is only one workable course of action and that is to take all the traffic will bear when the taking is good . . . that the ethical moralizing with oughts, shouldn'ts and don'ts is an effort to mitigate in some manner the brutality of the conflict and is a method used mostly by those who do not possess sufficient power to enforce their own will." F[erdinand] A[ugustus] Silcox, "Discussion," *ibid.*, XIV (February, 1929), 25.

[2] *Proceedings of the Society of Industrial Engineers, Eighth National Convention, April, 1922*, pp. 33–34.

sidered management under a Russian or an American regime. And, in fact, the *Bulletin of the Taylor Society* welcomed
the achievements of scientific management in communist
Russia and fascist Italy. Since the Taylorites worked primarily in American industry, the separation between administration and management furthered an acceptance of the
existing social system in America.[3]

During the 1920's, appeals to subordinate the profit motive
to the service motive became increasingly rare in the pages
of the *Bulletin of the Taylor Society*. The disruption of stable
production schedules by uncertain economic conditions remained one of its serious interests. But now the solution
seemed to rest more and more clearly in the hands of the
businessman and the powers that be. The chief executive,
through measures within the factory or broad business co-
operation outside of it (programs of the second type were
popular in the late 1920's), was expected to iron out some of
the ups and downs of the business cycle.[4]

The separation of administration from management was
rejected by men like Morris L. Cooke and Henry S. Dennison, to whom moral law seemed as much a matter of fact as
the law of gravity: either could be disregarded only at one's
peril. Actually, Cooke's view was closer to Taylor's and to
the general outlook of Taylor's generation. To the modern
observer, the fusion of fact and value underlying the early
history of scientific management is invalid and dangerous,
but so is their complete dissociation. The particular danger
which troubled Cooke was that this separation would lead to

[3] Elton Mayo, "A Supplement to 'The Great Stupidity,'" *Bull. Taylor
Soc.*, X (October, 1925), 225; "The Association of Russian Engineers,"
ibid., IX (April, 1924), 94; H. S. Person, "Pimco, Prague," *ibid.* (October, 1924), p. 198; V. Mouravieff, "The Central Institute of Labor,"
ibid., XIV (August, 1929), 168 ff.; Eleanor Bushness Cooke, "The
Third International Management Congress Held in Rome, Italy: A Report," *ibid.*, XII (October, 1927), 488; Wilfred Lewis, "Master Planks
in the American Industrial Program: Closure of Discussion," *ibid.*, XIII
(February, 1928), 49; [H. S. Person], "Comment," *ibid.*, VIII (April,
1923), 41.

[4] H. S. Person, "Scientific Management and the Reduction of Unemployment," *ibid.*, VI (February, 1921), 50, 52; David Friday, "Risk as
a Retarding Factor in Industry," *ibid.* (April, 1921), pp. 81 ff.; H. S.
Person, "Scientific Management and Cartels," *ibid.*, XII (June, 1927),
393; H. B. Brougham, "Must Prosperity Be Planned?" *ibid.*, XIII (February, 1928), 5 ff.

a sanctioning of the status quo. Though Cooke himself soon gave up hope for immediate measures of social reform in society at large, he remained a reformer in the realm of industry. This was true also of the ex-socialists who came to scientific management after the war and helped to develop the field of industrial relations. The personnel worker, thought Ordway Tead, was "a missionary for the idea that profit alone does not justify industry, that regard for the personality and for the richness and fullness of life for the rank and file of the workers of society is a necessary concern. . . ." [5]

In addition to the new distinction between management and administration which prevailed at the Taylor Society, important changes, both in the membership and in the activities of the Society and in Taylor doctrine, appeared during the 1920's. There was a general loosening of the canons of orthodoxy. In 1922, Persons announced that one need not "be a 'Taylor man' or represent a 'Taylor plant'" to join the Society. Membership now meant only that one was interested in management as a science, desired to promote investigation in that field, and was "open-minded and appreciative of the great contributions to the development of better management." [6]

Now the staff members of the large corporations flocked to the Taylor Society. These officials usually had no intention of revamping their firms in accordance with the stringent requirements of the Taylor System; rather, they would reshape the mechanisms of Taylorism to fit into the existing structure of their companies. [7] Members of the "Human Engineering Department" of General Electric, statisticians from DuPont, and plant managers from Western Electric and A.T.&T. began to take part in Taylor Society activities. Student branches

---

[5] Morris L. Cooke, "Discussion," *ibid.*, V (June, 1920), 128, 129; Henry S. Dennison, "Who Can Hire Management," *ibid.*, IX (June, 1924), 106; Morris L. Cooke, "The Influence of Scientific Management upon Government — Federal, State and Municipal," *ibid.* (February, 1924), p. 106; Ordway Tead, "The Field of Personnel Administration," *ibid.*, VIII (December, 1923), 239. Tead accepted the separation of administration and management but was not willing to grant all the major duties of administration to the chief executive.

[6] H. S. Person, "What Is the Taylor Society?" *ibid.*, VII (December, 1922), 225.

[7] See, for example, Steward M. Lowry (of Proctor and Gamble), "Discussion," *ibid.*, XIII (April, 1928), 82.

of the Taylor Society at the best business schools introduced scientific management to the future officialdom of the large corporations. These new elements swelled the membership of the Taylor Society, but "Taylor men" and representatives of "Taylor plants" remained in control.[8]

Most of the changes in the doctrines of Taylorism were more thoroughgoing. Most conspicuous of these doctrinal revisions was the decline of the gospel of production. The gospel of production had been a characteristic amalgam of moral and economic principles which preached the virtues of hard work, expanding production, low unit cost, and class harmony based on a judicious distribution of the ever increasing industrial product. In the 1920's, however, interest in production gave way to a new interest in sales. The depression of 1920–21 brought with it talk of a buyers' market, the disappearance of frontiers, and the coming of a mature economy. A sales section was set up in the Taylor Society which tried to transfer Taylor's principles of production to this unfamiliar field. There were discussions of the predetermination of consumer demand and the use of scientific methods to replace stunts and "magnetic personalities." "Was there any real difference," they asked, "between producing goods and producing orders?"[9]

It would seem that the notion of a mature economy might have shaken the belief in class harmony which for Taylor rested on continually increasing production. Actually, no one at the Taylor Society seems to have drawn this conclusion. In part, this can be ascribed to the fact that the image of the worker had also changed so as to make less necessary Taylor's social bond of growing prosperity. The worker

[8] This becomes apparent from a survey of the membership of the Board of Directors of the Taylor Society as well as from the discussions at the society.

[9] H. S. Person, "Shaping Your Management To Meet Developing Industrial Conditions," *Bull. Taylor Soc.*, VII (December, 1922), 213–15; Henry P. Kendall, "The Problem of the Chief Executive," *ibid.* (April, 1922), pp. 45–46; [H. S. Person], "Comment," *ibid.* (August, 1922), p. 125; Willard E. Freeland, "Sales Organization and Methods," *ibid.*, VI (December, 1921), 248 ff.; Harry R. Wellman, "Sales Planning, 1922," *ibid.*, VII (April, 1922), 46; John M. Holcombe, Jr., "A Case of Sales Research," *ibid.* (June, 1922), p. 112; "News of the Sections," *ibid.*, VIII (December, 1923), 246; L. J. Conger, "The Tie-up of Sales and Production," *ibid.* (August, 1923), pp. 138–39.

around whom Taylor built his system had been fitted out with desires native to the American middle class. He had been described as a man of few talents, but one who hoped to rise to the top in income and prestige. Taylor insisted on dealing with workers as individuals and on allowing each to go as far as will power and capacity could take him. Taylor's factory had been a hierarchy of character and abilities.

The Taylorism of the 1920's found the worker to be quite different. "The worker has a psychology all his own. We are absolutely wrong in judging the psychology of the worker from ours," declared N. I. Stone, who but a few years earlier had busied himself with annotations of Marxist classics.[10] (Perhaps it was especially easy for the ex-Marxist, who had once accepted the notion of class consciousness, to lead in the adoption of the notion of class psychology.) The worker was no longer thought to be an individualist. He was most comfortable, and could be dealt with most productively, in a group. He usually had little desire to rise or to increase his income by very much. What he did want was security and enough pay to satisfy his comparatively limited wants. Moreover, the Army Psychological Tests seemed to show that the average American had the mental age of a thirteen- to fifteen-year-old and truly needed an official in the factory who could take this into consideration. This was the job of the booming profession of personnel management.[11]

While the image of the worker as an "economic man" grew dim, the image of the chief executive as an "economic man" became clear. The chief executive had been almost ignored in the Taylor System. It had been Taylor's express purpose to set up a factory which could run effectively without an outstanding executive on top. He had invited the highest ranks

[10] N. I. Stone, "Discussion," *ibid.*, VI (April, 1921), 75.

[11] H. H. Farquhar, "A Critical Analysis of Scientific Management," *ibid.*, IX (February, 1924), 24; [H. S. Person], "Is Your Organization a Group?" *ibid.* (August, 1924), pp. 161–62; Henry P. Kendall, "A Decade's Development in Management," *ibid.* (April, 1924), p. 60; Morris L. Cooke, "Some Observations on Workers' Organizations," *ibid.*, XIV (February, 1929), 3. Among the books which played a part in this shift were Whiting Williams, *What's on the Worker's Mind* (New York: Charles Scribner's, 1921); Mary Parker Follett, *The Creative Experience* (New York: Longmans, Green, 1924); Henry Herbert Goddard, *Human Efficiency and Levels of Intelligence* (Princeton, N.J.: Princeton University Press, 1920).

of the factory to take an extended vacation and leave things to the planning department.[12] This upstaging of the chief executive of the firm reflected the nearsightedness of the consulting management engineer and was of considerable importance. It allowed the purposes of the firm and the source of power to appear ambiguous and thus invited suggestions of expert leadership, industrial democracy, and the ascendancy of a service motive over the profit motive. As part of the newly found distinction between administration and management in Taylorism, however, the chief executive reappeared distinctly, and with him came statements of the controlling importance of profits in the firm.[13]

There was no lapse into the older and simpler hard-shell business creeds in the 1920's. The Taylorites could no longer be fully in, nor of, the business community. The abiding effects of the mingling of Taylorites and reformers in the years before the war had made such a position unlikely. Close contact with progressive thinkers had brought the Taylor Society abreast of the newer intellectual trends. Even in the 1920's, when they left active reform programs behind, the Taylorites seemed to be particularly aware of the influence of society on the factory and the factory on society. The over-all direction of the changes which took place in the 1920's owed much to the new circumstances in which the Taylorites found themselves. Yet the extent and manner of these changes had been deeply influenced by the experience of the Taylorites before the war.

The most far-reaching influence that the progressives had upon the development of scientific management was their bringing the notions of democracy that prevailed in the progressive era to bear upon the doctrines of Taylorism. The Taylorites had come to grips with these criticisms and had absorbed them without abandoning their prescribed factory regime. This served to safeguard the system against more radical attack. It provided a perspective for coping with the

[12] See chapter ii, above; also "Testimony of Morris L. Cooke," *U.S. Commission on Industrial Relations*, 64th Cong., 1st Sess., Sen. Doc. 415 (Ser. Vol. 6931), 2680.
[13] [H. S. Person] "Comment," *Bull. Taylor Soc.*, VII (April, 1922), 37; Henry P. Kendall, "The Problem of the Chief Executive," *ibid.* (April, 1922), pp. 39–46.

problems of running a business system in which final authority rests on top, within a political society in which final authority rests below.

Taylorism, in turn, had had a significant influence upon progressive thought. It had carried the ethics of professionalism, so appealing to the middle class of the progressive era, into the heartland of "commercialism," and seemed to open the possibility of insinuating the college-bred into important positions. The trend away from old-fashioned reform, which had relied upon an appeal to conscience, and toward newer styles of reform, which looked to social control and manipulation, had found corroboration in scientific management. Furthermore, Taylorism had crystallized the sentiment for social control into a concept of planning.

During the politically barren years of the 1920's, the Taylor Society provided an oasis for future New Dealers. Much of what was absorbed there appeared in the next decade of reform. Rexford Tugwell, who came to Taylor Society meetings in the 1920's,[14] liked to say that the greatest economic event in the nineteenth century was Taylor's holding a stop watch on a group of shovelers at Midvale Steel. What America needed, he thought, was a Taylor for the economic system as a whole.[15]

Taylorism had come a long way from the yards of Midvale. It had been cast into a program for the entire factory, it had found a band of zealous advocates, it had been brought to the American public in the efficiency craze, and it stayed with some of the leading progressive thinkers and doers. Taylorism had influenced the progressives, and the progressives influenced Taylorism. The results of this interchange were important and long-lasting, and some of them are still with us.

[14] Among the other visitors who later figured prominently in the New Deal era were George Soule and John Maurice Clark. There were many lesser personages. Morris L. Cooke became head of the REA during the New Deal, and H. S. Person held a variety of minor posts.

[15] Arthur M. Schlesinger, Jr., *The Crisis of the Old Order, 1919–1933* (Boston: Houghton Mifflin, 1957), p. 194. The planning department of the Taylor System, which dealt chiefly in material efficiency and worked through a central planning room, pointed toward a concept of planning which neglected market mechanisms and the choices of those planned for or against. The influence of this notion of planning is evident at various points in New Deal reform.

Bibliographical Note

In writing this book, I have drawn upon the work of many scholars. The following remarks deal only with the works that were most directly useful.

CHAPTERS I–III

The study of Taylor and his system might well begin with Taylor's own words. A convenient compilation of his more important statements is in Frederick W. Taylor, *Scientific Management: Comprising Shop Management, The Principles of Scientific Management, Testimony before the Special House Committee* (New York: Harper, 1947). The most useful bibliography of the early literature on scientific management and efficiency makes up the concluding essay in C. Bertrand Thompson, *Theory and Practice of Scientific Management* (Boston: Houghton Mifflin, 1917).

Frank Barkley Copley, *Frederick Winslow Taylor* (2 vols; New York: Harper, 1923), is an enthusiastic biography, a product of an industriousness and intelligence worthy of its subject. I checked the biography at a number of points with the material in the Frederick Winslow Taylor Collection at the Stevens Institute of Technology in Hoboken, New Jersey, and found Copley quite accurate. Copley met Taylor and had the opportunity to talk with Taylor's family and friends. This made available a type of knowledge which the Taylor papers alone can never reveal.

Horace Bookwalter Drury, *Scientific Management* (3d ed.; New York: Columbia University Press, 1922), Milton J. Nadworny, *Scientific Management and the Unions, 1900–1932* (Cambridge, Mass.: Harvard University Press, 1955), and Hugh G. J. Aitken, *Taylorism at Watertown Arsenal* (Cambridge, Mass.: Harvard University Press, 1960) are all thorough and reliable. They asked and answered important questions which were prerequisite to the issues I chose to discuss. Daniel Bell, *Work and Its Discontents* (Boston: Beacon Press, 1956), is a brilliant series of reflections and *aperçus* on efficiency, whose chief shortcoming (inherent in the genre) is the difficulty of knowing when and where the insights are no longer trustworthy.

Daniel Hovey Calhoun, *The American Civil Engineer* (Cambridge, Mass.: Massachusetts Institute of Technology Press, 1960), discusses the history of American engineering before the Civil War, and Edwin T. Layton, "The American Engineering Profession" (Ph.D. dissertation, University of California at Los Angeles, 1956), covers the years 1900–1940. There is no study of American engineering in the crucial years between 1865 and 1900, the period of professionalization, and it is necessary to go to engineering journals, which are staid but informative. Also, there is no recent study of the campaign for the adoption of the metric system in America. The conservation movement, however, has attracted many scholars, among them Samuel P. Hays, whose *Conservation and the Gospel of Efficiency* (Cambridge, Mass.: Harvard University Press, 1959) is helpful and seems to dovetail with many of my findings.

The secondary literature on the developing notions of "system" in the late nineteenth and early twentieth centuries is relatively sparse. Most of it can be found in the pages of the *Business History Review*. Alfred D. Chandler, *Strategy and Structure: Chapters in the History of the Industrial Enterprise* (Cambridge, Mass.: MIT Press, 1962), which ties the evolution of business organization to market developments, appeared too late for use here. For information on the industrial betterment movement, one must go chiefly to contemporary accounts. H. F. J. Porter, "The Rationale of the Industrial Betterment Movement," *Cassirer's Magazine*, XXX (August, 1906), and Samuel Crowther, *John H. Patterson, Pioneer in Industrial Welfare* (New York: Doubleday, Page, 1923), were useful for my purposes.

The early days of the Taylor Society are described in Robert T. Kent, "The Taylor Society Twenty Years Ago," *Bulletin of the Taylor Society*, XVII (February, 1932), 39–40, and Milton J. Nadworny, "The Society for the Promotion of the Science of Management," *Explorations in Entrepreneurial History*, V (May, 1953), 245–47. Kenneth Bjork, *Saga in Steel and Concrete: Norwegian Engineers in America* (Northfield, Minn.: Norwegian-American Historical Association, 1947), contains the best available biographical sketch of Carl G. Barth. Taylor's two other direct disciples have uncritical but usable biographies: L. P. Alford, *Henry Laurence Gantt: Leader in Industry* (New York: American Society of Mechanical Engineers, 1934), and

Edna Yost, *Frank and Lillian Gilbreth: Partners for Life* (New Brunswick, N.J.: Rutgers University Press, 1949). Milton J. Nadworny, "Frederick Taylor and Frank Gilbreth: Competition in Scientific Management," *Business History Review*, XXXI (Spring, 1957), is a careful study which presents important material.

CHAPTERS IV–VI

My principal source for the efficiency craze has been the copious periodical press of the progressive era and, more specifically, many short-lived efficiency magazines available to the modern scholar through the Inter-Library Borrowing Service. For the response of the public school administrators, I have relied heavily upon Raymond E. Callahan, *Education and the Cult of Efficiency* (Chicago: University of Chicago Press, 1962); although his thesis is not completely convincing, his review of the evidence is of considerable value. Milton J. Nadworny, *Scientific Management and the Unions, 1900–1932* (Cambridge, Mass.: Harvard University Press, 1958), describes the response of organized labor and is especially good in the period before Taylor's death. It is surprising that such an interesting and influential figure as Melville Dewey does not have a satisfactory full-scale biography. His papers are at the Butler Library of Columbia University and are well catalogued.

My view of the intellectual history of the progressive era has been influenced particularly by Henry F. May, *The End of American Innocence* (New York: Alfred A. Knopf, 1959), a major work which says a great deal that is new and important about the period. With most students of progressivism, I have benefited from Richard Hofstadter's brilliant and stimulating book, *The Age of Reform* (New York: Alfred A. Knopf, 1955), as well as Morton G. White's incisive *Social Thought in America: The Revolt against Formalism* (Boston: Beacon Press, 1957). George E. Mowry's *The Era of Theodore Roosevelt* (New York: Harper, 1958) and Arthur S. Link's *Woodrow Wilson and the Progressive Era* (New York: Harper, 1954) are both standard works and quite useful. However, the "Progressive Profile" drawn by Professor Mowry seems to bear less resemblance to the progressive reformers if one turns away from California and its particular experience.

Alpheus Thomas Mason, *Brandeis: A Free Man's Life* (New York: Viking Press, 1946), is a sympathetic biography, indispensable for an understanding of Brandeis and contributing much to the broader picture of progressivism. Alfred Lief, *Brandeis: The Personal History of an American Ideal* (Harrisburg, Pa.: Stackpole Sons, 1936), fills in interesting details on Brandeis' early mugwump views. The Louis D.

Brandeis Collection at the University of Louisville Law School, Louisville, Kentucky, has untold and uncatalogued riches. The papers re-
main, for the most part, just as Brandeis left them in his file cabinets.
Those interested in the development of the ideology of professionalism
during the progressive era should read the classic statement by Brandeis' friend, Abraham Flexner, "Is Social Work a Profession?" in
Proceedings of the National Conference of Charities and Correction
(Chicago: Hildmann Printing Co., 1915), pp. 576–90. On Croly,
Lippmann, and the *New Republic*, I found David W. Noble's *The
Paradox of Progressive Thought* (Minneapolis: University of Minnesota Press, 1958), sensitive to the complexities and ambiguities of the
material, and Charles Forcey's *The Crossroads of Liberalism* (New
York: Oxford University Press, 1961) valuable for its thoroughness
in research and documentation. Marquis Childs and James Reston,
(eds.), *Walter Lippmann and His Times* (New York: Harcourt, Brace,
1959), and David E. Weingast, *Walter Lippmann: A Study in Personal Journalism* (New Brunswick, N.J.: Rutgers University Press,
1944), present useful biographical information.

My study of the influence of scientific management on the political
practice of the progressive era has gained much from Dwight Waldo's
The Administrative State (New York: Ronald Press Co., 1948).
Among the contemporary materials, I have found such important,
neglected books as [Edward Mandell House], *Philip Dru, Administrator* (New York: Heubsch, 1913), and Robert Moses, *The Civil Service
of Great Britain* (New York: Columbia University Press, 1914), quite
stimulating. The records of President Taft's Commission on Economy
and Efficiency are at the National Archives, and, as might be expected,
they are well indexed.

CHAPTERS VII–IX

The American experience in World War I generally has not been
given the attention it merits. Aside from Frederic L. Paxson's *America
at War: 1917–1918* (Boston: Houghton Mifflin, 1939), which is a
good, conventional historical narrative, most of the standard works
present a mass of undigested and indigestible material. The memoirs
and biographies of the major participants do have valuable insights.
See Ray Stannard Baker, *Woodrow Wilson: Life and Letters*, Vols.
VII, VIII (New York: Doubleday, Doran & Co., 1939); Anne W.
Lane and L. H. Wall (eds.), *The Letters of Franklin K. Lane* (Boston:
Houghton Mifflin, 1922); Josephus Daniels, *The Wilson Era: Years
of War and After, 1917–1923* (Chapel Hill: University of North
Carolina Press, 1946); David F. Houston, *Eight Years with Wilson's
Cabinet, 1913 to 1920* (2 vols.; New York: Doubleday, Page & Co.,

1926). Robert K. Murray's standard work, *The Red Scare* (Minneapolis: University of Minnesota Press, 1955), has a good chapter on the Boston Police Strike.

No one can write sensibly about Veblen without drawing from Joseph Dorfman, *Thorstein Veblen and His America* (New York: Viking Press, 1941). David Riesman, *Thorstein Veblen* (New York: Charles Scribner's Sons, 1953), is a provocative counterweight to the usual hagiographic studies. Morton White, *Social Thought in America* (Boston: Beacon Press, 1957), chap. VI, which describes Veblen as "The Amoral Moralist," has influenced my view. Edwin Layton, "Veblen and the Engineers," *American Quarterly*, XVI (Spring, 1962), 64–72, discusses this strange alliance from a viewpoint different from mine. The same author's "Frederick Haynes Newell and the Revolt of the Engineers," in *Journal of the Midcontinent American Studies Association*, III (Fall, 1962), 18–26, presents valuable information on the short-lived post-Armistice radicalism among engineers.

The most revealing book on Commons is still his autobiography, John R. Commons, *Myself* (New York: Macmillan Co., 1934), but Lafayette B. Harter, Jr., *John R. Commons* (Corvallis: Oregon State University Press, 1962), adds some useful data. Commons' ideas are seen at their best in Kenneth H. Parsons, "John R. Commons' Point of View," reprinted as Appendix III in John R. Commons, *The Economics of Collective Action* (New York: Macmillan Co., 1950), pp. 341–75.

My comments on Taylorism in the twenties rest largely on a close reading of the *Bulletin of the Taylor Society* in that period and upon the Taylor Society, *Scientific Management in American Industry*, edited by H. S. Person (New York: Harper, 1929), a semiofficial platform of the Taylorites which sums up the major changes in doctrine. Loren Baritz, *The Servants of Power* (Middletown, Conn.: Wesleyan University Press, 1960), presents an interesting review of the development of industrial psychology in the twenties, and Milton J. Nadworny, *Scientific Management and the Unions, 1900–1932* (Cambridge, Mass: Harvard University Press, 1955), is again useful in the realm of labor relations.

• INDEX

Acheson, Dean, 129 n.
Administration: and control, 85, 87, 95, 114; and expertise, 85, 87, 89, 95, 104–6, 143 n.; separated from politics, 100–1, 104–6, 111, 117, 172 n.; and legislation in World War I, 117–18; separated from management, 160–63, 166
Aitkin, Hugh G. J., 68 n., 169–70 n.
American Federation of Labor: opposition to Taylor system, 67–69; postwar program, 123; opposition to "industrial democracy," 130–31; battle against radicalism, 137; disdained by Veblen, 142; rapprochement with Taylorites, 149–50; see also Gompers; International Association of Machinists
American Industries, 70, 71
American Society of Mechanical Engineers: Taylor becomes president, 7; Taylor joins, 8; and professionalism, 9–11; and metrics, 12–13; and conservation, 13–15; rejects Taylor's paper, 18; Taylor's continued interest, 31; ascendancy of "progressives," 143–44
American Telephone & Telegraph Co., 163
Americanization program, and efficiency, 61–62, 125
Architectural Record, 83, 84
Architecture, profession of, 83–84
Ardzrooni, Leon, 143

Babbitt, Irving, 65
Baker, Newton D., 69
Baritz, Loren, 173 n.
Barth, Carl G., 50, 170 n.; "Taylor's most orthodox disciple," 34–35; con-

centrates upon factory problems, 36–37; private opinions, 37 n.
Barth, J. Christian, vii
Bates, J. Leonard, 14 n.
Beard, Charles A., 115 n.
Bell, Daniel, 170 n.
Bellamy, Edward, 150, 151 n.
Bendix, Reinhard, vii
Bergson, Henri, 91
Bernard, Luther L., 60 n.
Bethlehem Steel Company, 35, 42
Beveridge, Albert J., 102, 137
Beyer, Otto, 144
Birnbaum, Lucille, vii
Blackford, Katherine M. H., 56–57
Blankenberg, Rudolph, 108–9
Bolsheviks: disliked Gantt, 47; Senate investigates, 135; Veblen on, 142; resort to Taylorism, 151; *see also* Lenin
Boston police strike: and postwar shift in popular sentiment, 136; links American labor movement to radicalism, 137
Brandegee, Frank B., 117
Brandeis, Louis D.: and Eastern Rate Case, 53–55, 61; and Taylorism, 53–54, 58, 80–82; youth and education, 75–76; mugwump to progressive, 76–77; "commercialism" and trusts 77–78, 81–82; on unions, 77; leadership and professionalism, 78–79, 81, 107 n.; "logic of facts," 79–81; on bigness, 80–82, 95, 98; special type of progressivism, 82; on "industrial democracy," 95–97, 124, 126, 128; tries to save U.S. Commission on Efficiency, 114 n.; biographies, 171–72 n.
Breshkovskaya, Catherine, 135
Bruere, Robert W., 152

meanings in the progressive era: personal
Efficiency, slogan of, ix, 55, 61–62, 70 n., 72, 119–20
Efficiency craze, 51–74; see also Church, efficiency in the; Government, efficiency in; Home, efficiency in the; School, efficiency in the
Efficiency exposition; see National Efficiency Exposition and Conference
Efficiency Magazine, 72
"Efficiency records," 114 n.
Efficiency societies, 60, 72–74
Efficiency Society [of New York], 72–74
Elitism, xii, 152 n.; Lenin, 24 n.; Gantt, 43, 48; Ferguson, 45–46; Brandeis, 78–79; Croly, 84, 85; *New Republic*, 87–88; 89; socialism, 91 n.; Lippmann, 92, 93–95; and administration, 104–5; Veblen, 142–43; Commons, 146; see also Experts; Professionalism
Ely, Richard T., 101 n.
Emerson, Harrington: at Eastern Rate Case, 53–54; management mechanisms, 56–57; moral exhortation, 56–57; popularity, 57; slogans, 62; joins Efficiency Society [of New York], 73 n.; works for efficiency in government, 108, 147; sheds idealism, 161
Emerson, Ralph Waldo, 76
Emery, James A., 70
Engels, Friedrich, 91 n.
Espionage Act, 135
Executive budget, 114, 115
Experts, xii, 104–5, 116, 122, 152 n.; Taylor system, 24–25, 28; Brandeis, 78–79; Croly, 84, 85, 89; *New Republic*, 87–88; socialism, 91 n.; Lippmann, 93; Cooke, 109–10; Commons, 146; see also Elitism; Professionalism

Fabian Society, 120
Federated Engineering Societies, 156, 157, 159
Feiss, Richard, 32
Ferguson, Charles: early career, 44–45; social outlook, 45–46; and New Machine, 46–47; utopian habit of mind, 143 n.
Feuer, Lewis S., 140 n., 143 n.
Figgis, Rev. J. N., 45 n., 126

Fitch, John A., 33, 129 n.
Flanders, Ralph, 149 n.
Follett, Mary Parker: early career, 126; view of democracy, 126–27; "group principle," 126, 127; functional principle, 127; influence upon Taylorites, 131; *The New State*, 126
Forcey, Charles, 172 n.
Ford, Henry, 140
Frankfurter, Felix, 30 n., 33, 79 n., 106 n., 129 n.
Franklin, Benjamin, 57
Friends, Society of, 3, 6 n.

Gantt, Henry L., 34, 50, 170 n.; emphasized social implications of Taylorism, 37, 42–44; early career, 42; and Veblen, 44–45, 143–44; starts New Machine, 44–47; wartime social program, 47–49, 158
Gay, Edwin F., 73, 109
General Electric Co., 163
Germany, 119–20
Ghent, William J., 151
Gilbreth, Frank B., 34, 50, 171 n.; develops motion study, 26, 38–41; and Taylor Society, 31, 41–42, 160; early career, 37; under Taylor influence, 37–38; break with Taylor, 38; his "one best way," 41
Gilbreth, Lillian M., 39, 171 n.
Godfrey, Hollis, 46 n., 108
Golden, John, 69
Gompers, Samuel, 67, 137 n.
Goodnow, Frank J., 60 n., 103–4, 105, 106
Government, efficiency in: U.S., Army arsenals and Navy yards, 68–69, 108; Croly on, 89; Lippmann on, 93–94; municipal, 108–13; national, 113–14; state, 115–16
Gregory, Thomas W., 135
Gronlund, Laurence, 150
Guild socialism, 45 n., 96, 131

Halsey, F. A., 1 n.
Hanson, Ole, 135
Harvard Socialist Club, 156
Hays, Samuel P., 14 n., 62 n., 170 n.
Herrick, Robert, 95 n.
High cost of living, 51, 134–35
Higham, John, 62 n.
Hillman, Sidney, 150

applications in factories, 26, 35, 68, 107, 110, 120–21; at Eastern Rate Case, 28, 29, 53–54, 80; shifts in emphasis, 29–30; named scientific management, 55; changes in doctrine, 129–30, 160–61, 164–66

Tead, Ordway, 131, 152, 163
Technical Alliance, 144, 157
Thompson, C. Bertrand, 154
Thorne, Clifford, 52, 54 n.
Tilden Commission report, 99–100, 107
Time study, 2–3, 24, 29, 40–42, 68–69, 148
Tolles, Frederick B., 6 n.
Towne, Henry R., 1 n.
Trade associations, 72, 158
Trade unions, 57, 61, 146; and "industrial democracy," 33–34, 130–31; and Eastern Rate Case, 54; and efficiency craze, 67; opposition to Taylor system, 67–69, 110, 148; under attack in postwar period, 137; became friendly toward Taylor system, 149–50; *see also* American Federation of Labor; International Association of Machinists
Training School for Public Service, 112
Tugwell, Rexford, 82, 161 n., 167
Tweed Ring, 99, 100

United States Army arsenals and Navy yards, 68, 107
United States Army Ordnance Department, 121, 129
United States Army Psychological Tests, 80 n., 165
United States Bureau of Efficiency, 114
United States Commission on Economy and Efficiency, 113–14, 115, 172 n.
United States Commission on Industrial Relations, 35, 128, 145 n.
United States Emergency Fleet Corporation, 121, 129
United States Immigration Commission, 80 n.
United States Shipping Board, 121

Valentine, Robert G., 33–34, 45 n., 96–97 n.
Van Dyke, John C., 78 n.
Van Hise, Charles R., 30 n., 147, 157 n.
Veblen, Thorstein, 44–45, 49, 133, 138–45, 173 n.; the "amoral moralist," 139; and Taylor, 139; dichotomy between business and industry, 139–40; on socialism, 140; and engineers, 140, 141–45; and World War I, 141; elitism, 142; his "Soviet of Technicians," 142, 143–45, 157; and Commons, 145

Vitalism, doctrine of: influence upon Croly, 86; influence upon Lippmann, 91–92, 93

Waldo, Dwight, 172 n.
Wallas, Graham, 90
Walsh, Frank P., 45 n.
War Industries Board, 118, 120
War Labor Board, 118
Ward, Lester Frank, 143
Waste in Industry Survey, 156–59, 160
Weber, Max, 6 n.
Wells, H. G., 94 n.
Wendell, Barrett, 76
Western Electric Co., 163
White, Morton G., 118 n., 171 n., 173 n.
White, William Allen, 123
Williams, Albert Rhys, 135
Williams, Ben, 154–55
Willoughby, William Franklin, 105
Wilson, Woodrow, 45, 46, 47; and Taylor system in arsenals, 69; on administration, 103 n.; on efficiency and democracy, 107 n.; and Taft Commission on Efficiency, 114; on civic singleness of purpose, 118; his war organization criticized, 119, 121–22; on "industrial democracy," 124; condemns Boston police strike, 136; congratulates Calvin Coolidge, 136 n.
Winchester Repeating Arms Co., 120
Wisconsin, University of, 106, 145 n., 147
Wisconsin Commission on Efficiency, 115
"Wisconsin idea," 106
Wobblies; *see* Industrial Workers of the World
Wolfe, Robert B., 33
World War I: as "an all-correlating moral adventure," 47, 118–19, 127; and progressivism, 117, 138 n.; administration supersedes legislation, 117–18; makes efficiency a patriotic duty, 119–20; and John Dewey, 119; reconstruction plans, 122–23; bibliography, 172 n.
Wyatt, Edith, 61, 69 n.